Our Community at Winchester

The City and Its Workers at New Haven's Gun Factory

JOAN CAVANAGH

GREATER NEW HAVEN LABOR HISTORY ASSOCIATION

NEW HAVEN, CT

Our Community at Winchester: The City and Its Workers at New Haven's Gun Factory is based on an exhibit produced by the Greater New Haven Labor History Association in 2013 about workers and the community they created at the Winchester Repeating Arms plant in New Haven, Connecticut, throughout the 20th century. Material has been added to the book based on new research. Some of the original information has been revised and/or expanded upon for clarity. The exhibit may be viewed at http://exhibits.winchesterworkers.gnhlha.org.

————————————————

Published by OctoberWorks, 1477 Ridge Road, North Haven, CT 06473

For inquires or to purchase books:
https://octoberworks.com/our-community-at-winchester

ISBN: 978-1-7321801-5-4

This book is dedicated in loving memory to the former garment workers and other early Labor History Association members whose commitment, energy and histories inspired, informed and propelled the organization at its outset; to the six former Winchester workers who shared their important stories with LHA volunteers as their lives neared an end; and to LHA's long-time "prime movers:" Nicholas Aiello, Louis W. Berndston Jr., William Carey, John Hiller, Mary Johnson, Elizabeth Murray, David Montgomery, Lula White and Joan Whitney, dedicated historian-worker-activists, who understood the importance of learning about the past in order to forge a better future.

We remember each of you with much gratitude. Your lives were a gift to all of us.

Winchester Lofts, one of several "re-purposed" factory buildings in the gentrified city of New Haven, Connecticut, 2020.

Contents

Dorothy Johnson and Lula White are sisters. They are both members of the Executive Board of the Greater New Haven Labor History Association. In 2010–2011, assisted by other board members and volunteers, they conducted oral history interviews with former Winchester workers about their experiences at the plant.

The two sisters were born in Alabama but raised in New Haven in the Dixwell/Newhallville neighborhood. In 1944 their father, Edward White, Sr., moved his family to Connecticut. He found work at the Armstrong Rubber Company; later at the Winchester Plant; and finally, at American Cynamid.

DOROTHY JOHNSON

"I can remember when I was a little kid I'd walk down Winchester Avenue with factories on both sides of the street. You had to get out of the way when the shift changed."

Dorothy went to school in New Haven and worked at Circuitwise in North Haven from 1977 until it closed in 2004. She was an inspector and later served as president of United Electrical Workers Union Local 299 from 1994 until 2004.

Reflecting on the demise of Winchester and the rise of "Science Park":

"A lot of the neighborhood people feel shortchanged because they are not being hired."

LULA WHITE

"Most of the people I grew up with had fathers who worked at Winchester…You could hear the Winchester whistle for miles away. [At the sound] we'd leave the Winchester School, go home for lunch, and then come back."

Lula attended school in New Haven and went to the University of Chicago on a scholarship. On July 9, 1961, the then 22 year old White was arrested in Mississippi as a Freedom Rider, joining the more than 400 Americans who challenged the status quo that sanctioned racially segregated bus and train stations. It was a time when black and white citizens resolved to not "cooperate with segregation laws anymore."

Reflecting on the demise of Winchester and the rise of "Science Park":

"Everyone we knew worked at Winchester. Now it's Yale."

Lula White was born in 1938 and passed away on September 10, 2019. She was a participant in the Freedom Rides to desegregate public transportation in 1961, a retired teacher and a long-time member of the Executive Board of the Greater New Haven Labor History Association.

Acknowledgments

The former Winchester workers and their family members who shared their stories with us are the heart and soul of this book and the exhibit.

Marcia Biederman

Arthur Bosley, 1921-2017, former president, Local 609

Marie Boulware

Barbara J. Butler

Robert Erff, 1933-2018

Craig Gauthier, former president, Local 609

James Foster, 1929-2013

Emmanuel Gomez

Mildred Hopkins

Edna L. Hudson, 1934-2018

Sen. Martin Looney

Al Marder

Claretha McKnight

Westley McElya, 1918-2004

Marge Ottenbreit

David W.P. Roy

Raymond Simms

Lawrence Young, 1923-2015

We thank our funding partners for the financial contributions that made production of the exhibit and/or the book possible:

International Association of Machinists and Aerospace Workers; the Phoebe Foundation; members and friends of the Greater New Haven Labor History Association; Connecticut Humanities; the New Alliance Foundation; Historic New England; the Doris McGlone Neumann Revocable Trust; and an anonymous donor.

We thank the following organizations, publications and individuals for their contributions to the content of the exhibit and/or the book:

For their invaluable research assistance and consultation, much appreciation goes to:

Jason Bischoff-Wurstle, Director of Photo Archives, New Haven Museum and Historical Society

Zachary Brodt, University Archivist, University of Pittsburgh

Laura Renee Brooks, Library Associate, Archives & Special Collections, University of Pittsburgh

James Campbell, former Curator, Whitney Library, New Haven Museum and Historical Society

Traci Drummond, former Southern Labor Archivist, Georgia State University Library

David Grinnell, Coordinator of Archives and Manuscripts, University of Pittsburgh

Frances Skelton, Reference Librarian, New Haven Museum and Historical Society

Laura Smith, Archivist, Archives and Special Collections at the Thomas J. Dodd Research Center

Lisa Vallen, Southern Labor Archivist, Georgia State University Library

For providing images and/or quotes, sincere thanks to:

The Connecticut Historical Society (Winchester women packing bullets, 1877)

Suzanne Cooney (photograph with story of McDermott's Tavern)

Maryann Davies (photographs of Winchester Safety Outing, 1946 and WELI interview, early 1950s)

Stanley Heller (photograph of Westley McElya)

Herbert Houze (early Winchester photos from his book, *Winchester Repeating Arms Company: Its History and Development 1865 to 1891*, 2004)

Mary Jo Ignoffo (quote and information about early history from *Captive of the Labyrinth: Sarah L. Winchester, Heiress to the Rifle Fortune*, 2010)

New Haven Museum and Historical Society (Bird's Eye View of the Winchester Plant, ca. 1915)

Joe Taylor and the *People's Daily World* (1979-1980 strike photographs)

Steve Thornton (information, text, and images from *A Shoeleather History of the Wobblies: Stories of the Industrial Workers of the World (IWW) in Connecticut,* 2014).

While not pictured in the book, various artifacts added immeasurably to the original exhibit when it was shown from December of 2013 to April of 2014 at its first venue, the NewAlliance Foundation Art Gallery at Gateway Community College. Many thanks to Charles Bimonte, the late Arthur Bosley, Mary J. Gregory, Edward Ulrich and the late Lawrence Young for lending their treasures.

Much gratitude is owed to Christopher Wagoner, Director of the William W. Winpisinger Center for Education and Technology, and Dr. Charles N. Micallef, Director of the Retirees, Community and Membership Services Department of the International Association of Machinists and Aerospace Workers, not only for helping to fund efforts to preserve the Local 609 records and tell the workers' stories, but for twice hosting presentations about the "Victory Lodge" and the exhibit at their Local Lodge History week-long workshop at Placid Harbor in Hollywood, MD.

In addition to all the Winchester workers who so graciously shared their stories, the exhibit and book would not have been possible without the help of Everett Corey, Directing Business Representative, International Association of Machinists District 236, and John Reynolds, former president of International Association of Machinists Local 609, who together insured that the Local 609 records were preserved after the Winchester plant closed in 2006, and who shepherded their transfer to the Labor History Association. Mr. Corey also helped facilitate the records' move to their final home, the Southern Labor Archives at Georgia State University in 2017, after the Labor History Association had ceased to serve as an archival repository.

We also thank Mr. Reynolds, two other former Local 609 presidents, David White and Craig Gauthier, and retired Winchester worker and union board member Emmanuel Gomez for their participation in a focus group discussion during the planning stages for the exhibit.

Frank Annunziato, first president of the Labor History Association, is much appreciated for taking the time to listen to and write about his 1990 interview with the late Westley McElya, which gives a worker's perspective on the events surrounding the lockout described in Chapter 4. Debbie Elkin, the organization's second president, produced a chronology of events at Winchester for the Labor History Bus Tour she led in 1999 which provided many of the entries up to 1979 on the timeline at the beginning of this book. She also offered important editorial comments about the first three pages of the introduction.

Company publications including *Winchester Life, Winchester News, Olin News,* and *Target* were extremely useful in giving a picture of the political, cultural, and economic changes at the plant in the 20th century. The *Machinist* and *UE News* (journals of the International Association of Machinists and the United Electrical Workers, respectively) provided vivid details from the point of view of union organizers. The *American Independent Newsletter* and *Modern Times,* found in the files of Local 609, added additional perspectives about the community response to the Local 609 strike. The Local 609 records themselves are a treasure trove, only partially mined for the purposes of the book and the exhibit. Material from two venerable New Haven news sources helped to fill in missing details about the relationships between the City of New Haven, the various companies that owned Winchester, and the developing Science Park. Thanks to *New Haven Independent* editor Paul Bass for permission to quote from articles and use photographs about Science Park and Winchester Lofts. The *New Haven Register* was an invaluable resource for articles about the many struggles at Winchester and its relationship to the City of New Haven. Gratitude goes to the newspaper's Executive Editor, Helen Bennett Harvey, who told us the newspaper celebrated its 200th anniversary in 2012.

Last but not least, much appreciation goes to Nesta Allen, the late L. W. Berndston, Jr., Bill Berndtson, Andrew Calandrelli, Sr., Monica McGovern, Alessandra Nichols and Peter Vollemanns for their assistance in the very labor-intensive process of transporting and setting up the exhibit at various times during its tour of duty, 2013-2017.

A Short Timeline of the Winchester Company in New Haven

1858: Oliver Winchester starts New Haven Repeating Arms Company.

1866: Winchester Repeating Arms Company formed with issuance of stock.

1870: Factory built at corner of Munson and Canal Streets.

1888: Winchester purchases Eli Whitney's gun company.

1898: Employment at 3,000 during the Spanish-American-Filipino War.

1917: Employment at 17,500 during World War I.

1931: Winchester acquired by Olin Corporation.

1942-1946: United Electrical Workers-CIO (Congress of Industrial Organizations) attempts to organize a union at Winchester are met with strong management resistance and ultimately fail.

1949: AFL (American Federation of Labor) loses vote in election held by NLRB (National Labor Relations Board) at Winchester.

1954: Olin Industries merges with Mathieson Chemicals to form Olin-Mathieson Chemical Corporation.

1955: International Association of Machinists-AFL wins union election, forming Victory Lodge 609: 4500 employees in bargaining unit. The AFL and CIO merge to become AFL-CIO.

1962: First strike at Winchester.

1969: 17-week strike.

1979: Winchester moves brass mill to East Alton, IL.

1979-1980: Six-month strike over piece work and incentives which the company was trying to cut. Much community involvement through the Citizens Ad Hoc Committee. Mayor Logue closes the plant for three days; there is much community activity (meetings, Christmas party where 1400 children each given a wrapped toy; committees to help people keep their homes, have food.) 1350 workers in bargaining unit.

1980: The City of New Haven pays $416,000 to purchase seven acres of land from United Nuclear for use in the proposed Science Park and offers a major incentive package to Olin Corporation, including construction of a new $10 million plant, to keep it in New Haven. The initiative fails.

1981: Olin sells the Winchester division to a group of investors including Winchester executives; renamed U.S. Repeating Arms Company.

1980s: Various sales and reorganizations of the company fail to keep the company from financial failure.

OCTOBER 1990: 500 employees laid off, New Haven plant closes "indefinitely" while "seeking new financing."

NOVEMBER 1990: Fabrique Nationale Herstal, a Belgian company (owned by Giat of France), which had previously owned 44% of the company through its subsidiary, Browning America of Morgan, Utah, buys out the other two shareholders and now has full ownership.

DECEMBER 1990: Workers begin "trickling back" as company reopens. New president predicts "turnaround".

1990s: Workers attempt to implement High Performance Work Organization but are met with management resistance. The emerging Science Park faces financial troubles, goes for more city and state funding.

MARCH 1994: International Association of Machinists Union President George Kourpias visits the Winchester plant for a two-day kick-off event for the High Performance Work Organization. The HWPO is part of a union strategy to involve workers in decision making in all the plants it represents throughout the country. Despite initial success, the effort is ultimately not successful at Winchester largely due to management resistance.

AUGUST 1994: Completion of new Winchester plant at Science Park.

MARCH 2006: The Winchester plant closes shop, throwing its remaining 187 employees out of work.

1999-2019: A series of entrepreneurial "start-up" companies, most with affiliations to Yale, move in and out of renovated parts of the old Winchester factory complex. By 2019, many have been replaced by new ones.

MARCH 2012: Inauguration of "first phase" of Winchester plant renovation: ribbon cutting at Higher One, which will occupy part of the old factory building on Munson Street.

JUNE 2015: Luxury apartment building, Winchester Lofts, opens in the renovated factory building at Munson Street and Winchester Avenue.

DECEMBER 2015: Investigation by the Federal Deposit Insurance Corporation concludes, with Higher One found guilty of deceptive business practices by improperly collecting $31 million in fees from students from May 2012 to July 2014.

APRIL 2016: Higher One denies it will leave New Haven, despite mounting debts from various lawsuits.

2018: Blackboard/Transact replaces the defunct Higher One in the space on Munson Street.

MARCH 2019: Blackboard announces that Transact is to be "spun off," having been acquired by Revenue Capital Partners. It is unclear what if any impact this "spin-off" will have on the company's presence in New Haven, although it has denied that there will be employee layoffs as a result.[1]

Christmas at Winchester

THREE years ago this month, this great, peace-loving nation of ours was catapulted into a terrible World War by the dastardly attack on Pearl Harbor by the madmen of Nippon.

We here at Winchester have done everything in our power to supply our fighting-men with arms and ammunition to defend our shores and to drive back the hordes of invaders from the free lands they had plundered.

Christmastide, 1944 finds our fighting-men still locked in a desperate struggle with these merciless tyrants, and we on the home front striving with every means at our command to keep the wheels of production turning and the badly needed supplies rolling to the fighting fronts.

In the midst of all this blood, sweat and tears, it is hard for us to catch the wonderful, happy spirit of the Christmases we once knew.

Our thoughts, naturally, are continually with our loved ones, who are serving in the Armed Forces all over this war-torn world. Hardly an hour goes by without a hopeful thought for their welfare and a silent prayer for their safe return.

My fervent and sincere Christmas wish to our 3,350 fellow-employees in the services and to all our Winchester family here at home, is that when the spirit of Christmas falls next year over the world, Peace will reign in the hearts of all men and nations and all our families will be reunited with their loved ones.

Let us look forward to a Happy and Victorious New Year!

Thomas J. S. Bonk

Works Manager

Image from Winchester Life, *ca. 1945*

INTRODUCTION

THE WINCHESTER PLANT was a major employer in New Haven, CT, throughout much of the 20th century. The tale of the rifle and the company that produced it has been spun in books, movies and on the internet for many years. The romance and legend of the gun have been repeatedly burnished in company histories, Hollywood movies and gun collectors' tales.

The story of the plant's interaction with its host community and its impact on the lives of its workers has been told to a much lesser degree, presented in fragments through the lenses of various media. Usually, articles in journals such as *Winchester Life*, *Winchester News*, *Olin News* and *Target* stressed the need for employee-management unity and emphasized Winchester's achievements, while those in local newspapers like the *New Haven Register*, the *New Haven Journal Courier*, the *New Haven Advocate*, the *New Haven Independent*, and, occasionally, the *Yale Daily News*, most often appeared at times of crisis, including during strikes, layoffs, and company threats to leave town. The *Machinist* (a publication of the International Association of Machinists), the *UE News* (a publication of the United Electrical Workers), the *People's Daily World*, *Modern Times* and the *American Independent Newsletter* also periodically covered local organizing efforts and struggles. Articles and images from all these sources and more were used in this book, along with oral histories conducted by volunteers from the Greater New Haven Labor History

Association in 1990 and between 2009 and 2013. In the modest hope that it will inspire other, more comprehensive efforts to fill out the picture, this book (and the exhibit from which it draws much of its material) begins to look at the stories of Winchester workers' experiences as employees at the plant, as well as the company's often fraught relationship with New Haven's citizens and political infrastructure.

The story is a complicated one, filled with contradictions. First, the primary commodity produced by Winchester's workers was a lethal one. Although the company ventured into production of other wares at times when its gun sales flagged, making everything from roller skates to watches, it was, in fact, a munitions factory, and it was never intended to be anything else. Guns were its reason for being. Neither the commodity produced or the company's practice of selling it to whomever would buy it, no matter the use to which it would be put or into whose hands it might fall, were rarely, if ever, challenged, at least publicly, by any of the workers' advocates (including their unions), by city officials, or by the workers themselves.

Thus, there was a deep contradiction between the consequences of what Winchester produced and the justified pride in craftsmanship, skill and the positive example of a strong work ethic exemplified by many of its workers.

From its inception, the company, like all munitions manufacturers, went abroad to solicit contracts, violated the spirit if not the essence of U.S. neutrality laws, and, at least once, crossed the legal line so blatantly that it faced a civil penalty. (See Chapters 1, 2 and 8.) Winchester made the bulk of its profits in the early 20th century before and between the world wars by marketing its goods to fuel a variety of conflicts, using sales practices and sleight-of-hand that continued throughout its history. One long-term temporary agency employee sent to work at the plant in the 1970s, Marcia Biederman, knew when she started her job that there was a federal investigation underway into the company's sale of guns to a sporting goods store owner in South Africa at a time when exporting weapons to the apartheid state was illegal. She learned and reported in her *New Haven Advocate* exposé that these weapons were, by circuitous routes, being resold to white South Africans who were arming to shoot black South African protesters. While many workers at the plant and members of the New Haven community were incensed when they learned of this practice, the punishment meted out, many felt, was not adequate to the company's crimes.

Thus, there was a deep contradiction between the consequences of what Winchester produced and the justified pride in craftsmanship, skill and the positive example of a strong work ethic exemplified by many of its workers. For example, before the days of automation, the late Lawrence Young, a skilled and accomplished African American woodworker, made his own tools and "finished" the guns that the company sold to various prosperous and well-known customers. He was proud of his expertise and glad that he had been able to find employment at a company where he could use it and make a decent living while doing so. Active in his community, he was able to provide well for himself and his family. Winchester, for all its many drawbacks as an employer, nevertheless surpassed anything he would have found in the Deep South where he was born. (See Chapter 3.)

There was also a wide gulf between the restrictive and self-interested practices of company officials and the creative and interactive community that developed within the shop and among its workers in New Haven, particularly in the Dixwell-Newhallville neighborhood. Many of the oral histories speak to the sense of family that sprung up among workers over time at the plant, reflecting not only on the various social activities that drew them together but also on the sense of pride people felt about going to work every day at a place where friends, family members and neighbors were also employed. "Everyone we knew worked at Winchester," said the late Lula White, whose father was a machinist there and who conducted many of the oral histories in this book along with her sister, Dorothy Johnson.

Before and during World War II, African Americans migrated to the North seeking better opportunities and hoping for less discrimination, exponentially increasing the work force at companies such as Winchester. As Lawrence Young describes in Chapter 3, they found opportunities that would have been unheard of in the South. But, as Young also makes clear, even the most skilled faced deep racism and prejudice. American industry tried to thwart the advancement and training of black workers in every possible way, and Winchester was no exception. Indeed, industry's strongest weapon against worker organizing was to play off different "classes" of workers (skilled vs. unskilled, old vs. young, black vs. white) against each other. In the case of the Winchester plant, this strategy enabled the company to keep unions at bay for more than 50 years, even at periods when employees at other plants were successfully organized.

Before, during and after World War II, Works Manager Thomas I. Boak, a leader in the anti-union National Association of Manufacturers, struck out viciously against the attempt of United Electrical Workers-CIO Local 282 to gain a foothold at the plant. In 1946 he fired or "locked out" over 200 workers from the Brass Rolling Mill who attempted several times to meet with him to address grievances and finally went on strike. The subsequent National Labor Relations Board case continued for years, and eventually the union dropped it "because of lack of organization." But it was taken up by a private law firm, Gold & Gold from New Haven, which represented the individuals involved and won a recommendation by the Trial Examiner that the employees who had been locked out be reinstated. (See Chapter 4, which includes Frank Annunziato's commentary on his 1990 interview with the late Westley McElya, one of those locked out.)

Perhaps the company's biggest miscalculation was its post-war requirement that everyone increase production without an increase in pay. Many of the workers we interviewed believed that this stance was what led to the union victory for International Association of Machinists Local 609 in 1955. Said the late Arthur Bosley, (see Chapter 5), who had served as a president of Local 609, "For the longest time, the unions could not get in. Many of the [skilled] workers had good jobs and did not see a need… Boak wanted us to increase production and that went for everyone, including the older workers. We knew that if the union didn't get in, we would have to increase production and not get paid…"

Many of the workers who were interviewed praised Local 609 for helping to level the playing field in a more positive way, reducing pay inequities between skilled and unskilled workers and making it possible for more African Americans to bid on the better jobs available rather than merely being consigned to the dirtiest, most dangerous ones. But they added that it was always an uphill struggle, and the stronger the union got, the more the company tried to break its power. Local 609 always had a strong African American presence among its rank and file, and by the 1980s and 1990s, the union was led by Blacks, many of whom were women.

> One stated goal of the High Performance Work Organization was to actively engage workers in improving both the quality and quantity of production.

In the last years of its history, the Winchester plant had an opportunity to involve workers in a nationwide effort spearheaded by the International Association of Machinists (IAM) that would supposedly bring their expertise to the forefront of managing the production process. One stated goal of the High Performance Work Organization (see Chapter 10) was to actively engage workers in improving both the quality and quantity of production. Craig Gauthier, once a president of Local 609, cites an example of how this was successfully implemented in Winchester's Assembly Shop, where workers redesigned the shop, doubling production, according to Gauthier, within three weeks. Predictably, there was management resistance, "because they felt we were taking power away." HPWO efforts had varying degrees of success in other IAM shops. At Winchester the effort failed, taking with it any attempt at product diversification that might have occurred.

Decade after decade, in its various corporate incarnations, the company extracted concessions from workers (no pay raises, sometimes pay rollbacks, many repeated furloughs and layoffs) by threatening to shut down, leave town or move many of its operations to other locations. It also gained tax abatements and loans from the City of New Haven in exchange for minimum employment guarantees or other agreements that were continually modified or abrogated. (See Chapter 11.) Worker concessions and generous city financial incentives did not keep production in New Haven, maintain a high level of employment, or, ultimately, secure a future for the plant in the city. When the company's final owner, the Herstal Group, closed the plant in 2006, without the six months' notice to its remaining employees required by its contract with the city, there were only 187 people still employed there. Those workers never received the back pay that they believe was due them.

Nor did the city's repeated concessions lead to a better life or continued economic growth for most of the members of the Dixwell-Newhallville community, or indeed, New Haven. "Science Park at Yale" today is populated by entrepreneurial "start-up" companies, many with affiliations to Yale faculty members, and Yale offices. It employs few members of the larger community. New Haven, CT, remains in the 21st century a relatively small city dominated by an elite institution privileged by massive tax exemptions and continuing to gobble up more and more of the town's real estate. Yale's shadow only lengthened in the first two decades of the new century after the demise of Winchester and the emergence of "Science Park" described in Chapter 12.

As part of the city-wide and national trend toward "re-purposing" old factory buildings by turning them into high-priced rental units, a portion of the old Winchester plant has been converted to "Winchester Lofts," with "market rate" (read: unregulated) rents ranging, as of the summer of 2019, from $1260 to $3150. (See Chapter 12.) Studios alone can price as high as $1630. The apartment complex, complete with a 24-hour fitness center, game room, and even a "pet spa," has 158 units, only 32 of which are available as "affordable housing," which offers lower rents ranging from $754 (for a studio) to $1407 (for a two bedroom), and had a wait list, as of September 2019, of 57. As of late 2019, the minimum income for the "affordable" units ranged from $21,168 for a studio to a maximum of $64,330 for a household of one, depending on the unit. Prices remain, of course, "subject to change without notice."[2]

The overarching issues and themes highlighted by the stories of Winchester's workers, the company's interactions with its host community, and the short and long-term results of those interactions are not particular to one plant, one group of employees, or one municipality. The contradictions evident in the story of this one plant in this one city are embedded in America's history, and are starker than ever today. The munitions industry has long enjoyed outsized political, social and economic influence, successfully lobbying for massive government contracts and often ignoring or skirting federal laws as it has marketed its goods abroad. Corporate interests in general have put profits ahead of the well-being of communities and employees, and their greed has often smothered the just aspirations of the country's workers, weakened or destroyed unions, and crippled the labor movement, while using government bailouts paid for by citizen tax dollars. Union leadership itself has not always acted in the best interests of its membership, thus facing rank-and-file agitation and rebellion. Workers have been impoverished by company shutdowns and downsizing while cities like New Haven have grown more and more unaffordable for their own inhabitants, catering in all the necessities of life, including housing and food as well as education and health care, to well-to-do elites and technocrats. Throughout it all, citizens have organized, pushed back, and tried to mitigate the impact of these assaults with varying degrees of success. Today, trying to understand this history and grapple with its implications for our future is more important than ever as we face the backlash against all social progress that is gripping our country.

—*Joan Cavanagh, June 30, 2020*

THE STORY OF WINCHESTER

WINCHESTER FACTORY 1859 - 1866, LOCATED AT 9 ARTIZAN STREET

Winchester Factory 1859-1866, Artizan Street Photo from Winchester Life, 1942

1

EARLY HISTORY

IN THE BEGINNING: 1852–FROM SHIRTS TO RIFLES

In 1852, Oliver Winchester, co-owner of the Winchester-Davies Shirt Manufactory located since 1848 at 59 Court Street, New Haven, CT, invested in the Volcanic Arms Company with profits accrued from his shirt making enterprise. When Volcanic Arms went bankrupt due to mismanagement, Winchester was able to purchase its machinery, backlog and patents. He hired Benjamin T. Henry, a mechanic from the shirt factory, who designed the first repeating rifle. During the Civil War, Winchester tried aggressively but unsuccessfully to interest the union army in the rifle.[3]

A BRIEF DETOUR, THEN RETURN TO NEW HAVEN

Winchester demanded that Henry, the New Haven plant superintendent, increase production, and, when the demand was not met, privately leased another factory in Bridgeport and hired another superintendent to run it.

Following the time-honored tradition of all arms merchants, Winchester and his representatives went abroad to solicit foreign clientele for their goods. One of his salesmen, Col. Thomas Emmett Addis, is credited in the company's own history as "pulling the fortunes of Winchester out of the hot coals of possible bankruptcy." He delivered 1000 '66 rifles and a half million rounds of ammunition ordered by Don Benito Juarez, leader of the Mexican insurgency against Spain, and apparently risked his own and others' lives to return to the company with the payment. Addis thus became "the direct representative of Winchester to many foreign countries later."[4]

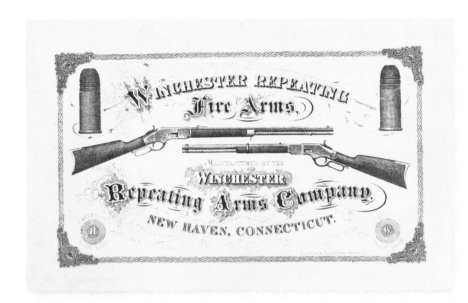

Ad from the company's 1870 catalogue. Image courtesy Herbert Houze, Winchester Repeating Arms Company: Its History and Development 1865 to 1981.

Taking advantage of one of Winchester's long absences overseas, Benjamin T. Henry legally incorporated the New Haven Company as his own Henry Repeating Rifle Company. In July 1865, Winchester filed papers of association for his Bridgeport plant with the state of Connecticut, making it the Winchester Repeating Arms Company. Henry's company soon went out of business, and in 1867, Winchester Repeating Arms was officially incorporated. It soon reopened in New Haven.

In 1870, Oliver and his son, William Wirt Winchester, convinced the skeptical Board of Directors of the new Winchester Repeating Arms Company to build a plant below Prospect Hill in New Haven, where Winchester and William Davies had just constructed their neighboring mansions. Mary Jo Ignoffo writes in *Captive of the Labyrinth: Sarah L. Winchester, Heiress to the Rifle Fortune*: "The main entrance [to the factory] faced the family mansion, just like Colt's, and all the workers knew that Oliver Winchester could stand in his grand parlor and gaze down on the production rooms, their smokestacks billowing testament to the company's profitability."[5]

It did not take long for the Winchester Repeating Arms Company to become New Haven's largest employer. Additions were made to the plant, and by 1895, the company employed 1,500 workers in a 400,000 square foot factory. On February 15, 1898, the U.S.S. Maine was blown up and sank in the harbor off Havana, Cuba. During the Spanish-American War that followed, the company directly supplied armaments to the United States government for the first time, doubling its employment to 3000 by the middle of May that year, with overflow workers occupying its auxiliary buildings at Lake Whitney on the site of what had previously been the Eli Whitney Gun Shop.[6]

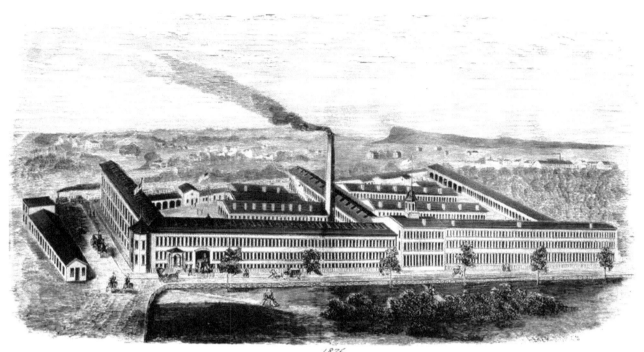

VIEW OF THE WINCHESTER REPEATING ARMS COMPANY'S WORKS, NEW HAVEN, CONN. U.S.A.

View of plant, 1876.

FEMALE OPERATIVES PATCHING AND PACKING BULLETS.

Female Operatives Patching and Packing Bullets ca. 1877. Image courtesy Connecticut Historical Society.

WE AIM FOR

ONE BIG UNION
FOR ALL WINCHESTER WORKERS
SHORTER HOURS BETTER PAY
INDUSTRIAL
FREEDOM
BETTER CONDITIONS

JOIN BROTHERHOOD
OF MACHINISTS
"EVERYBODY IS DOING IT"

WE ARE FIGHTING

LONG HOURS SHORT PAY
SINGLE TIME FOR OVERTIME
INDUSTRIAL
SLAVERY
SPY SYSTEM
BIG DIVIDENDS

SEND YOUR APPLICATION TO
BROTHERHOOD of MACHINISTS
34 PARK ROW NEW YORK.

Images courtesy Steve Thornton, A Shoeleather History of the Wobblies: Stories of the Industrial Workers of the World in Connecticut.

2

WINCHESTER IN THE EARLY 20TH CENTURY

Both the company's poor employment practices and its penchant for selling its wares to fuel conflicts abroad were evident by the beginning of the 20th century. As early as 1898, the International Association of Machinists (which had already begun attempting to organize the plant) had reported in its monthly journal that an order for 10,000 of the "latest pattern of military rifles and 5,000,000 rounds of ammunition was placed with the Winchester Arms Company by the Russian government, the company having had an agent negotiating with that government for several weeks."[7]

The Machinists' organizing efforts, which were largely focused on the national struggle to win a nine-hour workday, were hindered at Winchester in the early 20th century by strong-arm management tactics and, apparently, by divisions among categories of workers which were fostered by company officials. IAM Fifth Vice President M. W. Landers, who was located in Hartford and was organizing in both Connecticut and Massachusetts, reported in the September 9, 1902 issue of the *Machinists Monthly Journal* that he had just visited the New Haven Local, 420, and was disappointed in the small attendance at their meeting: "On account of the successful strike of the trolley men after a few days out, one would think that a great impetus would be given labor organizations, but it takes more than example to influence the intelligent (?) machinists." He complained that "the attitude of the Winchester Arms Company on the question of the rights of wage-earners to organize is deserving of more publicity than has been given it," and suggested that "they should be made to pay for the ill-treatment accorded the workers of our organization. Over a year ago when the nine-hour agitation was on, they let a number of men go so there would be no attempt made in their shop to better conditions, and that has been their position up to date: the superintendent will cause the discharge of any man known to be a member of the I.A.M." Landers recommended that "as much of their trade is in the west, it would be in the interests of the cause if the locals in that country [sic] would make note of the fact that the Winchester Arms Company is opposed to organized labor."[8]

In November and December 1902, and subsequently, the IAM placed Winchester on its list of "unfair" companies, stating: "This firm has operated on the ten-hour basis and has constantly discriminated against union labor, and especially against members of our Association. Members should urge upon their friends not to purchase firearms or ammunition manufactured by this firm until such time as they operate their plant under fair conditions and permit the workmen to affiliate with labor organizations if they desire to do so."[9]

In 1912, the Industrial Workers of the World made a brief union organizing attempt at the plant. In his book, *A Shoeleather History of the Wobblies: Stories of the Industrial Workers of the World in Connecticut*, Steve Thornton wrote that "Organizers… were in New Haven in 1912, just months after their celebrated 'Bread and Roses' strike victory in Lawrence, Massachusetts. [They] went public by distributing thousands of copies of the IWW's Machinist Bulletin to workers at the Winchester Repeating Arms Company."

The General Secretary of the International Brotherhood of Machinists, Robert M. Lackey, wrote an article for the *International Socialist Review*, November 1912 issue, entitled "How the Winchester Repeating Arms Company Rifles Its Workers," in which he described the means by which the company's owners and stockholders attained their wealth and contrasted the opulence they enjoyed with the conditions to which they subjected their workers:

> *The Winchester Repeating Arms Company is the largest manufacturer of firearms and ammunition in the world. Its plant covers 59 acres in the heart of New Haven…From 5,900 to 6,400 workers are on the payroll…Its products are shipped to every corner of the globe. Winchester goods are in great demand for sporting purposes, but wars are a very important source of revenue. Frequently, mysterious shipments are made to unknown destinations. They may be for a revolution in China, South America, or Mexico.*
>
> *[The company] is interesting because of the tremendous dividends paid the stockholders [and] the poor pay, long hours and tyrannical treatment given the employees…Ten hours constitute a day's work. Overtime is paid for as straight*

Robert M. Lackey, "How the Winchester Repeating Arms Company Rifles Its Workers," International Socialist Review, November 1912. Image courtesy Steve Thornton, A Shoeleather History of the Wobblies: Stories of the Industrial Workers of the World in Connecticut.

PLANT OF WINCHESTER·REPEATING·ARMS·COMPANY

HOW THE WINCHESTER REPEATING ARMS COMPANY RIFLES THE WORKERS

By ROBERT M. LACKEY
General Secretary Brotherhood of Machinists

time. A worker who is two minutes late is docked 1 3/10th hours on the week's pay...Every employee is watched like a prisoner and quickly fired if suspected of the least leaning toward unionism. The piece-work system has probably been carried out to a greater extreme than in any other American factory... Truckers are paid by the weight of their load; sweepers by the square foot; and the men who gather the cuspidors and clean the windows are paid by the piece. Frequent cuts are made but never all over the factory at one time. The company is too wise for that. A reduction is made in one department at a time but every department is due for about one cut in every two years.[10]

By 1914, with the onset of World War I in Europe and while the United States was officially neutral, the company received over $16 million in military orders from

Britain, Belgium and France; by the end of 1915, orders increased to nearly $50 million. Between 1914 and 1917, Winchester grew from 5,000 to 17,000 employees.

Focused now on winning an eight-hour workday as part of an international struggle to achieve that goal, the Machinists' organizing campaign continued at the plant as World War I geared up. In 1915, successful strikes had occurred in companies in Connecticut and throughout the Northeast in pursuit of that goal. In the January 1916 issue of *Machinists Monthly Journal*, organizer G. A. Doyle gave a stark report on conditions at Winchester and the treatment of workers who attempted to change them:

> One week ago Monday the men in the screw machine department of the cartridge side of the Winchester Arms Co. New Haven had their chairs taken away from them by order of the superintendent in charge of the department. The men decided to send a committee into the office to ask for the return of the chairs and also the eight-hour day. The members of the committee were promptly discharged by the firm and the 200 immediately walked out, although there were only three organized men in the department.

Bird's Eye View of the Winchester plant, ca. 1915. Image courtesy New Haven Museum and Historical Society.

Male production workers, interior of Winchester plant, ca. 1915. Photo courtesy Herbert Houze, Winchester Repeating Arms: Its History and Development from 1865 to 1981.

Shortly after, another department, which the firm a short time before had given an introduction to a 25 percent cut, came out in sympathy, and in three days 900 were out, which included girls and unskilled help.

This company is called a "penitentiary" by some of the workers there, and it is well named…In some departments the workers have to pay for the tools they use, such as drills, etc. If they scratch the work they pay for it, and if they fail to punch the clock they are fined; in fact, some of the workers at the end of the day figure up to see whether they owe the firm money or not."[11]

The company strategy of playing groups and categories of workers off against each other, although it obviously did not prevail in the case of the "sympathizers" who had walked out, often served to suppress dissent. Doyle asserted that "there are in this factory more human 'leeches' or spotters than in any other factory in this country, and every worker mistrusts the one next to him." Of the 200 who had initially walked out, he said, "a good many have jobs in other cities at 20 cents more an hour than they received at Winchester's," while "others have gone back to organize the workers."[12]

The strike of the "sympathizers" only lasted a week, at which point J.J. Egan, another IAM organizer, had "advised them to go back and start an organizing campaign." Even after stating that "we have a very good lodge there and things look good to me," he warned of the daunting task ahead because of the need to convert many of the workers to the cause as well as deal with management: "This company employs 19,000, so you see that it will be a big job for the one that gets the eight hours, *as there were never many union men in the plant and it is a case of go out and show the men as well as the boss.*"[13] (Emphasis added.)

Nevertheless, organizer J.A. Wickham struck a note of requisite optimism in his August report, stating that "it will not be long before New Haven is an eight-hour city," and asserting that "all eyes are centered on Winchester's plant." But he also reminded his readers that "we are in a state controlled by the Manufacturer's Association," thus, "the law does not favor us."[14]

In the middle of August, the IAM pressed its demand for the eight-hour day at three New Haven companies: Eastern Screw, Geometric Tool, and Winchester. "In each case the shop committees were discharged without a hearing and, of course, we were forced to strike these companies," Wickham wrote in his October report. He noted that "at the Winchester plant we had taken a strike vote and received 5,000 replies, besides numerous letters and pledges in favor of the eight-hour day, and assurances that they were ready to strike if necessary…We 'pulled' the best mechanics and have the shop pretty well disorganized in spite of the claim made by the newspapers that 'it was a fizzle.' They are now using Trades School boys, plumbers and all kinds of roustabouts to fill the places of the strikers. And as in every other instance, the machinists are fighting this battle alone. The polishers agreed to go along with us," he added, "and the men of the local were willing, but one of their organizers advised them to stay in. Those employed on the rifling job were also to go out with us but failed to do so on account of the action of the polishers. However, we are keeping up a strong fight at the Winchester plant, and every day additions are made to the army fighting for eight hours."[15]

The buildup to U.S. entry into World War I led to a spate of government orders from New Haven's munitions factories and an influx of new workers came into the city, producing a serious housing shortage by May of 1916. Many of the new Winchester employees had to look for homes in the outlying areas, "'all along the shoreline road.'" Deeper problems, and divisions among Winchester workers and within the community, followed the official U.S. declaration of war on Germany on April 2nd, 1917: people classed as "enemy aliens" were among the company's now 15,000 strong work force. New Haven's Chief of Police ordered a census taken at the plant, and those from Germany and Austria who had not taken out naturalization papers were immediately suspended prior to "further investigation." In addition, "all employees [were] required to answer certain questions...[Those] claiming citizenship in the United States were permitted to go, with the understanding that naturalized citizens must produce their naturalization papers within a stated time." The *New Haven Evening Register* chose to view the cooperation of the employees and the efficiency and speed with which the census was carried out as "a fair indication of the patriotic spirit which pervades the big Winchester plant from one day to another."[16] But it also could be viewed as an example of a darker spirit, fear of the "other," which is so easily conjured up at times of national crisis or despair, and which is invoked to protect the interests of those in power.

In addition to stirring up employees' suspicions of each other, the new war justified extreme measures within the larger community. The city police closed the streets around the factory to public use, and a week later, the Department of Justice issued a directive that "enemy aliens" were not to be permitted to live near munitions plants. There may or may not have been a more liberal interpretation of the latter order in New Haven, where some of the "enemy aliens" went to the Chief Attorney's office, soliciting help and advice after they found they were being not only barred from employment, but blacklisted from housing.[17]

A Woman Suffrage speaker greets Winchester workers at the plant's entrance, ca. 1916.
Photo courtesy New Haven Museum and Historical Society.

In the early 20th century, other issues besides the ongoing struggle against the company's unfair labor practices and the local implications of the war in Europe made their way even to the gates of Winchester. In addition, the culture of the plant itself and its relationship to the city of New Haven began to take shape.

Since the beginning of the century, a sense of community had begun to emerge both within and outside of the plant. Before and during the war, New Haven's Newhallville-Dixwell neighborhood in particular began to organize itself around the company's presence.

Employees at the company began to gather for social occasions and businesses like McDermott's Tavern grew up in the area to cater to Winchester's employees.

BACK IN THE LONG, LONG AGO . . . Here are the boys of the Barrel Job, class of 1908, enjoying a day of Hi Jinks at the fastidious Sea Cliff Inn, Morris Cove. You will note the boys had on their best "bib 'n tucker", including iron hats, straw fedoras and brilliantly polished celluloid collars. Many of these employees have passed away but we were able to identify some of the boys who are still employed in Winchester, thanks to Frank Vincent and Charlie Snyder. Front row, No 5, Frank Vincent; No. 7, Eddie Griffiths; No. 9, Jim Henry; No. 13, Charles Snyder. Top row, No. 3, Al Weirsman; No. 10, G. R. Watrous; No. 11, Al Young; No. 13, Arthur Parker. Can you name any of the others?

Image from Winchester Life, *1942, looks back at the "Boys of the Barrel Job, class of 1908," posing here at Sea Cliff Inn.*

McDermott's Tavern and its proprietors, ca. 1919. Peter and Rose McDermott emigrated from County Leitrim, Ireland. Their tavern on Ashmun Street was an important gathering place for Winchester workers from 1911 until 1951. Photo courtesy of Suzanne Cooney.

The Winchester plant would undergo many permutations throughout the 20th century as it was bought and sold on several occasions, with multiple changes in management and the waxing and waning of its workforce depending upon the national political and economic climate. But the patterns of its interactions with the community, with organized labor and with its own employees had already begun to be set in its earliest years. So, too, had the chasm between the aspirations of its workers and its own business practices, which would only grow over time.

Women making Browning machine guns—general view of polishing shop, Winchester Repeating Arms Co., New Haven, Connecticut, ca. 1917-1918. U.S. Army Signal Corps photo.

3

WEAPONS ARE THE WAY:
FROM CONTRACTION TO EXPANSION
IN 20 YEARS

1917-1935 WAXING AND WANING: THE AFTERMATH
OF WORLD WAR I

Winchester's war time expansion did not prove sustainable, nor did its subsequent foray into the civilian market. Faced with surplus production capacity, it ventured into the consumer goods industry, producing a variety of items, including kitchenware and hardware such as knives, refrigerators, batteries and roller-skates. These enterprises did not come close to matching the profitability of gun production, and the company was deeply in debt from the borrowing it had done to finance its massive, almost overnight, growth during World War I.

When the Great Depression intervened, Winchester went into receivership and the Olin family entered the picture. Western Cartridge, owned by Franklin Olin, acquired it at a bankruptcy auction on December 22, 1931, and, in 1935, formed the Winchester-Western Company. His son John became First Vice President of Winchester-Western and head of the Winchester Division. The Olin family quickly returned the Winchester company to its original mission, the production of arms and ammunition. According to a report on the number of employees in "New Haven's Manufactories and Mechanical Establishments in 1936 and 1937," the plant had 3100 workers, 2,015 men and 1,085 women, as of 1936. Apparently even during the Great Depression, munitions production remained somewhat profitable. When Olin reorganized its many businesses in 1944 to form a new corporate "parent," New Haven's gun factory became the "Winchester-Western Division of Olin Industries."[18]

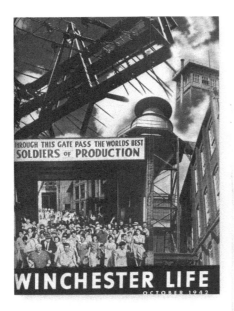

All images from Winchester Life, *1942-1944.*

WORLD WAR II: UNPRECEDENTED EXPANSION

Between 1939 and 1945, Winchester went into high gear once again to meet production demands as the U.S. prepared for and then fought the next war. Employment at the New Haven plant reached an all-time high of more than 20,000 during World War II.

> ## "I finished guns for President Roosevelt, President DeGaulle, and mostly all the presidents and prime ministers that came to Washington. I was the one they'd always come to, to finish the gun."

LAWRENCE YOUNG

Born in Eatonville, Arkansas, one of 9 children. His father worked in a saw mill and was his role model. But he had to leave school at 16 to help support the family, so his father got him a job at the mill. He contacted the local branch of the Civilian Conservation Corps, which President Franklin Delano Roosevelt had started to help create jobs to stimulate recovery from the Great Depression. The pay was $36 a month and his father got $30 of it. "But I got $6!"

When the U.S. entered World War II in 1942 he was too young to go into the military, so he enrolled in the National Youth Administration and was sent to a large trade school in Little Rock along with some friends.

"We had to go to school at night because the white boys went to school during the day."

Four of the six friends completed school and were sent to another trade school in Unionville, Ct. He was sent to interview at a factory in New Britain but the opening was for a machinist; he was a woodworker, and he didn't take the job. He and his cousin were then taken to Winchester in New Haven.

"We were the first two [Blacks] ever hired in the woodwork department at Winchester." There was a lot of prejudice against them as skilled black workers. Skilled white workers did not want to teach them how to do any of the work.

It didn't matter: "I already knew how to do it."

Shortly after he was hired, in 1943, he went into the military. He was stationed in Southampton, England during the German bombing, prior to the allied invasion, then was part of the supply line following the invasion force.

There was a lot of racism in the military: "They always told us we were second class citizens. But I didn't feel that way."

After the war, "No one welcomed the Black troops back to the South. I didn't really have anything to look forward to [except] going back to my job in Connecticut." Returning to Winchester, he was proud to see that he was on the honor roll of employees who had served in the war, prominently displayed on the side of the building.

He worked at Winchester for 43 years and was never laid off.

On the differences (and similarities) between life in the South and life in Connecticut: "It was like night and day. In the South, we were afraid all the time. They could hang you."

By contrast, "when I started at Winchester, I was free to sit where I wanted and I was making good money. But you always had to do more than anyone else to do the job, because I am Black."

Whites didn't want Blacks making more money than they did. And, indeed, "Winchester was segregated...but it was better than where I came from. As long as I stayed in my place, it was alright."

How did you feel about the work you did at Winchester?: "I felt good because it was something I wanted to do. I followed my dream [to be a woodworker.] I was making 60 cents an hour. Where I came from, you made a dollar a week. I liked wood working."

While most of Winchester's African American employees did the "dirtiest" and lowest paying of jobs, including cleaning the machines and sweeping the floors, Mr. Young as a skilled wood worker held one of the highest paying jobs.

"When I started...I did all the work by hand. I worked on the most expensive stocks at Winchester... I finished guns for President Roosevelt, President DeGaulle, and mostly all the presidents and prime ministers that came to Washington. I was the one they'd always come to, to finish the gun."

"Later on, after automation set in, we all did piece work."

Even during the war, there was still time for a little fun. The Winchester "Victory Playhouse" produced "Abie's Irish Rose" in 1943, with a cast and crew of Winchester workers. And the Winchester Repeating Arms Softball Team "remained undefeated" in the Y.M.C.A. Industrial Competition.

The struggle to construct sense and meaning from the loss of so many lives as the war neared its end took many forms, at Winchester as throughout the country.

Images from Winchester Life, *1942-1943.*

ABIE'S IRISH ROSE . . . One of the finest performances ever held in the Winchester Victory Playhouse was presented on the afternoon and evening of April 1, 1943 by the Victory Players before an audience that packed the theatre to capacity and turned away more than 300 eager patrons at the door. The successful laugh-comedy was expertly directed by Marion Conway, Winchester Female Counsellor. Settings were by Fred McKerness.

The cast did a splendid piece of work in interpreting their difficult parts and their excellent acting made for a most enjoyable evening. Those taking part in the play were: Sydney "Golly" Goluboff, Terrence O'Donnell, Viola Roberti, John Pleines, Sarah Leventhal, Joseph St. Clair, Frank Gargiulo, George Chapman, Billie LaVorgna, Mary Barney, Mickey Pickard, Katherine Thornton and Florence Nelson.

All images below and on opposite page are from Winchester Life, *1944-1945.*

THE W.R.A. SOFTBALL TEAM . . . Undefeated in the Y.M.C.A. Industrial league competition. All decked out in new uniforms, the squad includes: Front row, left to right: Nick DeStefano, Mgr.; Tony Assenzia, Frank Proto, Frank Durso, James Barry, Ed Twohill and John Kolago. Back row, left to right: James Camp, Ken Olsen, Mike Cantarella, "Tut" DeFrancesco, Joe DeAngelis, William Mahon, Vic Bialecki, and Coach Mickey Dolan.

OVER $200,000 CONTRIBUTED BY EMPLOYEES TO WINCHESTER WAR MEMORIAL HOSPITAL FUND

Employees' Committee Hope To Equal $250,000 Contribution By Company

The loyal workers of Winchester ended their 10-day plant-wide campaign for funds for the proposed Winchester War Memorial Hospital Fund with an overwhelming subscription totaling more than $200,000. The campaign has been so successful that the Employee Committee predict that the Hospital War Memorial Fund will equal or better the company's previous contribution of $250,000 through donations by employees who as yet have not had an opportunity to make out their pledges.

Herbert A. Smith and Lawrence E. Dickovick, Co-Chairmen of the Winchester War Memorial Hospital Campaign, were extremely pleased with the final results and credited the success of the drive to the 300 or more Division and Department Chairmen and to the ever ready generosity of our employees to all worthwhile community projects.

In a joint statement issued when the final returns were in they said: "We are all gratified that our fellow-workers have again accomplished one of their typical championship jobs. It certainly is an outstanding accomplishment when some 300 hard working men and women can organize and present this plan to our thousands of loyal workers and achieve such success in the short space of 10 days. We have had a great many drives for worthy causes during the war in this busy plant, but we believe that this one tops them all and indicates a full appreciation by our fellow-workers of the importance of adequate hospital accommodations and the seriousness of the community's lack of such essential facilities."

"We want to thank each and every loyal Winchester worker," the statement continued, "for the splendid spirit of co-operation and for their heart-warming generosity. All of New Haven will long remember your magnificent gift."

Works Manager Thomas I. S. Boak, who is serving as Chairman of the Grace-New Haven Building Fund Committee, was very gratified with the work of the Employees' Committee and the fine response by our workers. Mr. Boak said, "Once again our Winchester workers have proved their loyalty and demonstrated their unselfish willingness to co-operate in worthwhile community efforts. To have the large sum donated by the company almost equaled and perhaps surpassed by our employees' contributions is an outstanding example of civic spirit. I want to thank the Committee and Department Chairmen for their fine planning and work and all employees who so generously contributed. It was a worthy task and was well done. I am proud of you all."

Christmas at Winchester

THREE years ago this month, this great, peace-loving nation of ours was catapulted into a terrible World War by the dastardly attack on Pearl Harbor by the madmen of Nippon.

We here at Winchester have done everything in our power to supply our fighting-men with arms and ammunition to defend our shores and to drive back the hordes of invaders from the free lands they had plundered.

Christmastide, 1944 finds our fighting-men still locked in a desperate struggle with these merciless tyrants, and we on the home front striving with every means at our command to keep the wheels of production turning and the badly needed supplies rolling to the fighting fronts.

In the midst of all this blood, sweat and tears, it is hard for us to catch the wonderful, happy spirit of the Christmases we once knew.

Our thoughts, naturally, are continually with our loved ones, who are serving in the Armed Forces all over this war-torn world. Hardly an hour goes by without a hopeful thought for their welfare and a silent prayer for their safe return.

My fervent and sincere Christmas wish to our 3,350 fellow-employees in the services and to all our Winchester family here at home, is that when the spirit of Christmas falls next year over the world, Peace will reign in the hearts of all men and nations and all our families will be reunited with their loved ones.

Let us look forward to a Happy and Victorious New Year!

Thomas I. S. Boak
Works Manager

MRS. ANNA COSSABOOM—DK1F
5 Sons in Service

MRS. ANNA WALEKEWIC—DK1G
3 Sons in Service. One Killed in Action—One Wounded

MRS. CLAIRE M. GOODWIN—ATM
3 Sons in Service

WINCHESTER WAR MOTHERS

Winchester is proud of the many hundreds of mothers of servicemen who each day take their places on our busy production lines and help turn out vital guns and ammunition for our fighting-men.

May 13th has been set aside as Mother's Day, but we feel that EVERY DAY is Mother's Day in this great Winchester arsenal because of the magnificent job our War Mothers are doing.

We honor their indomitable courage, their patience and the many sacrifices they are making in order to help their loved ones, on far away battle fields, receive the vital munitions that may save the lives of countless American boys and bring them safely home.

MRS. ELLEN EUREKA—DK7F
3 Sons in Service

MRS. RITA CARR—DK7F
3 Sons in Service

MRS. MARGARET GEMMELL—BFE
4 Sons in Service

MRS. FLORENCE GALE—DG1R
4 Sons in Service

Winchester Honor Roll

Number of Winchester Employees Now Serving in the Armed Forces

3,270

19 former fellow-workers have died while serving their country in the Armed Forces. 12 are either missing in action or prisoners of war.

John A. Behuniak	ANN
Joseph A. Bernardini	ATF
Richard E. Bieltz	ATG
James W. Biondi	BFE
Ellis G. Bradley, Jr.	ANF
James H. Brooks	DBA
Byron C. Brown	ATM
Erminio S. Cassella	DK3F
William C. Coutts	ATM
Salvatore D'Auria	DK1G
David D. Dinwoodie	ATF
Walter J. Martin	DK1B
Marie T. Fazekas	DG2P
Robert P. Funaro	DLB
Stanley L. Gricsing, Jr.	ATF
James J. Griffiths	DGB
Norman Hakanson	ATG
Victor H. Harelle	DB2M
Alfred Hutton	ATG
Stephen S. Jedyank	ATF
Franklyn Jones	DK1F
Richard C. Joy	ATP
Michael Kakalow	ATP
Lawrence LaPan, Jr.	DB1M
Antonio LaVorgna	DG2B
Walter J. Martin	DLB
Joseph P. McHugh	ATM
Dorothy P. McKiernan	DK1B
Leslie C. Mercer	ATG
George Merwin	ATG
Donnell J. Molloy	ANE
John E. Monahan	ATM
Girardo Morrandino	DLL
Eldred C. O'Banks	DK2M
William J. Perrone	DK1B
Francis J. Pfnausch	ATF
William H. Pleines	ATD
Andrew Rizzo	DK1B
Richard Robinson, Jr.	DG1A
Emery E. Schmittgall	DB2M
Vito A. Sgro	DLB
Morris VanEs	DG2B
Nicholas J. Vischio	DG2B
Mary L. Wilson	DK1F

ANNEAL & WASH

Have you seen Jack Charonan, the turtle collector, sporting a new crop of red hair? Eddie Hohn paid us a visit the other day. He just finished Boot training at Sampson, N. Y.

"Chic" Heaphy was home for a visit recently also. He's a member of the Sea Bees. Bill Dwyer looks in the pink after being laid up for a few weeks. Glad to see you back, Bill.

Have you heard of that new outfit called "The Curbstone Brigade"? Al Clemente is the first bona fide member.

We hear Pat Dianni's son, Walter, is entering Yale this fall. Good luck, Walt.

How to break a window with one's fist? See George Dyson, instructor.

We hear S/gt. Billy Quitman is now stationed in the Hawaiian Islands.

OUR HONORED DEAD

Winchester Employees Throng Victory Square to Pay Homage to Valiant Dead

MEMORIAL Day, May 30, 1944, will long be remembered by our thousands of Winchester workers who gathered during their noon hour in the plant's Victory Square to take part in an impressive and reverent ceremony conducted by the Winchester Ex-Servicemen's Association. The exercises were under the direction of Past Commander Ellis Bradley and consisted of a colorful parade composed of our Plant Protection armed guards, John Brennan, drill master; the Winchester Band, Warren Sprague, leader; colors and color guard and members of the Winchester Ex-Servicemen's Association, Henry Lynch commanding. Reviewing the parade were the families of Winchester boys lost in this war; members of the Winchester Women's Service Unit and invited guests from the armed forces and officials of the factory.

Following the parade a short speaking program was conducted under the direction of Chairman E. A. Wall. Past Commander Ellis Bradley opened the speaking program with a stirring oration. Thomas I. S. Boak, Works Manager, then delivered the principal address and pointed out that this Memorial Day held a deeper significance for us all as many of our boys were about to face death in a titanic struggle with our enemies.

Prayer was then offered by Chaplain George P. Chapman, while a quartette composed of Ronnie Cargill, Victor Valente, James Mitchell and Lewis Knaut sang "Lead Kindly Light." The roll of our Winchester Honored dead was then called while a flower was placed in a wreath at the base of the monument that stood in the center of Victory Square, upon which were the names of the 19 Winchester young men who have given their lives for their country.

The speakers' stand and the imposing monument were created by Artist Fred McKerness, and were masterpieces of artistry.

The ceremonies were concluded with the playing of Taps, followed by the singing of the National Anthem by Fred Tatten as "Old Glory" was raised from half mast to the top of the flagpole over the main office.

Our workers received fervent inspiration from these ceremonies and returned to their work benches and machines with renewed determination to produce more and more supplies for our gallant and heroic fighting men.

We have resolved that those who have died here have not died in vain.

19

IN MEMORIAM
1882—Franklin Delano Roosevelt—1945

Program of solemn exercises in commemoration of the death of President Franklin Delano Roosevelt held in Victory Square at high noon, Saturday, April 14, 1945, by the employees and officials of the Winchester Repeating Arms Co. in New Haven, Conn., Division of Olin Industries, Inc.

Scott Buckley, Master of Ceremonies   Winchester Band directed by Warren Sprague
Mixed Chorus directed by Lewis Knaut and May Bradley Kelsey Ball
Taps sounded by Albert Miller
Prayer by Winchester Ex-Servicemen's Chaplain, George P. Chapman
National Anthem sung by Antoinette Civitelli
Tribute by Works Manager Thomas I. S. Boak
Color Guard—Ex-Servicemen's Association, Women's Service Unit, Plant Protection Unit
Speakers' Stand Decorations by Fred McKerness

This excellent photograph may be framed for use in your home if you so desire. Photo by Harris and Ewing.

All images are from Winchester Life, 1944-1945

A memorial gathering for President Franklin D. Roosevelt, who passed away several months before the war ended, was held outside the Winchester plant on April 14, 1945. Works Manager Thomas I.S. Boak, an intractable foe of unions or any form of worker organization, addressed the crowd in "Victory Square" with words of high praise for the man behind the New Deal, who had signed the National Labor Relations Act which created the National Labor Relations Board, and who had stated at the San Diego Exposition of 1935, "It is now beyond partisan controversy that it is a fundamental individual right of a worker to associate himself with other workers and to bargain collectively with his employer."[19] The NLRB was called upon several times by the United Electrical Workers in the 1940s to play a role in Winchester's labor struggles, including Boak's heavy-handed lock-out of 200 of his employees in 1946, as well as in later years. (See Chapters 4 and 5.)

Part of the huge assembly that filled Victory Square during the memorial exercises. Works Manager Thomas I. S. Boak is shown on the platform and in the insert as he paid high tribute to our late President, Franklin D. Roosevelt.

Winchester Safety Council Outing, 1945. Photograph courtesy of Maryann Davies.

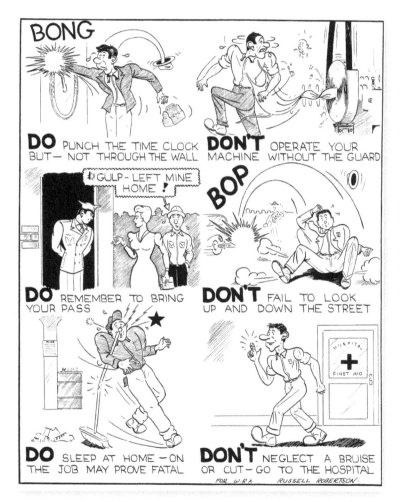

Image from Winchester Life, *1945*

Winchester Workers at McDermott's Tavern. Photograph courtesy Suzanne Cooney. She wrote: "Day and evening shifts had their meals at McDermott's... In the back room of the bar there was a kitchen. Meals were prepared there by Rose [McDermott], with the help of employees, many of whom lived in the neighborhood...On Friday, paychecks were cashed at the McDermotts'. The per check cashing charge was 10 cents. Peter's son-in-law, James P. Cooney, helped with check cashing on the evening shift...Peter ran the tavern from about 1911 until 1951... The business was then bought by Ed Blakeslee and ran for several years as Blakeslee's tavern."

UE NEWS

NEW HAVEN EDITION

UERMWA-CIO   9   69 CONGRESS AVE.   SATURDAY, JULY 18, 1942   Telephone 8-5071

BUY DEFENSE STAMPS BONDS

KEEP 'EM FLYING

THIS IS THE TIME

Today our fellow workers and buddies are stationed throughout the world, fighting shoulder to shoulder with the Armed Forces of the United Nations in a life and death fight against the Rome-Berlin-Tokio Axis to decide whether we shall live as free men and women or become the slaves of a Hitler dictatorship and its Quislings.

Not a man or woman in our country, whatever the color of his skin, his religion or his creed, can say today: "This war is none of my business." This war is everyone's business because Hitler's brutality has made it so.

We in the UE-CIO have recognized this for many months. And we have recognized also that the Axis CAN BE LICKED THIS YEAR, if we mobilize our forces and STRIKE NOW WITH A SECOND FRONT IN EUROPE. By taking the offensive NOW we can force the Axis to its knees and make it yell "Uncle."

Every day the Government of our nation, and the American people are recognizing more and more that ORGANIZED LABOR IN America has done, and is now doing a tremendous job in mobilizing and equipping our country to win the war. Now, with the need for an offensive against the Axis so pressing and so important for our whole future, our responsibility is even greater, and there is no doubt that organized labor stands ready to PRODUCE, PRODUCE AND PRODUCE, WORK, WORK, WORK, to smash the Axis in 1942.

WHY JOIN NOW?

Many workers ask the question: "Why should I join the UE now? With the war on, can't we all just glue our noses to our machines and work and produce? Organizing a union might hold up production . . . this isn't the time to organize."

The answer to that question is: IT IS JUST BECAUSE OF THE WAR THAT IT IS MORE IMPORTANT TO JOIN THE UE-CIO TODAY THAN IT HAS EVER BEEN BEFORE.

It's true that anything might hold up production today is harmful to our war effort, and to the whole future of the workers of America. That's exactly why our union has pledged that it will set aside its right to strike for the duration . . . and the UE-CIO has kept that promise, and will continue to keep it. Yet we know that in many open shop plants, like Winchester's and High Standard, stoppages of work has occurred! Why? Because the open shop methods of these companies, their cutting of piece rates, their complete inability to give the workers security on the job, and their failure to give the workers a workable way of settling their grievances have forced the workers to use the only weapon left to them to settle those grievances.... to stop work.

WHILE YOU ARE IN AN OPEN SHOP, STOPPAGES OF WAR WORK ARE LIKELY TO OCCUR ANY DAY IN THE WEEK. IT IS ONLY THROUGH A UNION LIKE THE UE-CIO THAT YOU CAN FIND A PEACEFUL WAY OF SETTLING YOUR GRIEVANCES WITHOUT LOSS OF PRODUCTION.

SO YOU'RE OFF TO THE ARMY?

Other workers tell us: "The UE-CIO is a good outfit if you're working in the plant, but I'll be off to the Army in a few months so what difference does the union make to me?"

Our answer to that one is: THE UE-CIO IS JUST AS IMPORTANT TO THE BOYS IN THE FRONT LINES AS IT IS TO THE WORKERS ON THE PRODUCTION LINES! THE MAN BEHIND THE MAN WHO TOTES A GUN IS ESSENTIAL TO VICTORY!

When you're at the Front, you'll need plenty of guns to "Give the Jerks the Works."

Workers who are members of the UE-CIO, in plants under contract with us, have been cited time and again for excellence in production. Production schedules in UE plants have gone way over the top. Why? First of all, because these workers have maintained a standard of living which keeps their morale high and their health good. Through their union they have been able to settle their grievances peacefully, without worry, without fear, and without loss of time.

Secondly, they have been able to pool their knowledge, experience and training to improve production in thousands of ways, with the confidence that their managements couldn't take advantage of these suggestions to cut rates and deprive them of their just earnings.

As an unorganized worker, YOU CAN NOT DO EITHER OF THESE THINGS. BUT AN ORGANIZED PLANT CAN CLEAN UP THE PRODUCTION PICTURE AND GUARANTEE MAXIMUM EFFICIENCY TO GET OUT THE GOODS AND KEEP 'EM ROLLING!

HOW ABOUT WAGES?

Many times a worker will ask: "I understand that the Government has frozen wages. How can the union do anything about my wages and living standards, especially since you people have set aside the right to strike?"

First of all, it is not true that wages have been frozen by the Government. The appeasers and enemies of national unity in America have tried to do everything they could to hog-tie labor, freeze wages, and put the whole burden of the cost of the war on the back of the workers.

In opposition to the appeaser's program, Pres. Roosevelt has proposed a 7-point program of price control, to spread the cost of the war on the principle of EQUALITY OF SACRIFICE, to stop profiteering on rent, food and other essentials, and to STABILIZE wages . . . not freeze them.

The Government has provided us with Governmental agencies, ON WHICH SIT REPRESENTATIVES OF ORGANIZED LABOR, to adjust wages and other disputes peaceably, to correct inequalities in wages, and help labor to bring up substandard wages. THE PRESIDENT OF THE UERMWA-CIO, ALBERT FITZGERALD, IS A MEMBER OF ONE OF THESE BOARDS. In other words, through the efforts of a big, established union like the UE-CIO you have the guarantee that your case will be given real consideration, and you have the ONLY POSSIBILITY OPEN TO YOU of adjusting your wages and working conditions so as to provide you with AN AMERICAN STANDARD OF LIVING.

ORGANIZED LABOR GOES TO WASHINGTON

This program as outlined by Pres. Roosevelt has, in most of its important points, been fought for by organized labor for many months, and IT MEANS YOUR BREAD AND BUTTER.

Fifth Columnists in our country are trying to break that program into bits, and substitute for it a program of squeezing the last drop out of the hides of the workers to pay for war, freezing wages, and tying labor hand and foot to keep us from making our contribution to the war.

THESE FIFTH COLUMNISTS HAVE BEEN FOUGHT SUCCESSFULLY SO FAR, MAINLY BECAUSE OF THE STRENGTH OF ORGANIZED LABOR. No unorganized worker can do anything effective to stop this drive. Yet if this drive is successful, every worker in America will suffer untold hardships, and the war will be lost.

It is ONLY THROUGH YOUR NATIONAL UNION, AND THROUGH THE ORGANIZED LABOR MOVEMENT, THAT YOU CAN FIGHT FOR THE DEFENSE OF YOUR RIGHTS AND YOUR COUNTRY IN WASHINGTON AND YOUR OWN COMMUNITY.

Pres. Roosevelt has recognized the importance of organized labor. Gen. MacArthur has recognized the importance of organized labor. And 41,353 new members of the UE-CIO who came into our union in the last three months—the largest number to come into our union in a three month period—have recognized the importance of organized labor. MORE THAN TEN MILLION ORGANIZED WORKERS IN THE U. S. A. CAN'T BE WRONG!

JOIN THE UE-CIO TODAY!!

4

NO UNION HERE

Beginning in 1941, buoyed by their success at other plants in the area and the increased demand for labor to produce armaments, the United Electrical Radio and Machine Workers of America (UER & MWA) began an organizing campaign at Winchester that, while ultimately unsuccessful, led to some dramatic moments and arguably paved the way for the victory of the International Association of Machinists, still some fifteen years away.

In May 1941, the 6,000 workers at Connecticut's other major producer of guns, Colt Firearms of Hartford, voted for union representation for the "first time in its 100-year history," according to *UE News*. In August, by a vote of seven to one, the United Electrical Workers handily defeated "a company-dominated organization" known as Independent Armscraft in an election conducted by the National Labor Relations Board. *UE News* explained that this meant UE was now "the sole collective bargaining agent for the arms, plastics and electrical divisions of the company," and called it the "second largest election to have been conducted by the NLRB in New England.[20]

Armed with news of this victory, UE stepped up its campaign at Winchester that spring, announcing that "10,000 employees of the famous Winchester Arms Company of New Haven are rapidly coming to the conclusion that for them the UE is more trustworthy than Winchester," and that "departmental and group meetings are being held throughout the plant and union committeemen are being chosen for those meetings in preparation for the organization of a functioning UE local in the plant." The newsletter article discussed Winchester workers' grievances and demands:

> Main grievance among the many that Winchester workers have centers about rates of pay, which are distinctly low... Winchester workers are already formulating demands for presentation to the company upon the completing of

their organizing job. They want time and a half for overtime after eight hours. It is not paid now, even Sunday work is being paid on straight time if it comes within 40 hours in one week. They want double time for Sundays and holidays and time and a half for Saturday work. They want 10% extra for the second shift and 15% for the third. They also want a new system of calculating pay, so that they can know from day to day what their wages will be. They can't tell now. They are also demanding an adjustment of day and piece rates so that people will be able to make out with normal effort. A particular grievance is that day work rates are way out of line with piece work-rates. To prevent accidents, now too common in the speed-up plant, workers are demanding safety measures. They also demand equal pay for equal work, a 50-cent minimum for girls and a 60-cent minimum for men, a 10 cent an hour wage increase and the day rate to be paid to piece workers for all lost time due to machine down.[21]

UE's initial optimism that the task of organizing Winchester workers could be accomplished in short order is evident in its response to the company's assertion that bullet-making "'is a natural woman's job.'" Apparently, the Connecticut governor, Robert A. Hurley, had lifted a ban on night work for women at the plant, but UE asserted that it would "soon be able to convince the company that night work for women and low pay for all the employees are not only not natural but definitely against good trade union policy."[22]

Other UE victories in Connecticut followed in July, 1941, when members of Unity Lodge 251 won a 10 cent per hour wage increase at a division of Pratt & Whitney Aircraft in West Hartford, and in New Haven at the Sargent Company, where workers voted for UE representation in December.[23]

Despite the victories won by labor during the buildup to U.S. entry into World War II and after, UE's progress at Winchester was rocky.

Despite the victories won by labor during the buildup to U.S. entry into World War II and after, UE's progress at Winchester was rocky. After the December 7, 1941 Japanese bombing of Pearl Harbor and the nearly unanimous Congressional declaration of war on Japan the next day, union organizers across the country used patriotic sentiment to advance their cause, arguing that war production would suffer if workers' conditions were not improved.

Michael Jimenez, a UE International Field Organizer working out of an office on Congress Avenue in New Haven, sent an undated letter on the Winchester Organizing Committee letterhead to various city organizations. It conveyed the sense of war urgency that the union consistently used to try to win public opinion to its side. Offering to send a speaker "to your next meeting," it asserted that "every citizen should be interested in the UE's campaign in Winchester," since "every family in New Haven wants to see Winchester produce more and more to insure their sons the necessary weapons to achieve victory over the Axis." The call by the President and Donald Wilson, War Production Chief, for increased output required that "the workers on the production lines must have the wages and working conditions on their jobs that will enable them to do their best" and "these workers must be protected against the rising cost of living." But "winning these gains and assuring the conditions that will guarantee more arms from Winchester for the battlefront depends on a disciplined and collective effort. Organization through a strong union like the United Electrical Radio and Machine Workers of America, CIO, can achieve this goal."[24]

Black workers were largely ignored or even discriminated against by mainstream labor organizers for more than half of the 20th century.

As the interviews with Lawrence Young (see Chapter 3), Westley McElya (see Sidebar, Chapter 4), Emmanuel Gomez (see Chapter 9) and others make clear, throughout the company's 20th century history, black workers faced discrimination no matter what their level of skill, and were usually given the dirtiest and lowest-paying jobs. While these interviews are specific to the experience at Winchester, such issues were by no means unique to that plant. In addition, black workers were largely ignored or even discriminated against by mainstream labor organizers for more than half of the 20th century. But at the start of U.S. engagement in World War II, they also became important to war production, and thus labor unions began, albeit tentatively, to advance their cause. Like other unions, UE now found it expedient to challenge racial discrimination.[25]

As part of the Winchester campaign, UE organizer Jimenez and Shop Steward Neil Scott reported on discrimination by plant management against black applicants for employment and black workers once hired. They charged that assurances given by Works Manager Boak to a Connecticut representative who appealed to the company to end any racial discrimination in its hiring practices had "grossly misrepresented actual conditions at the plant." Instead, there were at least nine points of discrimination to be found against "Negroes" [sic] in hiring and in working conditions there:

1. At the Winchester employment office, the Negroes are segregated and forced to wait out in the cold until all other applicants are interviewed.

2. Skilled Negro applicants are not hired according to qualifications and references like other skilled workers, the policy being that all Negroes can only be hired as common laborers.

3. 99% of the Negro employees are doing laborer's work in spite of their ability to do other work.

4. Negroes are employed only for the heaviest and unhealthiest jobs at lower rates than other workers.

5. The few that are on machines and semi-skilled jobs have been given the jobs that require a maximum of physical exertion. In these cases, Negroes are paid lower rates than others doing the same work.

6. Negroes are not given the opportunity of job training in the Winchester apprenticeship plan on an equal basis with other workers.

7. There is no Negro representation on the Winchester Employee's Representation Plan, though some Negroes have been in the service of the firm for the last 37 years.

8. The company has permitted use of company bulletin boards for the posting of printed matter which was intended to incite racial hatred.

9. In spite of the high merits and capability recognized by the firm in some Negro employees, none has ever been appointed to a foreman's position in the plant.[26]

Employee efforts on behalf of UE met with vicious company resistance, led by Works Manager Boak, and UE argued that this resistance was impeding war production. The March 21, 1942 edition of *UE News* reported that the UE Organizing Committee had sent a letter to President Roosevelt stating that the company's refusal to bargain was hampering production of the Garand rifle, and thus, the war effort. The letter told FDR that the Winchester plant was evincing an "unpatriotic attitude" and cited "ten departmental work stoppages, slow-downs and sit-down strikes" among "workers in the New Haven plant, totaling 15,000" in 1941 that resulted from "management inefficiency and profiteering." It argued that "every one of these disputes affected our national defense program…" Having conducted "a survey of conditions in the plant, we found that in spite of your repeated pleas for increased production, the Winchester Repeating Arms Company has and is hampering our war effort by shattering the morale of the workers by consistent union busting efforts." In addition, it was operating "major parts of plant facilities on a one shift basis, e.g. in the Garand Rifle Department, in which production is at 60% efficiency." The letter also asserted that "from the time the Winchester workers began joining UER & MWA the management has interfered, coerced, intimidated and fired workers in violation of the National Labor Relations Act." Finally, it urged the President to "have someone sent here to investigate the situation."[27]

> In addition, it was operating "major parts of plant facilities on a one shift basis, e.g. in the Garand Rifle Department, in which production is at 60% efficiency."

At least one case of workers discharged because of their union advocacy was brought before the NLRB in 1942. At a hearing in New Haven held between March 28th and April 2nd, the Board in a preliminary report found that three workers, Michael Amato, Charles Thompson and Ernest A. Cruz, had been fired for just that reason, and, in Amato's case, that the company had also blacklisted him, making it impossible for him to gain employment elsewhere. A press release issued by the New Haven office and printed in *UE News* remarked that "this is one of the first cases where an official agency of the government has been led by the force of evidence to conclude that a Connecticut manufacturer is guilty of blacklisting," adding that Trial Examiner C.W. Whittemore had been "forced to express serious doubts as to the authenticity of certain evidence presented by the company, including sections of testimony presented by the Works Manager himself, T.I.S. Boak." The Board recommended that the company "cease and desist" from any form of discrimination or harassment to "discourage membership" in UE "or any other labor organization of its employees" and from any other "manner of interfering with, restraining or coercing its employees in the exercise of the right to self-organization, to form, join or assist labor organizations, to bargain collectively through representatives of their own choosing, and to engage in concerted activities for the purpose of collective bargaining or other mutual aid or protection as guaranteed in Section 7 of the National Labor Relations Act."[28]

U E NEWS

WINCHESTER EDITION

FOR DEFENSE BUY UNITED STATES SAVINGS BONDS AND STAMPS

UERMWA-CIO   9   69 CONGRESS AVE.   THURSDAY, MAY 28, 1942   Telephone 8-5071

GOOD NEWS FOR NEW HAVEN WORKERS!

WINCHESTER ARMS LOCAL 282

National Office Charters Local For Winchester

The meeting of the Winchester Stewards' Council which was held on May 26th hailed the announcement that as of May 19, 1942, the workers of Winchester have been granted a charter, setting up their own organization and local in the United Electrical, Radio and Machine Workers . . . the **Winchester Arms Local 282.**

According to enthusiastic reports coming from delegates from the major divisions of the plant, the establishment of this local has already been a big help in stepping up the organizing campaign.

The Stewards' Council then proceeded to elect temporary officers for the Local, until such time as a contract is signed with the management and a permanent organization is set up.

The officers who were elected were: President, George Short; Vice-Presidents, Owen Berio, Winston Stewart and James DiCaprio; Secretary-Treasurer, Cornelius Scott; Recording Secretary, Florence Fox; Members-at-Large to the Executive Board, George Houlihan, Joseph Weiss, Florence Alderman, Vahe Zorthian, Edgar Beauvais, Anthony Cocchiara

The meeting also was addressed by Field Organizer Michael Jimenez who spoke on the newest developments in the Winchester organizing campaign. As numerous grievances were brought out by various delegates, all active union members were urged to report these grievances in writing, and further to report every case of attempts by foremen to discriminate against union members, so that the union could take action through the proper authorities to stop them.

The Winchester Stewards' Council at this meeting went on record unanimously "in support of the rising demands of the American labor movement" for the opening of the Western Front. Stating that "failure at this time to emulate the examples of the heroic Red Army, the Chinese Army and our Allies" would be fatal to our cause, the resolution of which copies are being sent to Pres. Roosevelt and Governor Hurley, concludes "let the guns and munitions we're producing now go to work on Hitler for Victory in '42."

HI-STANDARD WORKERS JOINING UERMWA-CIO

The High Standard Organizing Committee, composed of High Standard workers, members of the United Electrical, Radio & Machine Workers of America, has reported very satisfactory progress in the organizational drive at both the Dixwell and Waterfront plants.

Key men in all departments are responsible for the signing up of application cards which are flowing into our UE office in a continuous stream.

There are many grievances which the High Standard employees are confronted with. They understand that organization of the majority of the High Standard employees must be attained in order to adjust these grievances properly. The United Electrical, Radio & Machine Workers of America, CIO, will carry out its program in High Standard for wages for an American standard of living, guaranteed piece work rates, equal pay for equal work, strict seniority, all out maximum production for Victory, and a union contract.

Many High Standard workers have expressed satisfaction for the UE-CIO, pointing out that being in a union with Winchester, Sargent and several other plants in the city is a guarantee in itself. All plants engaged in the manufacture of guns, munitions, etc., such as Colt's, Smith & Wesson, Remington, and Winchester, will be in the same union—the UE-CIO. This is where every High Standard worker belongs.

EVERY W. R. A. WORKER A UE-CIO MEMBER

Sargent Local Helps Lick Hitler

The Sargent Local 243 of the UE-CIO was one of the first union plants in New Haven to take a big step forward toward improving war production by setting up a joint Union-Management War Production Council in the Sargent plant this week.

The Council, which is composed of five union members and five management representatives, with an additional subcommittee of ten, met last Tuesday at the suggestion of the union, rolled up its sleeves and got to work.

One of the first problems the Council will face is the job of speeding up conversion from peace-time hardware products to war work.

Additional problems the Council will attempt to solve are improved methods of work, improved planning, better utilization of machinery, training and retraining, increased self-discipline, improved morale.

The Council will meet once a week to make additional suggestions, and check up on the plans already made.

State Representative To Speak At Gate

Rep. Nicholas Tomassetti of the Conn. State Assembly will address two shop gate meetings at the Winchester plant next week. The meetings are scheduled for the lunch periods at noon on Friday at Munson Street and Winchester Avenue.

Rep. Tomassetti who is one of the staunchest supporters of organized labor in the Conn. Assembly will speak on "How Winchester Can Do More To Beat Hitler."

POWER PLANT BOYS GIVE GOOD TIP

For the last three months many New Haveners have been wondering why the Winchester Plant is lit up at night in many departments where no work is being performed. The rumors are that it is done to give the impression that everything is going "full blast." But it really looks suspicious to look in the windows in Tracts A and B and see no one working at night and all the lights on. Your suggestion "AN ALL OUT EFFORT—All lights and power off, when not in use. Save and we shall not slave" is darned good.

Now let's hope something is really done about it.

EVERY W. R. A. WORKER A UE-CIO MEMBER

PRODUCE FOR VICTORY IN 1942!

RAISES ARE FINE - - - BUT WE'RE STILL JOINING THE UE

The few raises that have been handed out recently in various departments at Winchester have not had the effect desired by management. Obviously given out to discourage membership in the UE-CIO, the results have been the contrary. No one has been fooled and it won't work. While we welcome these wage increases, it is an insult to the intelligence of the Winchester workers for management to think that this is going to stop the union's successful drive.

Reports from all departments are that the interest in the union has increased instead of decreasing, because the workers are distrustful of any raises that are not guaranteed by a written contract. All workers know that these small raises cannot overshadow the fact that employees lack all the benefits provided for in a union contract.

The consistent flow of union applications into the office of the UE-CIO is continuing ever increasingly. The slogan to "Keep 'Em Signing" is a living reality.

UE - CIO PROGRAM

1. Wages for an American standard of living. 2. Guaranteed piece work rates. 3. Equal pay for equal work. 4. Strict Seniority. 5. All-out for maximum production to win the War. 6. A Union Contract.

It is apparent from later issues of the *UE News* and from correspondence that the company did not comply with the NLRB directive to reinstate the workers, although Michael Amato was elected unanimously as chairman of the Winchester Organizing Committee at its May 2, 1942 meeting. At the same meeting, the Committee also passed a resolution linking the national call for increased war production to the need for their union at Winchester. "The Winchester sub-standard wages," the Committee wrote, "constant cutting of piece work rates, and bad working conditions, and the resulting lack of unity and discipline among the workers" as well as "certain inefficiencies of management" served to "hinder good morale and top production." Since "we have seen that in organized plants workers are able to improve their experience and skill to greatly increase production, therefore,

> Be It Resolved: That we, the Winchester Organizing Committee of the United Electrical, Radio & Machine Workers of America, CIO, in order to best carry out the program and policies of President Roosevelt for Victory over Hitler in 1942, pledge ourselves to work untiringly to organize the workers of Winchester. United, we can win the means and incentive to produce, produce and produce for victory.

> Be It Further Resolved: That we will work to weld this organization of Winchester workers together with the millions in the CIO under the leadership of President Philip Murray, to carry on a powerful offensive for freedom and security for American workers and the entire American people."[29]

On May 19th, 1942, UE members at Winchester were granted a charter from the National Office as "Winchester Arms Local 282." At the Winchester Workers' Council on May 28th, the Stewards' Council "proceeded to elect temporary officers for the Local, until such time as a contract is signed with the management and a permanent organization is set up." The Council also "went on record" as unanimously supporting "'the rising demands of the American labor movement' for the opening of the Western Front. Stating that 'failure at this time to emulate the examples of the heroic Red Army, the Chinese Army and our Allies' would be fatal to our cause, the resolution, of which copies are being sent to Pres. Roosevelt and Governor Hurley, concludes 'let the guns and munitions we're now producing go to work on Hitler for Victory in '42.'" In June, the full membership "voted unanimously" to join the growing labor movement demand for a Second Front in Europe.[30]

The flurry of union activity at Winchester in May continued throughout the summer, with predictable company responses.

The *UE News-New Haven Edition* reported in June that the company had "pulled another trick out of the old bag to stop UE-CIO's successful campaign." The "trick," in the shape of "'new'" grievance machinery "'developed'" by Winchester "has not been done as the company contends 'in furthering the company's policy' but because the company has been under pressure from various sources on the UE-CIO's insistence." It asserted that "several Government officials have been to see the Winchester management…because we have demanded that the Winchester workers be provided with an adequate grievance machinery." In a separate story, the newsletter reported on a visit from State Representative Nicholas Tomassetti to the union's shop gate meeting, quoting him as urging workers who had not yet "signed up" to do so "in the interests of the nation as a whole…I, who have been fighting for the interests of the workers of this state, urge you to join the union, not only to help you to improve your condition, but also because I know that when you are organized, you can make a substantial contribution toward victory of our nation over Hitlerism."[31]

The UE claimed other victories that summer. When a company supervisor "violently assaulted" a UE Steward, for example, "a protest was sent to Mr. Boak charging him with being the instigator of [the] attack because he has encouraged and complacently given approval to all the anti-union acts which have been going on at the plant. In part the protest said: 'We hold YOU responsible for this bodily attack and demand Mr.Cassella be given immediate satisfaction by the immediate dismissal of the assailant.'" The article claimed that "two hours later, the supervisor was OUT."[32]

In July, the UE demanded, and got, the reinstatement of three workers that the company had fired for "sabotage." In fact they had, according to the union, "been arbitrarily dismissed for leading a fight to adjust piece work rates and maintain a good level of production." When the company made a proposal for a slight rate increase for piece work, workers at a department meeting had decided the proposed increase was inadequate. When the three leaders of the dissent were fired the day after the meeting, the UE sent wires to the NLRB and "other agencies and got action FAST. A final conference was called between the dismissed workers and the Company and resulted in the reinstatement of the workers."[33]

At the end of July, Boak cut out piece work rates entirely for workers in the Brass Rolling Mill (a job always known as one of the dirtiest and hardest in the plant), an action that led to a drastic reduction in pay, followed by a work stoppage on the 3-11 shift by workers who unsuccessfully demanded a pay raise. But at the same time, the Works Manager was "compelled" as a result of the "constant pressure" of the NLRB and the UE to post a plant-wide notice making it clear that its workers had every right to join a union if they chose. It quoted from the National Labor Relations Act, "which states, 'Employees shall have the right to self-organization, to form, join or assist labor organizations, to bargain collectively through representatives of their own choosing, and to engage in concerted activities for the purpose of collective bargaining or other mutual aid or protection.'

"It then goes on to state: 'The Western Cartridge Co., Winchester Division, recognizing the rights of its employees as set forth above, states that it:

"'1. WILL NOT IN ANY MANNER INTERFERE WITH, RESTRAIN OR COERCE ITS EMPLOYEES IN THE EXERCISE OF THESE RIGHTS.

"'2. WILL NOT DISCOURAGE MEMBERSHIP IN THE UNITED ELECTRICAL, RADIO & MACHINE WORKERS OF AMERICA, CIO… BY DISCHARGING OR THREATENING TO DISCHARGE ANY OF ITS EMPLOYEES FOR JOINING OR ASSISTING THE SAID UNION…

"'3. WILL NOT IN ANY OTHER WAY DISCRIMINATE AGAINST ANY OF ITS EMPLOYEES IN REGARD TO HIRE OR TENURE OR EMPLOYMENT OR ANY TERM OR CONDITION OF EMPLOYENT FOR JOINING OR ASSISTING THE SAID UNION…'"[34]

Make Yourself 500,000 Times Stronger---JOIN NOW
United Electrical Radio & Machine Workers of America
Affiliated with the Congress of Industrial Organizations

I hereby request and accept membership in the above named union, and authorize it to represent me, and in my behalf to negotiate and conclude all agreements as to hours of labor, wages, and all other conditions of employment.

Signature ....
Sign your name—Do not print

Address.. City........................

Employed by.. Dept................

Date.................... Occupation.................... Shift....................
(Fill out and return to UERMWA-CIO, 69 Congress Ave., New Haven)

This coupon appeared in every UE News-New Haven *edition published in the summer of 1942. The* UE News *ran special Winchester and New Haven editions during 1942 at the height of its organizing campaign.*

Boak apparently also responded to all the "pressure" by offering workers a 3% bonus, which was derided by the union as an "old, open shop tactic."[35]

On August 2, 1942 delegates representing "50,000 ordnance workers in UE shops in process of organization by the UE" met at the Hotel Garde in New Haven for a discussion of "common problems." In addition to the Winchester plant, delegates attending represented workers from Colt Patent Firearms Co., Smith and Wesson, A.S. Woods, A.S. Campbell, Remington Arms Company, Auto Ordnance, High Standard Manufacturing Company and United Shoe Machinery Company. The delegates passed a resolution stating their joint commitment to prosecuting the war effort, adding that "the UE is rapidly becoming the organization of the Small Arms Ordnance Workers of Connecticut. Thousands of these workers are joining the UE and seeking to establish their right to bargain collectively on wages, hours and conditions of employment." At this meeting and in the resolution, Winchester was singled out as being a

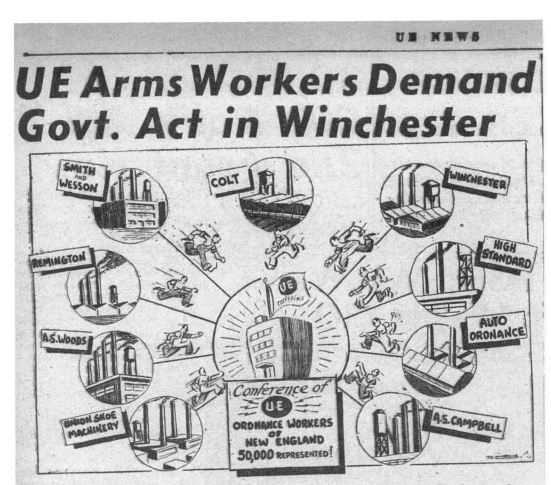

UE Arms Workers Demand Govt. Act in Winchester

NEW HAVEN, Conn., Aug. 10—Representatives of 50,000 New England ordnance workers in UE shops in process of organization by the UE met for the discussion of common problems at the Hotel Garde, in this city, recently.

Delegates attended from the Colt Patent Firearms Co., Smith & Wesson, A. S. Woods, A. S. Campbell, Winchester Repeating Arms Co., Remington Arms Co., Auto Ordance, High Standard Manufacturing Co., and United Shoe Machinery Co.

UE News Vol. 4 No. 33 (August 15, 1942), 4.

particularly recalcitrant employer, "following their old business as usual opposition to the self-organization of their workers." While UE had repeatedly tried to "bring order out of chaos" at the plant, and "to settle the grievances of the workers without stoppages," the company had "responded with the most complete and arbitrary rebuff." Moreover, "the UE-CIO has repeatedly called to the attention of the War Labor Board, the War Department and all other relevant government agencies the chaotic state of production and morale in the Winchester plant, but has to date been given no adequate consideration" by these agencies. The resolution "sharply criticized" this failure to act, and called on the War Labor Board to "immediately come into the picture and fulfill its duty…and to compel the Winchester Repeating Arms Company to practice patriotism and justice in its dealing with the Winchester workers."[36]

By the end of August, the company still hadn't complied with the NLRB order to reinstate the three workers dismissed the previous winter, despite being given a "final" NLRB order on August 16th, with a ten-day deadline. Instead, the Winchester management decided to take the case to Circuit Court. The union, meanwhile, had been trying to get the case "certified" to be taken to the War Labor Board. In a letter dated August 31st, Local 282 International Field Organizer Martin Hourihan appealed to "All Local Unions" to send wires to the Board and to the U.S. Conciliation Service in support of that goal, explaining, "the War Labor Board… would not consider certification while the National Labor Relations case was still pending. Now, however, because the final decision has come down, and the company refused to abide by it, we feel that we have a very good chance to have this case certified." The bigger issue which should motivate Locals to "take an active interest in this case" was that

> This company is one of the worst open shop concerns in New England, and it is our feeling that if we can break them, the entire CIO movement in Connecticut will make a great stride forward. Because of the company's attitude towards the union and towards the workers themselves, production is not within 40% of the potential of the shop. Due to the piece rate and bonus systems in force in the shop, the workers are afraid to make an all-out effort on war production. We all know that with a Union in the shop, that these bottlenecks can be overcome.[37]

In September of 1942, the Labor Department agreed to certify the case to the War Labor Board. A Winchester delegation, accompanied by delegates from Colt Firearms, Smith and Wesson and Auto Ordnance, all of whom had UE contracts, met with a panel of the WLB, which agreed to look into the "Winchester case." After the meeting, the War Department and the U.S. conciliation service sent investigators to New Haven.[38]

In January and February of 1943, the case status was twice reported as "ready for a directive order of the Board."[39] As of April 22, 1944, it was listed under "Status of UE cases in Washington," as one of four cases "awaiting compliance action."[40]

There is no further reference to Winchester in UE publications until the December 25th, 1944 issue of the *UE News National Edition*, which reported that the company still had not rehired Michael Amato, who was one of those fired back in 1942, and added that Thomas Boak had been issued a contempt of court citation: "Manager Thomas I.S. Boak, manager of the New Haven Plant of the Winchester Repeating Arms Company, was especially singled out in an order of the U.S. Circuit Court of Appeals, adjudging him, the Winchester Company, and the Western Cartridge Company, parent company of Winchester, to be in contempt of court:

It'll Take a Strong Union To End Winchester Tyranny

BULLETIN

NEW HAVEN, Dec. 3—Mayor William Celantano of New Haven recommended last night before a crowded meeting of the Board of Aldermen that a Committee of Five be set up to investigate the issues in the Winchester dispute.

Workers from the Winchester rolling mill, who have been locked out by the company for three months for protesting the firing of three union leaders, packed the meeting room and enthusiastically applauded the Mayor's recommendation. The Aldermen's Committee was set up at the meeting and announced it would begin soon to conduct hearings.

By BETTY GOLDSTEIN
UE NEWS Staff Writer

NEW HAVEN, Conn., Dec. 2—"The best Christmas present I could get would be for the company to settle. But we don't need any Santa Claus—we got to hit that picketline."

The stern-faced men that met at UE headquarters here Sunday morning in the third month of the lockout at the Winchester Repeating Arms Co. said "Amen" to that one. And went over their plans once more to throw an even tighter picketline around the huge plant that now stands as the largest fortress of the open shop left in New England.

Winchester locked its gates against the 440 rolling mill workers in September when they dared to protest the firing of three of their fellow workers whom they'd elected to a union committee to take up their grievances with the boss. But as I heard it from the Winchester workers that was merely the last chapter in the long, long story of the Winchester company's attempt to rule its workers as slaves under dictatorship rather than as citizens in a democracy.

NEVER HAD A SAY

The Winchester workers have never had anything to say about their working conditions, never had any way to get their grievances listened to. During the war the rolling mill workers literally worked both day and night, the same men both day shift and night shift, three and four weeks without any relief. These men believed wholeheartedly in the war, but no human being could stand such a load. They got together and elected a grievance committee to see Works Manager T. I. S. Boak about rotating shifts. Twice they came together to meet with management about this, and twice Mr. Boak didn't show up.

WORK OR GET OUT

The third time Boak came—and the men can still hear the insulting, deliberate sound of his voice when he said: "I'm running this shop, I do as I please. You can put your passes here and go home —or go back to work." The men went back to work, still working days and nights.

The rolling mill workers remember how once they decided they'd have to have more money. They went into the washroom and asked Boak down to hear their demands. Boak came and complimented them on their efforts in producing seven million pounds of brass a month, told them they shouldn't take time off from their machines this way, and that they shouldn't worry their work wasn't appreciated—weren't they getting their bonus from the foremen of a cigar and two cigarettes apiece every month?

"We laughed our heads off," Nick Bruno recalls.

"I said 'we can't feed our families on cigars and cigarettes.' But they wouldn't give us a raise. So I decided to join the union."

SAME FOR EVERYBODY

It was the same way for everybody. Felix Mastracchio drove a crane, and his eyes were being ruined. There was no ventilator or fan and all the smoke accumulated near the ceiling. "My pal Pete and I used to go up to the boss all the time and ask him about that ventilator, and he kept saying 'it's coming.' But that ventilator still hasn't been installed."

NAM TRICKS

"We work seven and eight days a week at one stretch, working over Saturday and Sunday, but we still get paid straight time as if we were on a 40 hour week," Louis Morton said: "I talked to the superintendent, and he told me if I didn't like it I could get a job somewhere else. And then we formed the committee, and he fired the three who went to speak for us. When we go back, we'll go back with the union."

The Winchester company knows all the tricks when it comes to trying to keep the workers from organizing a union. Its bosses are recognized for their ability along those lines. Boak, for instance, has been a director of the Natl. Assn. of Manufacturers. Maybe it was there he learned the trick that was tried in Winchester several years ago when an active union member was put down in a subcellar working in water up to his knees. (That union member had guts—he told them he wouldn't quit, they'd have to fire him if they wanted to get rid of him.)

The community of New Haven is on the side of the workers in the Winchester lockout, and backing up their demands that the company reinstate all the fired workers, including the three fired for union activity. From the AFL truck drivers and the railroad brotherhood members who won't drive material into the plant across the UE picketlines to the Yale professors, small business men and religious leaders who are forming a Citizens Committee, the attitude is pretty unanimous that Winchester's persecution of its workers is a blot on the whole community.

The Board of Aldermen of the city of New Haven has unanimously passed a resolution submitted by the union calling upon Mayor Celantano to intervene in the Winchester dispute. The court here refused to grant the Winchester company an injunction to prevent the workers from picketing. The State Unemployment Compensation Board has ruled that the Winchester workers must get unemployment insurance, holding that this was a "lockout" although the company tried to prove otherwise.

So far the company has refused to meet directly with the union, and has refused to take back the men it locked out without discrimination.

It takes a strong man and a convinced one to stand watch these cold days and nights at the many exists and entrances to the Winchester rolling mill which

"MY EYES BURNED all the time from the smoke," said Felix Mastracchio, crane driver at the Winchester rolling mill. "We kept asking them to put in a ventilator or a fan but nothing was done. They won't do anything for us until we have a union."

"SEVEN DAYS one week, eight another," is the way men worked at the Winchester mill, explains chief picket captain Louis Morton. "We'd work over Saturday and Sunday, but they still paid us straight time like on a 40-hour week. We need that union."

must be guarded to keep the company from bringing material in or out. The Winchester rolling mill workers are strong men and they are convinced from their own bitter experience of many years that the only way a man can live and work in decency with this company is with the strength of a union behind him.

A LEADER from the first days the workers began to organize at the Winchester plant, Nick Bruno, war veteran, remembers how they called him in the office to fire him, but said he could stay on if he "quit the union and took some of the boys with you."

"I GOT FIRED for fighting for my rights as an American citizen," said Angelo Conte, inspector. "If you took a grievance to a superintendent, that's the last you heard of it. So we organized."

LOCKED OUT BECAUSE THEY PROTESTED the firing of three of their fellow workers for union activity, the workers of the Winchester rolling mill in New Haven stand in solid ranks at the gates of the largest open shop fortress in New England. The Mayor, Board of Aldermen, civic and religious leaders are united in pressing the company to open these gates and end its last desperate attempt to keep the workers from organizing.

UE News Vol. 8 No. 49, December 7, 1946, 9.

Boak was ordered to reemploy Michael Amato, former Winchester employee fired because of UE activity at the plant. Boak's contempt of court consisted in his long refusal to obey an order of NLRB even though [UE] had been successful…in appeals taken right up to the U.S. Supreme Court. Western Cartridge, Winchester Arms, and 'in particular, Thomas I.S. Boak,' are ordered by the court to 'purge themselves of their contempt' within 10 days. Further refusal to comply can lead to a fine or a jail sentence.[41]

From this point on, the Winchester company dropped off UE's national map until October of 1946, when a report with the dateline "New Haven, October 14" described a series of events that UE Field Organizer Vincent Romeo, addressing a citizens' rally, called "the climax of a five-year attempt by [Works Manager Thomas I.] Boak to keep the workers from joining the union." The rally was called in response to a lockout by the company of rolling mill workers who protested the firing of three UE committeemen for unspecified "union activity." Civic, labor and religious leaders, including Congressman James P. Geelan, Clark Brown representing the Religion and Labor Foundation at Yale Divinity School, Allen Twitchell of the Independent Citizens Committee, CIO Regional Director Edward J. McCrone, Ralph Zingerella of Amalgamated Clothing Workers, and Dexey Wilkerson of the National Negro Congress "vigorously denounced" the lockout. And the Rev. Willard Uphaus, speaking on behalf of the "AFL Central Labor Union" (presumably the Central Labor Council of New Haven?) was paraphrased in the article stating, "No hard won labor victories in this area will be secure until this last fortress of anti-unionism falls."[42]

According to the article, "three weeks ago, the 440 Winchester rolling mill workers sent a committee of two vets and an old-timer to take up some grievances with [Boak]." These employees, about half of whom UE said were veterans of World War II, " get only straight time for Saturday and Sunday work, and have no grievance machinery except stooges appointed by Boak to take up complaints." Predictably, Boak refused to grant the committee an audience. The day shift protested with a 15-minute sit down after lunch, and Boak proceeded to fire the three men. Then, "when the next shift took it up with an eight-hour sit down, Boak locked the gates of the mill before the night shift could act. Solid UE picket lines now have the mill closed down tight against Winchester's refusal to reinstate the [fired workers.]"[43]

Winchester attempted to get an injunction against the continued picketing, but it was denied in Superior Court, possibly due to community protest. The company's action in initiating the lockout—and the workers' continued resistance–seems, according to UE, to have provoked strong community support for the workers. At a public meeting held at the African Methodist Episcopal Zion Church in early November of 1946, "the Negro

UE PICKETS mass at the huge Winchester Arms plant in New Haven where the rolling mill has been closed down three months by a company lockout because workers protested the firing of three men for union activity. This plant is in the process of organization.

See page 9 for story on how UE members have won the support of hundreds of New Haven citizens in the drive to end the long open shop reign at Winchester.

UE News *Vol. 8 No. 49, December 7, 1946, 9.*

[sic] community pledged its support to the union" and "the minister of the church spoke on the fight for Negro rights to jobs in Winchester...Other speakers at the UE-sponsored meeting represented the National Association for the Advancement of Colored People, the National Negro Congress, the Religion and Labor Foundation, the AFL Musicians Union, and UE International Representative Richard Linsley."[44]

At one of the New Haven community meetings (probably the one described above), a union organizer (probably Linsley or Field Organizer Vincent Romeo) outlined the issues that the UE had been dealing with at Winchester in its five-year campaign, putting the lockout in this larger context but also explaining the immediate actions that had provoked it. The union, this official told his audience, had been thwarted in its attempts to organize Winchester employees since 1941 by the company's continued "defiance of the laws of our country by discriminating against and spying upon its employees and [firing of] people at will for union activity...The National Labor Relations Board has found Winchester guilty of all of the above named unfair labor practices."[45] The UE organizer continued:

> The events which brought about this dispute occurred as a result of Mr. Boak's failure to listen to the just grievances of his employees in the Winchester Brass Rolling Mill. In the early part of this year a new work schedule was put into effect which required the men to work on Saturdays and Sundays for straight time pay. The men involved tried to avail themselves

of the so-called company grievance procedure for a period of months but the company... ignored their protests...

The overwhelming majority of these men, members of our union, the UE-CIO, held several meetings and decided to extend their lunch period for fifteen minutes and the men gathered that afternoon at 12:15 and the committee spokesmen tried to convince management to listen to their grievances. But Mr. Boak...refused to listen to their pleas and ignored them completely. That very same afternoon the three committee members from the 7-3 shift...were summoned to the company's offices and were fired. The second shift, 3-11... refused to work from lunch time until the end of their shift as a protest against these unjust dismissals. The complete third shift, 11-7, was not permitted to enter the plant. They found locked gates when they reported for work.

The following day, Sunday, the gates were still locked. On Monday men who reported for work were told that they could not enter through the usual gates but were instructed to report to the personnel office where their passes would be changed...

That same week, the company sent a letter to some employees stating that a new work schedule would be put into effect which would eliminate Sunday work and would pay time and one half for Saturdays which indicates that the company could have adjusted the grievances earlier and thus eliminated this dispute...

Furthermore, a score of other men were fired and they received releases stating that they had participated in an illegal work stoppage...

Our union has endeavored for the past twelve weeks to bring about a just settlement of this dispute and has called upon the U.S. Conciliation Service, the State Board of Mediation and Arbitration, church groups, citizens' groups and Mayor Celentano for a fair and just hearing. But in each and every instance Mr. Boak and the Winchester Company have refused to arbitrate these issues.[46]

The union official reminded his audience that "everybody in the community is affected by the kind of industrial relations that exist within that community...If good wages are paid, a better standard of living will exist in the community. Good wages mean decent homes, better health standards, less sickness and worry, more purchasing power and full employment." He declared that "Mr. Boak may control or advise the affairs of the National Association of Manufacturers, but he will never control the will of the people or deprive them of their fundamental freedoms. This is

WESTLEY MCELYA (1918–2004)

By Frank Annunziato

Photograph taken by Stanley Heller

This text is based on an interview conducted by Dr. Annunziato with Westley and Anita McElya in 1990. Annunziato was a co-founder with Nicholas Aiello of the Greater New Haven Labor History Association, and was its president at the time of this interview.

Westley (Wes) McElya was no labor agitator when Winchester hired him in 1941. He had just married and needed steady employment. Winchester's was the right place at the right time because on December 7, 1941, the Japanese empire attacked Pearl Harbor and the next day the United States entered World War II. Winchester, producer of "the gun that won the west," began to fabricate munitions to help the allies defeat the fascist axis powers. Wes started as a "material handler, carrying supplies throughout the plant." The US government considered his work vital to the war effort and never drafted him.

Wes was born in 1918 and spent his early years in the New Haven public schools. He learned about the basics of American history but felt that there was little to no technical education. He also felt that as an African American, he should have had more black teachers to be role models. He could only remember one or two. For him, as for many African Americans, Joe Louis "was our hero."

After he left school, Wes went to work in New Haven area restaurants, as a busboy. He and his friends often went to Harlem where they saw the best African American performers in the country. He taught himself to tap dance and developed his own niche: he tap-danced while jumping rope. This theatrical skill brought him jobs in the New Haven area and New York.

After Franklin Roosevelt's 1933 election victory, the United States government provided better employment opportunities. Wes was accepted into the Civilian Conservation Corps (CCC) and later the Works Progress Administration (WPA) and worked throughout New England, with black and white co-workers. He was impressed that all workers were treated equally by these federal agencies. He often performed for his co-workers, the tap dancing he had learned in Harlem and in the New Haven area.

Winchester Repeating Arms, one of New Haven's oldest employers, was located in a historically black neighborhood. As World War II approached, Winchester management began hiring more workers. Black men began to be hired. Within a few years, black women would also find jobs at Winchester's.

Wes worked his way up the ladder until he became an overhead crane operator in the rolling mill. The war continued until 1945. While Winchester's began to lay off some workers, the rolling mill was not affected. Management began to be less careful with hours and schedules. Workers did not know from one day to the next when they had to report to work and how long they had to work on a particular day. At one point in 1946, the workers became angry about this arbitrary treatment and stopped work. They demanded to speak to the General Manager, [Thomas I.] Boak. The workers had a designated spokesperson. Mr. Boak became irritated that he was summoned by the workers. He began to verbally attack the workers' spokesperson, who had just returned from serving honorably in the war. The rest of the workers jumped to their spokesperson's defense. This event was during the 11 to 7 shift. There was no progress made at the meeting. The next day, Mr. Boak shut down the rolling mill. A company lock out began.

The workers enlisted the support of the United Electrical (UE) Workers union. Through the union, they hired the Gold and Gold law firm. For the first time in his life, Wes McElya was part of a union. He wore his picket sign and was delighted when trucks and trains refused to cross the worker picket line.

Little did the workers know how strongly Winchester management disliked unions. In 1948, two years after the 1946 confrontation, the National Labor Relations Board ruled in favor of the workers. The Winchester management appealed the case to the federal courts. The case dragged on until 1952. Then, Winchester capitulated and settled. All the locked-out workers were allowed to return to work. Winchester's had to pay the sum of $300,000 to 101 of the workers who were locked out of the rolling mill. Winchester had to post notices around the shop, saying that no discrimination would be tolerated against any of the workers who came back to work.

The lock out of the Winchester workers from 1948 to 1952 was possibly the longest work stoppage in New Haven history.

Wes McElya received his portion of the $300,000 and returned to Winchester's for two more years. He was able to find work at Yale New Haven and St. Raphael's hospitals. When he left the hospitals, he was hired by Southern Connecticut State University for twelve years, until his retirement after so many years of strenuous work.

a free America. There is no room here for industrial dictatorship…The only remaining issue which must be resolved is the immediate reinstatement without discrimination of the 200 members of our union who have been unjustly locked out of their jobs." He urged the citizens to write to the President of Olin Industries, John M. Olin, in East Alton, Il. to issue this demand "as a consumer and New Haven resident. Do your part. Help to get these workers back on their jobs before Christmas."[47]

Despite these dramatic remarks, by July of 1947, the matter was still unresolved. Furthermore, the union itself had now decided that it would advise the "individuals involved" to proceed with the case before the NLRB on their own. Vincent J. Romeo, International Field Organizer, made a motion on July 29th to "withdraw the case without prejudice to the individuals involved," which was granted by the Trial Examiner. The case was continued by a New Haven lawyer, Marvin C. Gold. A letter sent by Gold on November 27, 1948, reported that "the Trial Examiner has found that Olin Industries, Inc., Winchester Repeating Arms Company Division has 'interfered with, restrained and coerced its employees in the exercise of the rights guaranteed in Section 7' of the National Labor Relations Act." The examiner essentially recommended the reinstatement of 106 named individuals.[48] (Presumably these were the people who had decided to proceed with the case.)

It is not entirely clear why the national union decided to "withdraw the damn charge," as suggested in a letter from its General Counsel, David Scribner in a letter to Alfred Smith, International Representative, UE-CIO in Bridgeport, CT, in July of 1947. Apparently, a decision had been made that UE's efforts at Winchester were fruitless. In December of 1948, Scribner reminded Smith that "my records show that about a year and a half ago, after we had put in about three years work on the War Labor Board stuff and the NLRB stuff, we decided because of the lack of adequate organization to drop the NLRB case." Learning of the Trial Examiner's decision favorable to the workers, Smith commented in a return letter to Scribner that "I don't know much more about this stuff than you know, except that, regardless of the NLRB decision, I doubt like hell whether this company will reinstate anybody, short of a directive by the U.S. Supreme Court."[49]

The case was appealed several times and wasn't finally settled until 1952, two years after Thomas I. Boak had left the company, when a number of the workers finally were recalled.

"I can remember my mother saying to me... [about a neighbor] 'He has a good job at Winchester.' This to my mother was achievement."

ALFRED MARDER

"Working at Winchester was tied to everything else I did." Al Marder was born in the back of a store on Spring Street in West Haven, and raised in New Haven where his parents had a "little impoverished store on Oak Street...It provided a very poor living for them." At one point, they had a four room house on Davenport Ave. in the Hill, where he "slept on a sofa." His mother, an immigrant, had had a short term job at Winchester, but she "never told me what she did." He also had a stepbrother who worked there later, at the same time he was at the plant. Marder's short time working at Winchester himself was "tied to everything else I did." Early on he became part of the "leftist youth movement" and became the chair of a peace group at Hillhouse High School, where "many of us came from poor, immigrant families. The topics of the day were social issues- the rise of fascism, discrimination...The Depression was the umbrella under which we operated."

"Winchester was part of my neighborhood...but it was not on the union's agenda...it was these other shops..."

While he was a junior in high school, the United Electrical Workers Union began trying to organize in the area, at Sargent's Manufacturing Company and other plants. He was "one of the few young people who had [access to his father's car]," and he would get up very early, push the car without starting it out of his family's yard in order not to wake his parents, and then go to distribute flyers with the union at these shops. Then they'd come back, push the car onto his family's lawn, and he would "go back to bed, fully dressed. This went on for months...Many years later, my mother said, 'You thought we didn't know what you were doing? But I told your father, 'no use trying to stop him, he's going to do it anyway.'"

As a member of the Youth Conference of the Young Communist League, Marder went to work at the Waterbury Brass & Smelter Plant. He remembered that they dealt with "all the issues...the fight for the eight-hour day, the fight for social security, decent wages, seniority, the end of discrimination...We were all socially aware."

By the time he was a junior in high school, Marder's family lived on Shelton Terrace., and "Winchester was part of my neighborhood... We got up and went to sleep by the sound of the whistle." Nevertheless, it "just stood out there" and "was not on the union's agenda."

That changed when World War II intervened.

WINCHESTER'S WAR BOOM

Al had graduated from high school and, despite his desire to "become a union organizer" and forego college, he was prevailed upon to reconsider. He went on to one year at City College in New York, considered "the Harvard of New York," attended by "children of immigrants all striving desperately to achieve...The competition was fierce." Al was more interested in being a student leader and an organizer than in paying attention to his studies. He was told by the administration "maybe it's better if you leave," because of his political affiliation and the "poisonous atmosphere" beginning to manifest in government investigations of the school system that would culminate in the "Red Scare" of the late 1940s and 1950s.

Winchester's war boom sparked the United Electrical Workers union's interest in organizing the plant. They now "realized that Winchester stood there and they were recruiting from the south and feeding the war effort abroad." UE organizers approached Marder after he returned to New Haven and asked him to apply there. He got a job as a laborer "carrying boxes of casings to the workers operating the machines" and was "under the strictest discipline not to talk to the union." His purpose there was to scout the situation out, to find "friends," and generally "get the lay of the land," as Lula White, interviewer, put it.

But after several months, Marder was "found out...of course. One day the company police came and said, 'You're through.'" Later, when he examined his own FBI files, he saw that the FBI had gone to the company with information about him and his likely motive for being there.

"I [later] realized...that the effort was unlike Brass Valley, Sargent's, Armstrong Rubber,] where we succeeded... Winchester was just a hold-out."

Marder later joined with UE's organizing efforts at Winchester from the outside, but "the atmosphere was not conducive...We didn't have those who were willing to take up the cudgels. We couldn't find them. ..[For] the flood of people [coming from the South who] were not New Haveners...[it was] the first factory job they'd ever had." And the war itself was another mitigating factor: "Once the war began, there was a general attitude that everyone had to pitch in to the war [effort]. That was the attitude even in the trade union movement: 'Don't press'...People bought into that...even though fortunes were being made and Roosevelt tried to impose a $25,000 pay limit for executives and the president of Sears Roebuck had to be thrown out" because he would not comply.

Interviewer Lula White cites the example of the auto workers as "kings of the labor movement," whose militancy in the union effort "gave Blacks access to the middle class" and produced strong Black leaders in the trade union movement. Al Marder says he "always wondered about Winchester's relationship to the autoworkers "because they too had come from the South. But look how militant they were."

Ultimately, the UE effort at Winchester was "not successful. I realized... that the effort was unlike the Brass Valley, Srgent's, Armstrong Rubber where we succeeded. Winchester was just a hold-out."

"Thank God For Peace!"

Men and Women of Winchester . . .

ALMOST overnight we have changed from a world at war to a world at peace.

In some corners of the globe it will naturally take somewhat longer for this to become an actuality. However, here at Winchester we are a plant at peace—already changed over to the manufacture of commercial products with a most aggressive approach to the intense competition facing us.

We can all agree, I'm sure, that this period of transition has already presented many problems, both for supervision and the working force, and no one can doubt that there are just as many ahead of us. You have all done a most splendid job during the war years. Let us not falter in our efforts to make an economic success of the peace for which so many fought and died.

There is room for everyone's opinion and common ground on which all differences can be settled. Only by the closest cooperation between employer and employee, labor and management, can Winchester in this post-war era resume her leadership in the Industry.

Let us strive cooperatively for prosperity and good-will. Let us create the kind of post-war industrial atmosphere to which our boys will be happy to return.

Thank God for the peace! May it be His Will that it will be an enduring peace.

Thomas I.S. Boak

"The Three Roadblocks"

It's not a pretty picture I'll paint for you today. Nine months after V-J Day, the greatest producer nation in the world is still confronted with shortages of everything—everything but words from Washington.

How is it possible that our country could turn out such an overwhelming flood of goods to smother the Axis—and yet can't turn out enough products now to smother inflation—or even to give us the things we want to buy? What are the roadblocks to our peacetime progress?

They are three: bureaucratic price controls, strikes and government extravagance.

One of the biggest and most stubborn roadblocks was the bureaucratic regimentation called price control.

Despite the fear propaganda being loosed by government "information specialists," let's be realistic about the O.P.A. In the first place, it was absolutely impossible for any man—or group of men—or government bureau—to sit in judgment on eight million prices and three million businesses.

Assuming the O.P.A. had the best of intentions, its officials were bound to make mistakes—plenty of them. And when mistakes are made on even the smallest component part of a major product—when that part can't be made because of price ceilings—the radio, or the refrigerator, or the washing machine you want, can't be made.

Under government-promoted rising costs and frozen ceiling prices, industry just could not swing into full production. Some firms were closing their doors—others going into high priced lines. Shortages continued to get worse and worse—and with them, inflation.

Thank goodness, with O.P.A. gone, the old law of supply and demand can now function in the American Way.

The second roadblock is strikes. Now, no one wants to see labor's right to strike taken from it. But whatever the justice or injustice of strikes, we have to admit that things just don't get made during strikes when men are on the picket line instead of the production line. It takes years of work at new wages for the employees to break even. And the public—as always—holds the bag. Nobody wins.

The best way to avoid strikes is to settle them before they break out in violence. In other words, real collective bargaining, instead of the "collective demanding" we've seen so much of lately. The key to labor peace is EQUALITY BEFORE THE LAW. Right now, management is answerable to the courts if it violates a contract, abuses free speech, or uses monopoly practices against labor. But, labor isn't—in most cases and in most states!

I believe that Congress should write a complete set of rules for genuine collective bargaining and the Administration should enforce them impartially.

The third roadblock is government extravagance. During the last *fifteen minutes* our Government has spent nearly two million of your dollars and my dollars—and our children's dollars. Aside from the high taxes now, this means an ever increasing government debt PLUS rich food for the giant "inflation."

Government fiscal policy during the war has been one equivalent to the printing of paper money. It borrowed most of its money from commercial banks—which, instead of laying the cash on the line, merely extended credit to the government. You know the results today, when you read that the money supply in this country has just about tripled.

We need a balanced budget immediately and a gradual repayment of the 274 billion dollar debt—beginning right now.

Only by sweeping aside these three roadblocks—price controls, strikes and federal extravagance—will this nation be able to move full speed ahead. It's up to us, the American people, to do that job through Congress.

Thomas I.S. Boak
Works Manager

Thomas I.S. Boak, Works Manager at Winchester Repeating Arms from 1932 until 1950. Boak, a 1914 graduate of Cornell University, had been a three-time Eastern Intercollegiate Wrestling Association champion during his college years. He was a long-time member of the National Association of Manufacturers. He died in 1969 and was selected as a charter member of the Cornell University Hall of Fame in 1978. Photo courtesy New Haven Museum and Historical Society.

Other images are from Winchester Life, 1945-1946.

5

A UNION HERE

As described in Chapter 4, in the immediate post-War years, Works Manager Boak continued his persecution of workers who had organized and supported UE 282, escalated his campaign against unions in the pages of *Winchester Life* as well as on the floor of the plant, and remained noncompliant in the face of NLRB findings about his practices.

The American Federation of Labor (AFL) apparently had also begun attempting to interest Winchester workers in unionizing by the late 1940s. Whether this was done in direct competition with its rival, the Congress of Industrial Organizations (CIO), of which the United Electrical Workers was an affiliate, is not clear.[50]

In September of 1949, Boak took his final anti-union shot in the pages of *Winchester Life*. He thanked his employees for having voted down AFL representation. He crowed: "The election, ordered by the National Labor Relations Board, has been held. The American Federation of Labor has had its 'day in court.' The official count was 2,897 'No's', 1,392 'Yes's.' I am deeply grateful for this overwhelming vote of confidence given management by the men and women of Winchester...To those who voted for no union, I express my sincere appreciation. To those who voted for the American Federation of Labor, I can only say that you have been overruled by the majority."[51]

By April of 1950, there was a new Works Manager, Berton E. Rogers, at Winchester, and by July, a newly created position of Industrial Relations Manager, filled by Robert I. Metcalf.[52] Metcalf became the company press spokesperson thereafter. While union advocates couldn't have been sorry to see Boak leave, one or two later expressed a sentiment to the effect that, at least with Boak, "you knew what you were getting."

1955-1956 THE BIRTH OF THE VICTORY LODGE

Winchester workers were finally successful in winning a union, despite ongoing company attempts to thwart it. International Association of Machinists Local 609 was called "the Victory Lodge" because it managed to prevail despite staunch management opposition which continued long after Boak's retirement.

Workers like Arthur Bosley, who eventually became the Local's first African American president, believed that it had been Boak's pre-retirement decision to institute post-war production speed-ups for all workers without pay increases that finally motivated the more "privileged" employees to take an interest in the union efforts which they had previously spurned.

In a last-ditch effort to thwart IAM's progress, the Olin-Mathieson Company filed a petition that was heard by the NLRB on September 8, 1955, at the New Haven Post Office. *Winchester News* reported that the company's legal counsel, attorney Benjamin E. Gordon, "told the hearing officer: 'I offer to prove that the employees of Olin-Mathieson have not at any time authorized the International Association of Machinists to represent them as a bargaining agent. The employees of the New Haven plants are being misled into believing that the question on which they might be voting is whether or not they want the International Association of Machinists to represent them, whereas it has been agreed among the IAM that such employees will be divided among 40 or more international unions to which they never had any intention of belonging.'"[53]

Winchester News, *September 16, 1955. Image courtesy IAM Local 609 Records, held at the Southern Labor Archives at Georgia State University.*

The company claimed that because the Connecticut Federation of Labor effort to get employee signatures on union cards, begun in June, designated only the American Federation of Labor as its sole bargaining agent, not the IAM, the IAM's petition for certification before the NLRB was not valid. The Secretary Treasurer of the CFL responded that the organization "represented 550 affiliated unions, including 40 international unions, and its purpose is to organize workers and place them into proper unions... He said whenever [the Federation} gets a call to organize, it refers the call to what it considers the proper affiliated union."[54]

A second issue in the hearing, probably of more serious concern to the company, was the composition of the proposed bargaining unit. The Machinists Union agreed to an amendment to their petition, which would restrict its unit to "'all hourly-paid production and maintenance employees, exclusive of guards, factory clerical personnel, office clerical personnel, professional personnel, and supervisors as defined in the [National Labor Relations] Act.'" This agreement reached, the NLRB then denied the Olin Mathieson Company's bid to reject the IAM petition.[55]

In December, 1955, the *Machinist*, IAM's newspaper, declared "the greatest union victory since the historic merger of the A.F.L. and C.I.O. in New York earlier this month" after a four to one majority of eligible employees voted in its favor, bringing "union representation to Winchester

"To me, Boak was the reason the union got in."

ARTHUR BOSLEY

Went to work at Winchester in 1943. Why Winchester? "Because I needed a job and I heard they were hiring." He worked there for 43 years in many different departments and was a gun inspector when he retired.

Bosley was the first African American to become president of Local 609. "The only reason I became president was because of the friendships I made."

On why the plant finally went union in 1956: "For the longest time, the unions could not get in...Many of the workers had good jobs and did not see a need. To me [Works Manager Thomas] Boak was the reason the union got in. [He] wanted us to increase production and that went for everyone, including the older workers. They all knew that if the union didn't get in, we would have to increase our production and not get paid. So they signed the union cards [too] and began participating."

On the impact of the union: "It made a big difference for Blacks, who were finally able to bid on a wider variety of jobs."

On other products made by the company: "The flashlight was the last to go before... they decided to just make guns."

On the demolition of the Winchester factory buildings after the company closed in New Haven: "When they tore down those buildings, those buildings resisted... It was well built."

New Traffic Rules on Pages 4-5

THE *WINCHESTER* NEWS

OLIN MATHIESON CHEMICAL CORPORATION · NEW HAVEN, CONN., NOV. 25, 1955 · VOL. IV, NO. 18

Company Takes IAM Petition to Court

Story on Page 2

Family Open House is a success! Shown in these pictures are the first groups to tour the Ammunition Plant on November 16. At the top, visitors watch assembly line belt in .30 Caliber Load and Pack. At lower left, it's time for a rest. Visitors spend a few minutes in the Ammunition Plant office. At right, visitors see operator packing shot shells after the loading operation. Names and story on Page 3.

The headline on the front page of the Winchester News *for November 25, 1955, was the ongoing company challenge to the IAM's authority, but the big story being promoted pictorially was the company's "Family Open House," where families of employees were treated to a tour of the company's ammunition plant. Image from Local 609 records.*

employees for the first time since the famous arms manufacturing concern was founded 89 years ago." It reported that 3,179 out of 4,162 eligible employees voted for the IAM.[56]

Winchester's Industrial Relations Manager, Robert I. Metcalf, expressed "disappointment" at the election outcome in a message "To All Employees" on the front page of *Winchester News*, but wrote that "the orderly manner in which the election was carried out shows that we can all work together harmoniously even when there are some differences of opinion," adding the usual company refrain that "the thing for us all to do now is to get on with the business of making fine quality products at the best possible price so that our jobs may be secured. That is where real job security lies."[57]

The Machinist, *December 8, 1955. Image from Local 609 records.*

MACHINIST EDITORIAL

The Machinist, December 1955. Image courtesy Local 609 Records.

A Lodge Is Born

EMPLOYEES of the Winchester plant of Olin Mathieson Chemical Corporation in New Haven, Conn., are preparing to go to the polls. The occasion will be a National Labor Relations Board representation election covering more than 4,000 production and maintenance workers.

It calls to mind elections in other shops years ago, when we were convinced union organization was necessary to cope with the power and resources of large companies.

It's true that some of us wondered whether we were doing the right thing. And, of course, we were deluged with the same general type of company literature trying to convince us that unions were unnecessary. In some cases, company stooges threatened us if we voted for the I.A.M. Others were called in and questioned by management. Rumors were planted prophesying dire action if the workers went union. And, attempts were made to buy votes by granting promising wage increases.

We wouldn't be surprised if the same thing is happening at Winchester today. Company tactics don't change much over the years. The approach may be a little different, but the goal is always the same—to lull employees into a sense of false security to discourage them from voting for a union.

Well, years ago we took the plunge and darned if we didn't discover that the union representatives had been telling us the truth all along. Companies that had threatened to move out of town if we voted union, didn't move after all.

They learned that having a union in the shop wasn't as bad as they'd feared. Everything wasn't peaches and cream, but eventually we were able to work out our problems through negotiations.

Next thing you knew, morale had improved, production increased, pay envelopes got fatter and profits continued to roll in. In short, everybody was making progress.

Some of these tough employers who had fought us with tear gas, bombs, armed management goons, etc., actually broke down and apologized for their actions. We won job and wage security, secured regular, negotiated wage increases. We improved hours and working conditions.

A few years later these same employers were coming to us asking for union label agreements. We were happy to oblige, because we believe in pushing the products of companies where I.A.M. members work. The more money these companies make, the more pay and benefits our members secure.

Well, we dare say, Winchester is in the early stages of the same experience we went through. When the vote is counted on election day, we'll find there's a new I.A.M. local lodge in existence—Winchester Lodge 609.

Winchester workers will face the same problems we did. And they'll solve them by working together, just as we did. The

Winchester News, December 16, 1955. Image courtesy Local 609 records.

Punch Lines

Real Job, Wage Security Are Now Within Our Grasp

By GENE PUNCH, Chairman of the Winchester Volunteers

At stake in our election, Dec. 15, are two key issues: wage and job security. For years we have worked without any guarantee of security in our jobs. Many of us didn't worry about it when times were good at Winchester, because we thought we had it.

Now conditions have changed. We're not getting those fat pay checks any longer. The company knocked out our piece work rates and substituted a merit review system. Personally, the changeover cost me $.45 an hour or a minimum of $900 a year. There is little chance that I will ever get that money back under present conditions.

All of us have seen or heard of huge wage cuts, widespread layoffs and unjust terminations. Those of you who felt the brunt of the company's actions had no recourse. You had to fight it out alone. None of this should have happened! We missed the boat when we failed to band together some time ago. However, that's all water under the bridge. Rather than worry about the past, we should be more concerned about the future.

Wage security must be won at Winchester, if our jobs are to have any value. We can get it through collective bargaining. This can be accomplished by spelling out the exact pay rates for each job in a signed union contract. Since no one party can change the terms of a contract without the consent of the other party, the company will no longer be able to lower wages without our agreeing to it. THIS IS WAGE SECURITY.

As for job security, that is even more important. I.A.M. members at Winchester will sit down with Union representatives to draw up what the employees want for seniority. Then we will vote to decide which type we wish to have. The company's triple-pronged seniority categories will no longer be forced upon us. In other words, we will have a voice in our job security.

Without a concrete seniority program of our own choosing—protected by a union contract—there is no security for anyone. Seniority affects us in layoffs, transfers, promotions, downgrades and recall after layoff. It is imperative that we have something to say about it.

To protect the wage and security features of our union contract, we will need stewards and committeemen in the shop. It will be the responsibility of these representatives to make certain that no one tampers with our rights.

Should any irregularities be found in the administration of the terms of the contract by the company, we will have recourse to a grievance procedure that will get results. We want justice!

Because layoffs have become a major problem at Winchester, steps should be taken to provide more stable employment. Severance pay plans have this as their prime objective, by stipulating financial penalties on the company for not establishing steady employment.

Under such a plan, the company would have to accept its responsibility to the workers. Failing to provide steady employment, the company would pay each laid off employee a lump sum settlement.

There's no doubt in my mind that this would help solve the layoff problem. Where such plans exist, the record shows that layoffs are fewer and jobs more secure.

The power to solve these problems lies in our hands when we cast our ballots. It's now or never! Either we are going to join together and work toward settling our problems, or we are going to be doomed to a continuation of present company policies.

I want to do something about it. How about you?

Here's IAM 10-Point Program for Progress

Here are highlights of the major contract proposals suggested for Winchester employees by the I.A.M. They are designed to bring badly needed progress and prosperity within the grasp of every Winchester worker.

1. Re-Timing of Jobs
Employees should have a voice in the setting of production standards to eliminate speed-ups without compensating increases in pay.

2. Automatic Progression
Regular pay raises every three months from the minimum rate to the "A" rate without merit reviews, empty promises and favoritism.

3. Genuine Job Security
Employees to decide which type of seniority they wish to have to give them maximum protection in matters of layoff, recall, transfers and promotions.

4. Overtime Equality
Equal distribution of overtime.

6. IAM Grievance Plan
Speedy and effective settlement of shop problems through an I.A.M. grievance procedure and arbitration of your grievances by a neutral third party when company fails to correct injustices.

7. Retroactive Pay Raise
A wage increase to bring Winchester pay rates in line with union rates of pay—retroactive to Aug. 25th.

8. Annual Pay Increase
Yearly wage negotiations to improve your standard of living and to afford protection from any future wage cuts by company.

9. Better Fringe Benefits
More paid holidays, improved vacations, paid sick leave.

Local 609 began negotiations with the company immediately after the December '55 victory. They concluded six months later, when workers ratified their "first ever" contract in "the company's 90-year history." Most significantly, the agreement provided for a union shop for the 4500 employees it represented, as well as "wage increases of 21 cents an hour over the next 18 months, improved vacation, holiday, pension and insurance benefits" and night shift premiums of 10 cents an hour for the third shift, mandatory rest periods, a 15 minute paid lunch, seniority protections, "a grievance procedure with full arbitration," and a flat $25 payment "for each employee on the payroll May 21…in lieu of retroactivity."[58] The era of the union had been inaugurated at New Haven's gun factory.

Local 609, International Association of Machinists Charter, February 1, 1956 and minutes of an early meeting of the Local, February 14, 1956. Images courtesy Local 609 Records.

> "[My father] would have said that the last nine years" (after the union came in) "were so much better than the first 16."
>
> —*Connecticut State Senator Martin M. Looney*

MARTIN FRANCIS LOONEY

 This photo of my father, Martin Francis Looney, was taken at the time of his retirement from Olin-Winchester in 1965. He operated a forklift there for 25 years, 1940-1965, interrupted by U.S. army service for six months, September 1942-March 1943.

He was born March 9, 1900 in Miltown, Maltbay, County Clare, Ireland, emigrated to the U.S. in 1927, and died in New Haven on April 29, 1972 at age 72. He lived in New Haven from the time of his arrival in the U.S. until his death.

My mother, Mary Mescall Looney, was born April 22, 1910 in Cooraclare, County Clare, Ireland, emigrated to the U.S. in 1929, and died in New Haven on May 28, 1991 at age 81.

They were married on June 20, 1942 in Brooklyn, NY, where my mother lived from the time of her arrival in America until her marriage. They settled in New Haven where I, their only child, was born in 1948.

—Connecticut State Senator Martin M. Looney
AUGUST 16, 2017

The union was important for the Dignity of the Workers

MARTIN FRANCIS LOONEY, UNION ORGANIZER

When the International Association of Machinists began its drive at the Winchester plant in the early 1950s, Martin F. Looney became an active union supporter and organizer. His son, Connecticut State Senator Martin Michael Looney, remembers:

Led early on by William S. Boak, "the personification of management anti-union efforts" and his sucessors, the company showed "clear favoritism toward those they saw as reliable anti-union votes." Looney had been counseled by friends and family who correctly feared company retribution "not to be so active" at his age, but, "he believed strongly that the union was important for the dignity of workers," and that "for industrial workers, there really was no way to avoid discrimination and abuses without it."

As his friends and family feared, after the first International of Machinists union vote failed in the early 1950s, in punishment for his activism, the company transferred Looney to a different job, moving freight. In his early 50s at the time, he was now "working with men twice his size and half his age." Recognizing the reason for his transfer, and the fact that "helping him was helping the union," the younger men, mostly African Americans, did what they could to ease the burden of the most strenuous tasks, "without drawing the ire of management."

Mrs. Looney worried about her husband during this time "because she saw the physical and emotional toll" the work itself and the struggle for the union were taking on him. Looney had high blood pressure and "it was a difficult couple of years."

In addition to wages, workers were concerned about safety issues and about discrimination against older workers. As they became increasingly aware of the "company strategy of divide and conquer" (pitting different classes, ages and ethnicities of workers against one another), "they didn't want to be complicit in what it was trying to do and were finally willing to take their long-term interests into account, rather than the short-term."

After the union was finally victorious in 1956, Mr. Looney got his old job back within a couple of months. Sen. Looney recalls the "great celebration and joy" his father experienced because of the victory, and notes that "our family's standard of living definitely improved."

MARTIN FRANCIS LOONEY, UNION STEWARD

For nine years after the union victory, until his retirement in 1965, Looney was a Local 609 steward. As an advocate for workers, he considered that the "highlight" of his tenure in this position was his handling of a complaint by an African American worker who had been "racially slurred" by a high-level manager. Looney documented the complaint and saw it all the way through the grievance process. The manager had to submit a written apology which was posted in the work-place.

Mr. Looney worked at the plant during only one of the big strikes after the union victory. In 1962, the issues were, according to his son, "wages, the level of increase being offered, benefits in terms of the health plan, work rules and protections of people in certain job categories."

What would his father have said to sum up his experience at Winchester?

"[My father] would have said that the last nine years" (after the union came in) "were so much better than the first 16."

> "[My father] was very passionate about the union. If he would drop the union stuff...he was offered the position of foreman, but he felt so strongly about [the need for] the union that he refused."

MARGE OTTENBREIT

Marge was born and raised in New Haven. Her father, William J. Slater ("Bill") "worked at Olin since he was 21. That's the only job I remember him having." He was a sheet metal worker and "didn't make the big pay of those working in guns and ammunition." He helped his brother get into the plant during World War II, making ammunition and gun parts for "long hours and big money."

Mr. Slater worked at Winchester for 38 years and retired on disability at age 59 after being scalded when a gang plank he was standing on gave way. He was given a retirement party, but "no big settlement."

Marge's brother also worked at Winchester on the night shift when he got out of the Navy, and participated in the Local 609 softball team.

On working at Winchester: "There was always some element of danger in what they were doing." But the job "gave [her father] stability. He had four kids and a wife to support...I never remember him taking time off for being sick. He was very loyal." Some members of management attended his retirement party.

About the union: Mr. Slater served as a Vice President of Local 609 under President Louis Oronzo and "was very passionate about the union." As a child, "I remember doing flyers at St. James' Church on why they needed the union." And the union made a difference. "You felt you had more protection. If something was wrong, you could speak up." When he was offered the position of foreman, he refused to take it but opted to remain with the union.

> "I praise the union because I know what existed before they came in."

RAYMOND SIMMS

Mr. Simms was born in New Haven, CT and lived there for 46 years. He worked at Winchester for 12 years; for Electrical Workers Local 90 for three; and retired in 1991 after working 25 years for the city of New Haven. His mother worked in the Battery Shop at Winchester for 15 years. His brother worked there for 20 years in gun assembly.

"They encouraged me to leave."

Working at Winchester: "As soon as I got out of the service, the first thing I thought about was Winchester." He was hired the day he applied in 1953. Under the G.I. Bill, he entered Olin's apprentice training program and received on the job training as an industrial electrician..."I was an apprentice and then became a Class C electrician. But I wanted to apply to upgrade to Class B. That's when the trouble started."

He had seniority and experience, but his boss "wouldn't budge" even after he filed a grievance with the union. Although he won the case in arbitration, the process took six months and he never received back pay.

About the union: "It was a blessing."

Before the shop was unionized, "there were very few jobs open to African Americans," and those were "back breaking and dangerous. It was a situation where you get up and hate to go to work."

"When the union got in, they had to start opening up all the jobs to African Americans who qualified. I praise the union because I know what existed before they came in."

WINCHESTER

Life

FEBRUARY 1952

The Plant Around Us

Cover of Winchester Life, *February 1952.*

6

THE 1950S
AT WINCHESTER

THE PLANT AROUND US

If management's attempts to crush worker organizing had become especially blatant and oppressive in the 1940s and early 1950s, family culture, worker pride in accomplishment, and a sense of community continued to be promoted in company publications from the "plant around us." The juxtaposition was no doubt intentional. Many workers shared these values even while resisting the company's transgressions.

In 1951, the company sponsored its annual "Winchester Employees Photo Contest." The results depicted not only cross-generational employment but the variety of ethnic groups who had worked at the company thus far into the 20th century, many of them immigrants. The African Americans who had swelled the workforce during World War II and after, on the other hand, were not as well-represented in the contest.

The famous "Winchester Club" was a local icon, and the factory whistle could be heard calling people to work for each shift throughout the neighborhoods surrounding the plant.

Family Album Photography Contest. Images from Winchester Life, *1951.*

"It was a city unto itself...It was like a big family. I got along with everyone in my family."

ROBERT W. ERFF

Mr. Erff was born in West Haven, CT, his father the Assistant Chief of the West Haven Fire Department. His mother stayed home because she "had to take care of six kids." Just out of the Navy in 1954, he went to Winchester in order to support his own growing family. (He and his wife have seven children.) He got his GED while working there: "They put on a class open to anyone in the facility."

He started in the Boiler Room: "On the weekend we blew the tubes on the boilers and the neighbors complained that their sheets were black."

"Most people had the opportunity to move up the ladder." Erff became the Assistant Supervisor of Power and Water, then Full Supervisor. He worked at Winchester for 44 years, retiring at 65 in 1998. "They were damned fair to me."

Erff "never worked on rifles." What else did Winchester make? "You name it, they made it...roller skates...flashlights...They made a lot of things and they were good at it." With Olin as the parent company, they "made a profit on the diverse products they made. They were shrewd people."

Memories of Winchester: "New Haven was good to Winchester. Winchester was good to New Haven."

It was a "family oriented group...Anything pertaining to education or your welfare, Winchester would listen to. A lot of people didn't see it. Maybe I only saw it because I was a young, green kid. They were very good to me and my family."

When he began, there were three shifts around the clock. The plant was a "city unto itself" in many ways, with its clubhouse, store and theatre. "We had our own fire department, [employing] three professional firefighters...a beautiful medical department (for a while we had our own ambulance)... We had our own electricians, plumbers and maintenance people. We didn't use outside contractors. We made our own electricity, and we had two 500 gallon oil tanks over on Gibbs Street..."It was like a big family. I got along with everyone in my family."

About the union: Before becoming part of management, he was a steward and later a Chief Steward in Local 609. "There might have been individuals who weren't treated well, but if you complained through a steward, you were heard.

"Some people felt they were being discriminated against. There might have been some [treated unfairly] but for some, it was their own fault.

"We [maintenance people] were doing alright without the union. Most of the maintenance people were treated fairly."

Still, he agrees that Local 609 achieved better pay and better working conditions. For example, "with the union, they made it a law" for workers in certain areas to wear safety goggles. And, before the union, many workers had operated under a quota system: "If they didn't meet their quotas, they'd just fire you on the spot."

On his transition from union to management: "At one time I was a steward [in the union] and the company, to get rid of me, wanted to put me in management. If you have a steward that's trying to benefit workers, they'll take you and you have to shut your mouth. It's quite common." In fact, most of the supervisors from Winchester began as hourly workers [although this was not true of those from Olin, the new parent company.]

"There was a little resentment [among his co-workers] when I became the boss man."

About having to remain on the job when other workers were on strike: He was already in "low management" at the time of the first strike in 1962. "We had a skeleton crew in the power plant to keep the heat up. We weren't doing anybody's job; we were just maintaining the facility.

"We were operating engineers. We took an oath when we got our licenses. You can't just leave the plant. None of the strikers bothered us because they wanted the place to be there when they came back."

On the demise of Olin Winchester: When the company started outsourcing work, "that was our downfall. We used to make everything. You start letting pieces out, then you start letting bigger pieces out."

How did you feel in 2006 when the plant closed?: "It hurt.

"This was a booming area for manufacturing. Now there's nothing."

WELI Interview with Winchester Employees. Photo courtesy Maryann Davies. Ms. Davies' father, Edward Doughan, pictured here second from left, worked at Winchester in the 1940s and 1950s and was supervisor of the Brass Casting Shop.

From trade school trainees to retirees, employees were often prominently featured in *Winchester Life*.

Eleven Who Retired

The pictures on this page were taken in connection with the Trade School story in June and then we found that we did not have room for them. We thought you would like to see them, however, so here they are: Top left: Courtland Wilson is studying a blueprint, part of the Trade School training being blueprint reading. Top right: Herman Koltermann is operating a milling machine. Bottom right: Lester Andrews is pictured checking the height of a piece of work with a dial indicator, instrument reading being part of the Trade School course.

Images from Winchester Life, 1950-1952. Courtland Wilson, pictured reading the blueprint as part of the training school course, helped to bring in the Machinists Union while he worked at Winchester, later becoming President of the Local NAACP and a co-founder of both the New Haven Black Coalition and New Haven's Hill Parents Association. He worked as Assistant Dean of the Yale Medical School and later at the Yale-New Haven Hospital in the Office of Government and Community Relations, and finally served as Executive Director of the Hill Development Corporation. A branch of the New Haven Free Public Library, named for him, opened in 2006.[59]

You Were Saying?

Do you rely on the factory whistle?

T. Jastremski   **Joseph Price**   **Oscar Kaizer**   **Lillian Rice**   **Arthur Hahn**   **Frank Dolceaqua**   **Michael Carusone**   **Louis Pace**   **John Patterson**   **George Coutts**

THADDEUS JASTREMSKI, Garage: "I don't wait to listen. I come in ahead of time . . . just don't want to be late. Sometimes I happen to hear the seven o'clock whistle but I usually go by the clock. I go according to the clock at three, too. I don't even remember ever hearing the three o'clock whistle. Is there one?"

JOSEPH PRICE, Rolling Mill: "I use the eight o'clock, quarter of seven, and five of seven. They're kind of a warning for me when I'm on the day shift. I usually get in early and listen for the whistles to keep track of the time. When I lived near here I always heard them. Even when I was on the other shifts, I used them to tell time in the morning."

OSCAR KAIZER, Carpenter Shop: "Why certainly. I listen for the seven o'clock and the noon whistles. I don't always hear the noon one . . . it depends on the wind. If we don't hear the whistle, though, we depend on the buzzer in the shop. Sometimes, too, with the machines going, the outside whistle is hard to hear."

LILLIAN RICE, Janitor Service: "Yes, I really do. The seven o'clock, 12 o'clock and 12:15 especially. That's right, I do listen for them every day. I would even if I was home."

ART HAHN, Machine Shop: "Sure. I hear the quarter of seven . . . gives you an idea of how fast or how slow to go. The five of means it's time to get set for work. And of course, the three o'clock when it's time to go home. At lunch, we stop at five of and with the machines stopped we can hear the noon whistle. Doesn't mean anything except that it's noon."

FRANK DOLCEAQUA, Pipe Shop: "You're not kidding I do. Which do I count on regularly? The ones in the morning . . . quarter of and five of. I try to park out in front in the morning so I get here early and wait in the car. I usually listen to the radio until the whistle blows. You know, if I'm late, I can hear the whistle all the way down Washington Avenue where I live."

MICHAEL CARUSONE, Production Tool: "Well, I'm kind of used to hearing them although I don't exactly listen for the morning whistles. I hear the noon one at lunch time. In the morning I make a practice of getting here on time. I'm used to that. Got used to it in the Army. I was a mess sergeant in the infantry."

LOUIS PACE, Model 50: "I depend on them for time. The morning whistles at 6:45 and 6:55 are the ones I depend on most. With machines running, we very seldom hear the noon whistles. At the end of the day, wash-up time is five of three so we can hear the three o'clock whistle when we're in the washroom."

JOHN PATTERSON, Gun Parts: "Yes, sometimes. I hear the quarter of seven whistle and leave my house by that whistle. Coming into the plant, I usually hear the five of whistle. For lunch I listen for the department buzzer. And I practically always hear the three o'clock."

GEORGE COUTTS, W-W Tool Room: "No, I don't depend on them and I wouldn't miss them. I hear the five of seven, seven o'clock, and three o'clock that blows when we leave here. It wouldn't make any difference to me if they didn't blow them."

Images from Winchester Life, *1958.*

The newly renovated Winchester Club. At the top is the recreation room. Lower picture is employee store. Insert shows how store looked before renovation.

WORLD PREMIERE

Shelley Winters, co-star of Universal-International's big western, "Winchester 73," is presented with one of the "stand-in" models of the famous "One of One Thousand" rifle by John M. Olin, President of Olin Industries. The presentation was made on the stage of the Shubert Theater, where the world premiere of the picture was held.

NEW HAVEN got a first-hand glimpse of what a Hollywood premiere is really like when motion picture dignitaries, Olin officials, Winchester employees, and hundreds of newspaper, radio and magazine writers, including reporters from Canada, England, France, Australia, and Mexico gathered in the Shubert Theater recently to view the pre-release showing of filmdom's story of a Winchester gun, "Winchester 73."

The schedule of activities to entertain the visitors began early in the afternoon with the arrival in New Haven of the "Premiere Special," bearing Shelley Winters, feminine star of the picture, and scores of officials and reporters. From the train they were whisked in waiting busses to the East Haven Rifle Range where Herb Parsons, Winchester-Western's world famous exhibition shooter, started the celebration with a demonstration of his marksmanship.

Gathered under tents, sheltering them from the heavy rainstorm which handicapped Parsons, and which he claimed was the worst he had ever experienced on such an occasion, the crowd expressed amazement at his marksmanship. Included in his program was the particularly amazing demonstration of shooting holes through coins tossed into the air. It was with this feat that Parsons played an important behind-the-scenes part in the filming of the picture on which he was technical advisor and gun expert—although on the screen it appeared to be Jimmy Stewart who shot the holes through coins.

Below left: At East Haven Rifle Range, Shelley Winters gets lesson on how to handle the big .44 caliber Winchester 73 from Herb Parsons. One of the world's fastest shooters, Parsons gave a demonstration of his marksmanship in connection with the world premiere of the motion picture "Winchester 73". Looking on are Olin Industries' officials (left to right): President John M. Olin,

Secretary R. R. Casteel, 1st Vice-President Spencer T. Olin, and (behind Parsons) Vice-President John W. Hanes. Below right: As Miss Winters and group arrived at New Haven railroad station they were met by Winchester representatives, headed by George L. Dawson, regional manager, who presented her with a bouquet of roses as she alighted from train. Movie officials also attended.

Premiere of the movie "Winchester 73" starring Jimmy Stewart and Shelley Winters at the New Haven theatre, the Shubert, in 1950. The movie burnished the romance of the gun, and the press premiere brought out Olin officials, Hollywood stars and the eight Winchester employees who crafted the "stand-in" models for the movie. The following evening, a special pre-release showing for Winchester employees was attended by 4,000 workers. Images from Winchester Life, 1950.

Winchester employees attended a special preview of "Winchester 73" as guests of the Company. Thronging sidewalk, lobby of Shubert Theater, thousands of employees came to see the picture which was built around one of famous Model 73 Winchester rifles. Because of the great number of employees who attended, it was necessary to give three consecutive showings to accommodate all.

After the exhibition the crowd moved to the Hotel Taft where a buffet dinner awaited them and, at eight P.M. the scene shifted again to the Shubert Theater where the picture was to be shown.

This was the point at which the celebration assumed the proportions of a real Hollywood premiere. Although the sweeping rainstorm succeeded in keeping the sidewalk clear of people, the lobby was jammed to capacity. When Shelley Winters made her appearance, the crowd, many of them seeking autographs, pressed forward to meet her. The floodlights of the newsreel cameramen and the popping flash-bulbs of the still photographers lent an added air of excitement to the scene.

Prior to the showing of the picture, Mr. John M. Olin, President of Olin Industries, called Miss Winters to the stage and presented her with one of the "stand-in" models of the gun for which the picture was named.

Among the many who attended the entire premiere celebration as guests of the Company were the eight Winchester employees whose craftsmanship aided in the making of the picture. They were the men who made the special "stand-in" models of the original Winchester 73 which "starred" in the picture. These men who made such an important contribution to the picture and who were justly included on the roster of honored guests are: Al Berzinis, Oscar Ludwig, Ted Iwach, Pat Devine, John Kusmit, Frank Durso, Jack Lacy, and Ed Doyle.

After the press premiere, on the following evening, a special pre-release showing of the film was held for Winchester employees. More than 4,000 attended as guests of the Company, and so great was the interest in the picture that the film was run three times in order to accommodate the entire crowd.

Right: Top photo shows part of the crowd of some 500 newspaper, radio and motion picture writers and officials who attended the buffet supper at the Hotel Taft, prior to viewing the picture. Bottom: The registration desk, built by Fred McKerness, Winchester artist and display designer, simulates that of an old-time frontier hotel. Set up in the lobby of the Hotel Taft, it was here that premiere guests registered. Desk clerks were dressed as frontiersmen.

Winchester Bows Out Of Skate Business; Not Compatible With Guns

"We're now out of the roller skate business," Vice President W. Miller Hurley, general manager of the Winchester-Western Division, reported last week. "We've sold the last of the inventory and we have the money."

Thus the company wrote "finished" on an enterprise that goes back over 30 years and was marked by many improvements in roller skate design to the advantage of the youngsters of the country, if not to the company.

Winchester's first experience in roller skate manufacture was in the 1920s when it was trying to find production lines to take the place of military arms. Even then Winchester roller skates were superior and were in fact the first nickel-plated skates in the country.

The line was dropped during World War II but in 1953 under the direc-tion of Harry Swain of Winchester-Western sales, was revitalized as a fabricated item, using the same tool-makers and assemblers as were used on such products as lipstick cases and flashlights. Unlike lipsticks and flash-lights, roller skates are made of steel and require larger presses and assem-bly units.

Our skate testing in 1953 drew a lot of national publicity and by 1954 we were in production with three new roller skate models. It was by far the best looking skate on the market and in most respects superior to anything

(Continued on page three)

Ghost Town effect of Winchester Avenue was apparent on April 17, seconds after the signal for "Operation Alert 1959," was sounded. Pedestrians waiting for the downtown bus took refuge in the Credit Union office and all traffic was halted until the end of the alert at 1:43 p.m. The test, which lasted for 10 minutes, was the local phase of a nation-wide Civil Defense training exercise.

Images are from Winchester Life, *1958-1959.*

OUR COMMUNITY AT WINCHESTER CONFRONTS THE COLD WAR

In the August 15, 1958, edition of *Winchester Life*, workers responded to the question, "What are our chances for World Peace?"

Of the 10 workers who responded to the question "What are our chances for world peace?," most seemed to feel that "beating communism" and "defeating Russia" were prerequisites to the goal of peace:

> Sal Capasso of the Casting Shop thought "Chances are pretty good' because 'we've called [the Russians'] bluff by sending troops to the Middle East."

> Robert Stackpole, Gun Assembly: "The way the President has sent troops overseas is helping world peace. We're calling Russia's bluff...Peace is being made right now by these different actions."

Nevertheless, Capasso, Vince Criscuolo from the Mill Stockroom and Leonard Cables from the Barrel Shop also expressed confidence in the work of the United Nations:

> Capasso: "The U.N. and Hammarskjold [Dag Hammarskjold, then President of the United Nations General Assembly] have been doing a pretty good job of finding out what the trouble is and trying to do something about it. I think the coming generation will see peace."

> Criscuolo: "I have confidence in the U.N. Everyone has something to lose—if one gets hurt, they all do. In the long run, we'll beat communism. We can take it by the numbers."

Cables: "I think they can work something out through the U.N. and get together, as in the summit meeting."

Others were cautious or pessimistic, still viewing Russia and/ or communism as the obstacles to world peace.

Fedora Surato, Model 50: "Russia seems to disagree a lot, but we can overcome communism and work something out if they are really sincere about wanting peace."

Eddie Estes from the Garage: "I think everybody's very selfish; like Russia—they want to take over the better parts of the earth. I don't see any peace in sight."

Some evoked religious faith as a means of "defeating communism:"

Henry Parker of the Battery Shop: "All of the nations can meet together and work things out by discussing it. I think we can overcome communism. We have to take care of our allies and pray a little harder. That's important."

Mary Gosch, 24-D Arms: "Until people learn to live together, I don't think there will be any peace. Our only hope is that our President will work for us. We're strong enough to beat communism by our religious faith alone. People of today have a lot of religious education."

Thomas Morsicato, of the Sheet Metal Shop, felt that peace was possible, but sadly, not at hand: "It could happen if all the nations got together and tried to get along with one another. As long as we and the allied countries keep strong and keep our standard of living, we can keep communism away from here. But the way things are, peace is far away."

You Were Saying?

What are our chances for world peace?

Sal Capasso　Henry Parker　Eddie Estes　Francis Quinn　Vince Criscuolo　Thomas Morsicato　Mary Gosch　Robert Stackpole　Leonard Cables　Fedora Surato

Image from The Winchester News, August 15, 1958, p.4.

Only Francis Quinn from the Receiver Shop mentioned the unprecedented weapon of mass destruction used by the United States in 1945 as a new factor, and he didn't appear hopeful that any lesson had been learned: "One country is just as afraid of war as another. They know what the situation with the atomic bomb is. They should do away with all the armies, but that will never work out. If people want a war, they're going to have one."[60]

Union members at work and play. Images from Local 609 Records.

Postcard

1964 GRAND LODGE CONVENTION
International Association of Machinists
IN SESSION AT THE DEAUVILLE HOTEL
Miami Beach, Florida — Sept. 8 to 18

Hi Gang,

Regards to the fellows + Doris. The weather is hot + (humid)

They really got us going down here along with night sessions. We all miss New Haven. Here is the picture they took of us, as you may have noticed Tommy got cut out and he is (mad) angry. Carl + Doris make sure you hold the fort.

Alvin-Tom-Lou

Victory Lodge 609
308 Ashmun St.
New Haven, Connecticut

Victory Lodge   Local No. 609
International Association of Machinists

Date May 27   1964

The Lodge was called to order at 8:33 p.m. and opened in due form.

The official roll call resulted as follows:

President C. Johnson   Conductor T. King
Vice President L. Romano   Sentinel T. Turck
Recording Sec'y M. Panicali Trustee F. Romano
Financial Sec'y D. DiNatale (absent) Trustee E. McCarthy
Treasurer P. LaTorraca   Trustee S. Zampano

Following pro tem appointments made

Minutes of last meeting were read and Approved - M. Ras - 2nd J. Christina.

Receipts from all sources for this meeting

Disbursements for all purposes made by this meeting   A regular membership meeting was held at the Labor Temple.

Pres C. Johnson presided

Communications were read.

Report of Comm.

Pres Johnson reported on an arbitration awards which was rendered by H.S. Wolfe on three cases. Two for the Company and one for the Union.

Tom Burns reported on a conference of the New England Conference of Machinists which took place at Rhode Island.

V. Pres L. Romano reported on a Labor Day Parade which is to be held on Sept 7, 1964, in which all unions affiliated with the Labor Council will participate.

New Business.

Nominations for delegates to the G.L. Convention which is to be held at Miami, Fla. in Sept. Those nominated were, Tom King (43) James Sabellico (48) Harold Lord (26) Ted Turck (32) Edward McCarthy (22) L. Romano (67) Mike Ras (48) Alvin Panicali (62) S. Zampano (10) John Golia (7) P. Adamaitis (12) C. Shannon (10) Nominations were suspended until the second shift.

7

THE 1960S
AT WINCHESTER

STRUGGLE AND CHANGE

The company strove to "modernize" its operations in the early 1960s.

The opening of the newly renovated Olin Research Center was celebrated in a special program which included a press luncheon at the New Haven Lawn Club followed by a press conference and tour of the facility. Mayor Richard C. Lee spoke of the "importance of Olin to the city of New Haven" and hastened to assure the Olin officials present that "'your investment in the city is not mistaken, and over the years the returns it will bring you are immeasurable.'"[61]

The Olin Research Center was part of the overall company modernization plan, scheduled for completion in 1964, that eventually would include other parts of the New Haven plant, but which also introduced a potential harbinger of doom: "construction of an entirely new brass and copper casting and rolling plant at East Alton [Illinois]."[62]

THE Olin NEWS
AT NEW HAVEN

OLIN MATHIESON CHEMICAL CORPORATION • NEW HAVEN, CONNECTICUT, MARCH 24, 1961 • VOLUME IX NUMBER 18

Blood Donors p.2
Renovation p.2
Catherine Walsh p.4
You Were Saying p.4
Winning Cagers p.4

Research Center Is Dedicated

W-W Gets $5 Million BOD Award

State Groups Hear Sowders

Mill on 4 Days for 6 Weeks

Tour 70% Subscribed

AFL-CIO Research Authority Slated To Speak April 6

Meet The Press!

Plans Progress for Formation Of United Nuclear Corporation

22 Inducted Into Research Society

Machinists File Petition To Represent Nuclear

Recovering

Second Award

Image from page 1 of The Olin News at New Haven, *March 24, 1961.*

Image from The Olin News at New Haven, *August 18, 1961.*

THE Olin NEWS
AT NEW HAVEN

OLIN MATHIESON CHEMICAL CORPORATION • UNITED NUCLEAR CORPORATION • NEW HAVEN, CONNECTICUT, AUGUST 18, 1961 • VOLUME X NUMBER 2

N.H. Brass Facility Will be Modernized

German Professor At RESA Seminar

Fab Grad Reunion?

Duckpin & Big Pin Leagues Coming

Yankee-Cleveland Tickets Available

More Multiple Gallon Donors

Protection Moving

Big Face Gets Big Lift

ENTER (AND EXIT) UNITED NUCLEAR

In March of 1960, workers at the Nuclear Fuels Corporation, a division of Olin Mathieson located in New Haven adjacent to Winchester, rejected a bid by the IAM to represent production and maintenance employees and inspectors at their plant. In 1961, the IAM filed an appeal with the National Labor Relations Board. At the same time, plans were announced to form the United Nuclear Corporation, "with the Olin Mathieson Nuclear Fuels operation as a major part."[63] The merger also included the Mallinckrodt Corporation of America and the Nuclear Development Corporation of America. The IAM did not, apparently, succeed in its efforts: information about a strike at the plant in 1968 shows that these workers were members of the Oil, Chemical and Atomic Workers Union, AFL-CIO, which had signed a contract with the company in 1965.[64]

Although not officially part of the Winchester factory, the New Haven United Nuclear plant operated at an adjacent site on Winchester and Shelton Avenues and Mansfield and Gibbs Streets from 1961 until 1976, when it transferred most of its work to its Montville, CT facility.[65] Its work was always classified, but in the early 1970s it was awarded several lucrative contracts to make nuclear reactor cores for Navy submarines produced at General Dynamics' Electric Boat shipyard in Groton, CT. The shadowy nature of the operation in New Haven, and the subsequent cleanup after its departure, aroused concern in the community at a time of high anxiety about nuclear weapons and power in the United States.

THE 1962 STRIKE

In 1962, with rumblings that a strike was in the offing, Olin-Winchester's management tried to convince union workers that a strike for better wages would threaten their job security.

In *Olin News at New Haven* dated May 25th, 1962, the company published a photo essay and a strongly worded editorial to try to dissuade its employees from taking this action. But by the time this newsletter was published, Local 609 workers had already rejected the company's strategy.

Negotiations in 1960 had apparently "gone down to the wire" as well but did not result in a strike. In 1962, talks between the company and the union had begun on March 26th, but a vote by participating members of Local 609 rejected the company's offer by a margin of 24 to one in early May, authorizing a walkout if no better agreement was reached. What became the first strike by the six-year-old Local began on May 28th and ended on July 16th.[66]

UNITED NUCLEAR CORPORATION

In and Out of New Haven, 1961-1976

1948 Nuclear Development Corporation is established in the post-World War II move to harness the atom for peaceful uses, aka nuclear energy.

1950s The Naval Products Division begins fabricating reactor fuel elements for the Naval Nuclear Propulsion Program at a facility in Montville, CT.

1961 United Nuclear is founded in a merger of Olin Corporation, Mallinckrodt Corporation of America, and Nuclear Development Corporation of America. It employs between 600-700 in New Haven by 1968. (Estimates differ.)

1965 Local 8-718 of the Oil, Chemical and Atomic Workers Union, AFL-CIO, signs a three contract with UNC.

FEBRUARY 1968 400 UNC production employees in New Haven, represented by Local 8-718, stage a brief strike over "seniority and reassignment of workers."

APRIL 1970 The Atomic Energy Commission (AEC) awards $64 million contract to UNC, "the biggest single contract ever handed a New Haven industry." New Haven employment gradually rises to approximately 725, as compared to 390 in Montville.

FEBRUARY 1972 The AEC awards a second contract for over $60 million for nuclear fuel components to be delivered over the next four years.

APRIL 1972 The company, having outgrown its capacity in New Haven, announces it will move "most of its operation in stages" to Montville by the end of 1974. Speculation is that the move is also related to the top-secret nature of its defense work.

MARCH 9, 1973 Local 8-718 goes on strike over issues of severance pay and pensions; accord is reach after 15 days of mediated negotiations.

BY 1976, UNC's New Haven operations have ceased.

Images from The Olin News at New Haven, *May 25, 1962*

According to the *New Haven Register*, the union was asking for a 3% wage increase (about six cents an hour), but at the end of 20 negotiating sessions the company hadn't budged beyond its initial offer of one cent. Lowell E. Krieg, the Olin vice president and the general manager of the Winchester-Western Division, was the company's press spokesperson during the strike, and his repeated mantra was that the plant must improve efficiency to remain competitive.[67]

On July 16th, at a union meeting at New Haven's Paramount Theatre, Local 609 members ratified a new contract, ending the strike. Calling it the "'the best offer we could get,'" the Local's president, Carl Johnson, "listed 22 points in the contract. Many involved changes in work rules and procedures. Management refused to alter a clause bothersome to the union. The union failed to have the clause 'in the opinion of the company' deleted from the seniority language. Johnson said remedial action may be found in pending arbitration cases."[68]

Which Would You Pick?
MORE MONEY? or JOB SECURITY?

When this picture was taken last month, negotiations were beginning. Since then, much time has been spent discussing the things which employees value most in a labor agreement.

The bargaining committee has tended to concentrate on economic issues. Company negotiators have urged that a man's job, itself, must also be considered. Members of Local 609 will have a choice to make on these important matters.

IN MAKING THIS DECISION, KEEP IN MIND:

Our sales people travel all over talking to dealers and those who buy our products. They say emphatically that we cannot act in New Haven as though nobody else in the world was making a gun.

They say, too, that a product customers consider over-priced stays on the shelves . . . today more than ever. People shop as never before, looking closely at materials, workmanship . . . and price tags.

WHAT MAKES A PRODUCT OVER-PRICED?

Four things have to be covered in the price of every product:
a) The raw materials that go into it.

b) The labor that goes into it.

c) Some return for the people who invest their money.

d) Money for new methods and machinery, new products, general modernization, to improve quality and reduce costs.

YOU SHOULD LOOK HARD AT ALL THESE THINGS

We are exploring new materials and finding new uses for them.

We are modernizing our plants. Corporate funds have been poured into New Haven by the millions. These funds must be repaid.

(Average Hourly Wages & Fringe Benefits)

Olin	New Haven	Conn.	U.S.
$3.16	$3.07	$3.02	$2.76

We are proud of our position in New Haven's wage picture. Any increase in our high wages could lead to a loss of markets and jobs.

When wages are already high, job security is more important than any wage increase.

Job security depends on sales and sales depend on products that can compete with others in the market place, both as to quality and as to price. The cost of our products thus becomes everybody's business and pricing them out of the market becomes a folly.

We have confidence in the New Haven operations. We believe there is a bright future and that it can be especially bright if we face it together: shoulder-to-shoulder.

SO, WE ASK: WHICH WOULD YOU PICK? **WHEN THE TIME COMES TO DECIDE, BE SURE YOUR VOTE IS BASED ON YOUR OWN DECISION.**

THE 1969 STRIKE

With the advent of the anti-labor Nixon administration, workers' struggles entered a new era. In New Haven, Local 609 went on strike again, this time for over three and a half months, beginning on July 15, 1969.

Articles about the strike appeared in the newsletter of the American Independent Movement, which had its New Haven headquarters on Orange Street. The articles spoke of the company's long anti-union stance and the hard-fought victories of its workers. Ruth Meyerowitz wrote that the 609 members had "rejected a company offer which would have destroyed many of the gains won by the workers over the past 13 years," adding that "although negotiations began more than two months before the contract was to end, the company held firm to its original offer, following a widespread management strategy of forcing lengthy strikes."[69]

"The union pointed out that a 5% wage increase was grossly inadequate," Meyerowitz wrote, "and that the company proposal for phasing out an incentive system would mean a wage cut for more than 1200 of its members during the three years of the contract. Other attacks on work standards by the company included a proposal to eliminate double-time pay on Sundays and to weaken security and pension provisions..."[70]

This image is from the Local 609 records, with no date. It is most likely from The American Independent Newsletter, New Haven, 1969.

Workers Strike Profit-Hungry Olin

by Ruth Meyerowitz

The 3,000 production workers at the Winchester Division of Olin Mathieson Chemical Corporation are currently on strike against an attack on both their standards of living and their union.

Stormy labor-management relations are not uncommon at Winchester. The company has a history of anti-union policies. For example, there was a seven week strike against the company in 1962. Moreover, it took six or seven major attempts to get a union into the plant. When the International Association of Machinists (IAM) was finally recognized as bargaining agent in 1957 it called the local "Victory" Lodge 609 to celebrate its hard-won triumph.

On July 16, 3,000 workers at the Winchester Division of Olin-Mathieson New Haven's largest industrial employer, voted to strike. The members of Victory Lodge 609 of the IAM rejected a company offer which would have destroyed many of the gains won by the workers over the past 13 years. The union pointed out that a 5% wage increase was grossly inadequate and that the company proposal for phasing out an incentive pay formula would mean a wage cut for more than 1200 of its members during the three years of the contract.

Other attacks on work standards by

Strikers keep vigil as Olin delays settlement.

Collective Bargaining?

Also at issue is Olin's way of negotiating. Although negotiations began more than two months before the contract was to end, the company held firmly to its original offer. In a press release June 25, union president Louis Romano revealed no agreement had been reached on a single issue. He accused Olin of attempting

pany seems to be following a fairly common American management practice of forcing long and costly strikes on unions in hopes that after several weeks the union must accept on the company's terms. Olin's hopes to force workers to question the value of a union which can get them little, if anything, more than the company was originally willing to

The long strike had a major impact on the larger community, which provided much support for its striking workers.

In a telegram of October 27, 1969 to the President of Local 609, Louis Romano, the Democratic candidate for Mayor, Bartholomew Guida, offered his services as a third-party participant in negotiation meetings to attempt to help resolve the impasse between the company and the union.

The union took out a full-page ad in the *New Haven Register* which appeared on the 103rd day of the strike, Sunday, October 26, 1969. On November 12, workers voted to accept a settlement which many felt left important issues unresolved and could hardly

A small number of the 500 delegates from the Connecticut State Labor Council Convention, held that September in New Haven at the Park Plaza Hotel, joined pickets on the line at Olin-Winchester. New Haven Journal-Courier, *no date visible. Image is a clipping from the Local 609 files.*

ᴋers Rap Union Actions

ᴇst Olin Talk' Fruitless'

NTHONY
ᴄff Reporter
session
officials of
d Victory
nal Asso-
AM), ap-
ᴐproduc-
ngs.
ᴅent of
local,
sion was
further
1.

said his
ᴆresented
ᴆich they
hours"
ᴆince ear-
without a

went on,
it made
ᴋe began
s rejected
he mem-

ᴛemate in
ly contin-
ᴛing signs
ying to
ᴇ elotment
ᴆding the pa-
Olin's striking

k workers who
picketing the
evening con-
when he ar-
ging that they
ᴆnformed about
ᴆgotiations

Journal-Courier Photo by Robert C. Child III

Labor Council delegates join pickets at Olin Wednesday.

Union Delegates Join Pickets At Olin Plant

be viewed as an unqualified win for the union. For example, although they would be given an opportunity of first bid by seniority on other jobs in the plant, nearly 400 workers would be cut from Olin's ammunition department, which the company claimed resulted from its inability to procure ammunition contracts during the strike.[71]

On the Line

Olin has offered its working members a very unfair contract. I feel this contract to be outrageous because a very large company like Olin can afford to pay its workers more.

Olin has workers, both men and women, black and white, who want to make a better life for themselves and their families. These workers would strive to better themselves, to learn more and to become better and more highly trained, if Olin would give them the chance.

But Olin will not pay a decent wage. Today, with the higher prices on everything, like rent, food and medicine, a worker has got to be at least six days on the job in order to give his family a decent life. This means he can't be with his family but one day, and then he's too tired to be bothered with their problems. He can't spend time with his family or in his community. He can't help with problems in his kids' school or in his own community. He's got to work all the time for his family just to keep up with the times. But Olin keeps on making more and more money.

We must demand Olin give us higher wages and better working conditions. We must get Olin to do away with job discrimination among all, to give a man or woman an opportunity to perform a job regardless of color or sex. We, the members of Lodge 609 can blaze ahead in the industrial field and can set a pattern for all the working people in this country to set their sights on.

. . . .

As a member of Lodge 609 of the International Association of Machinists, I am writing this in hopes that other members of this union will understand how wrong Olin is in their bargaining offer to us concerning our contract. For example, the medical offer is very unfair and has been for some time. They are offering labor grades 1 through 3 $75.00, and the rest of the labor grades remain the same.

This means that after ten days out sick, members in the lower labor grades get the same $55 or $60 a week as before.

It takes as much for the rest of us on medical roll to live as it does the top labor grades, with the same higher cost for doctors, medicine and hospital care. We the people in labor grades 5 through ten will suffer as we have in the past, I feel that the company should realize this, for they have been sick and have felt the higher costs in the medical field. I feel that this is an issue that we the members of Lodge 609 and other members of union lodges are very concerned about, and the people should know the type of issue we are faced with.

I hope that they understand and support us.

A concerned union member.

This paper was published by the American Independent Movement.

THIS PETITION WAS CIRCULATED BY PEOPLE FROM AIM. IN A SHORT TIME AS MANY AS 240 COMMUNITY LEADERS AND SMALL BUSINESSMEN SIGNED TO DEMONSTRATE THEIR SUPPORT FOR THE OLIN STRIKERS. THE NAMES OF SOME OF THOSE PEOPLE ARE PRINTED BELOW.

We the undersigned are businessmen, ministers, and community leaders in New Haven. We are concerned that the Olin strikers, our friends and neighbors, have been forced into a prolonged seven week strike by the Olin Corporation. We believe that the company offer in a time of rising prices and higher taxes is inadequate. We think that the company's style of bargaining is high-handed and arrogant. It refused to meet with and tried to ignore the union, Victory Lodge 609 of the International Association of Machinists (IAM). It ran expensive propaganda campaigns in the newspapers. It tries to bribe the strikers into an early settlement by withholding vacation pay until a new contract is signed. We support the strikers' fight for a decent standard of living.

GRAND AVENUE AREA

Palm Beach Restaurant, 384 Grand Ave.
Wil Mor Pharmacy, 396 Grand Ave.
Giorgio Liquor Store, 398 Grand Ave.
Grand Pharmacy, 309 Grand Ave.
Burns Restaurant, 303 Grand Ave.
Cumberland Farms, 304 Grand Ave.
Empire Wines, 298 Grand Ave.
Cepeda Plastic, 288 Grand Ave.
Grazzy's Restaurant, 284 Grand Ave.
Supreme Department Store, 266 Grand Ave.
Hamilton Poultry Market, 232 Short Beach Rd. East Haven
Petis Hardware, 258 Grand Ave.
D'Amato Sea Food, 250 Grand Ave.
Baracles Pharmacy, 248 Grand Ave.
Connie's Fashion Beauty Salon, 244 Grand Ave.
De Felice Service Station, 208 Grand Ave.
Sals Sandwich Shop, 188 Grand Ave.
Sunoco Service Station, 187 Grand Ave.
Riverside Laundry, 251 Grand Ave.
Brillante Grocery, 255 Grand Ave.
Fair Haven Furniture, 263 Grand Ave.
Cramas Hair Styles, 271 Grand Ave.
Connecticut Auto Parts, 273 Grand Ave.
Fortuna's Bake Shop, 258 Grand Ave.
Perrotti's Farm Market, 108 Grand Ave.
Grand Apizza, 117 Grand Ave.
Fair Haven TV Service, Grand Ave.
Milano's Meat Inc., 93 Grand Ave.
Cassellas Sign Store
U and M Surplus
Pequot Pharmacy, 106 Grand Ave.
Fair Haven Cleaners, 387 Grand Ave.
Bartirmo's Bakery, 389 Grand Ave.
Walts Bar and Grill, 393 Grand Ave.
Unger's N.H. Tile Co, 575 Grand Ave.
Mack's Barber Shop, 43½ Grand Ave.
Fish Market, 3914 Grand Ave.
Ferro Fish and Chip, 361 Grand Ave.

DWIGHT AREA

Greenhouse Food Shop, 1181 Chapel St.
New York Delicatessen, 1207 Chapel St.
Spic and Span Cleaners, 1379 Chapel St.
J.B. Shoe Repair, 1337 Chapel St.
Castaway Cafe, 1279 Chapel St.
The Skin Trader, 1335 Chapel St.
Swingin' Door Cafe, 1333 Chapel St.
Leon's Barber Shop, 1391 Chapel St.
Jo's Lending Library and Book Shop, 1241 Chapel

DOWNTOWN AREA

Bread & Roses Coffeehouse, 538 State St.
Vollano's Jewelry, 508 State St.
Popular Package Store, 514 State St.
Barranquitas Restaurant, 516 State St.
Gary Stevens, Inc., 150 Orange St.
Beauty Court Salon, 113 Court St.
Carrolls, 820 Chapel St.
E.S. Stores, 810 Chapel St.
Criscuolo's Beauty Boutique, 422 State St.
Court Restaurant, 418 State St.
Chef's Restaurant, State & Court Sts.
Fashion Salon, 140 Orange St.
American Optical, 9 Elm St.
Lundblads, 41 Elm St.
Milford Optical Co., Inc., 259 Orange St.
Dunkin Donuts, 81 Church St.
Bond Clothes, 57 Church St.
American Shoe Repair, 56 Orange St.
Universal Jewelers, 65 Orange St.
Zemel Brothers, 160 Orange St.
People's Hemstitching, 159 Orange St.
Delisle Music Center, 265 Orange St.
Blairs, 74 Orange St.
Triestino State and Court Liquor Shop, 417 State
U.S. Vacuum Store, 405 State St.
Clover Stores, 431 State St.
Red's News Stand, 112 Elm St.
Airmar Travel Service, 746 Chapel St.
Goldie & Libro, 756 Chapel St.
Elaine's Inc., 822 Chapel St.
A & M Discount Stores, 868 Chapel St.
Lowenthal's, 861 Chapel St.
Tifon Jewelers, 833 Chapel St.
Morse Shoe Store, 827 Chapel St.
Morton's Shoe Store, 823 Chapel St.
Carol-Ann Dresses, 813 Chapel St.
United Men's Shop, 799 Chapel St.
Merle's Record Rack, 819 Chapel St.

KIMBERLY AVENUE AREA

Gem Liquors, 65 Lamberton St.
Pepe's Market, 61 Kimberly Ave.
Tip Top Market, 74 Kimberly Ave.
Paramount Barber Shop, 467 Greenwich Ave.
Advocate Press, Inc., 75 Daggett St.

DIXWELL AVENUE AREA

Aubrey Williams, 89 Dixwell Ave.
Vincent Marchese, 79 Dixwell Ave.
B & L Record & Gift Shoppe, 79 Dixwell Ave.
Reaves Barber Shop, 73 Dixwell Ave.
Prouite's Clothes, 71 Dixwell Ave.
Rite Way Tailors, 53 Dixwell Ave.
Lake Variety, 29 Dixwell Ave.
Crisma Fashions, 336 Shelton Ave.
Joe & Jessies, 322 Shelton Ave.
Butler Package Store, 230 Shelton Ave.
Taylor's Watch Repair, 219 Shelton Ave.
Herman & Thurman's Barber Shop
Florentino Beverages, 172 Dixwell Ave.
Jones Barber Shop, 308 Dixwell Ave.
Star Restaurant, 315 Dixwell Ave.
Cozy Corner, 329 Dixwell Ave.
Cash a Check, 3 Shelton Ave.
Dorner & Sykes Inc., 346 Dixwell Ave.
Junction Liquors, 344 Dixwell Ave.
Farrell Drive In, Dixwell Ave.
Fair Department Store, Dixwell Ave.
Capitol Market, 168 Dixwell Ave.
Fashion Flair, 271 Dixwell Ave.
Tony's Fish Market, 249 Dixwell Ave.
Fiorentino's Confectionary, 180 Dixwell Ave.
Marty's Barber Shop, 241 Dixwell Ave.
Goodwill Rehabilitation, 245 Dixwell Ave.
Big Jim's Record Shop, 247 Dixwell Ave.
Superb Restaurant, 257 Dixwell Ave.
Jimmy White Cleaners, 256 Dixwell Ave.
Carla's Togs, Dixwell Ave.
Henny's House of Style, Dixwell Ave.
Davis and Waller Pharmacy, 287 Dixwell Ave.

MEMBERS OF COMMUNITY GROUPS

Frank Annunziato, Fair Haven Betterment Association
Thomas W. Trizzi, Jr., F.H. Betterment Assoc.
David Adams, F.H. Betterment Assoc.
Carol Tripp, Fair Haven Betterment Assoc,
Anthony Acapora, Grand Lodge
Wesley Sackson, Action, Inc.
Thomas Mason, Action, Inc.
Dorothy E., Dixwell Legal Rights Association
Phyllis, Dixwell Legal Rights Association
Jean Walker, Dixwell Legal Rights Association
Janet Glasson, Dixwell Legal Rights
Loretta Henderson, Dixwell Legal Rights
Joseph S. Harris, Dixwell Legal Rights
Ruth O. Robinson, Dixwell Legal Rights
Ida Bruce, Fair Haven Parents' Ministry
Lois Ford, Fair Haven Parents' Ministry
Cassandra Daniel, Fair Haven Parents' Ministry
Hilda Morning, Fair Haven Parents' Ministry
Janet Murphy, Fair Haven Parents' Ministry
Airba Gomez, Fair Haven Parents' Ministry
Paul Spicer, Freedom Now, Inc.
Willie Counsel, President, Hill Parents' Association
W.C. Jones, Dixwell Soul Station, Director
Virgil Gomez, Dixwell Soul Station, Co-Director
William Jones, Progressive Democrats
Dr. Paul Taylor, Kappa Alpha Psi
Patrick Loggins, Black Educators
Alphonso Tindael, Director, Dixwell Community House
Isabel Russel, University Park Community Council
Doris Morrison, University Park Federal Credit Union
Yvonne Moran, C.P.I.
Leroy Anderson, Widow Son Lodge
Joe McCauley, Jr., 19th Ward Democratic Comm.

AIM Editorial

WORKING PEOPLE ARE IN TROUBLE – at Olin, in New Haven, and all over the country. The business – controlled press blames "greedy" workers for inflation. The facts tell a different story: the average worker can buy less for his family than he could three years ago because of higher prices and taxes. But the profits of the big corporations like Olin keep on rising.

THE UNION TRIES TO DEFEND WORKERS AGAINST THE CORPORATION. The union tries to improve the workers' standard of living by fighting to get the profits distributed to the workers who produced them, not to the rich stockholders. It tries to improve working conditions and to protect the workers from getting pushed around by the company – from speed-up, arbitrary rulings, and discrimination.

AIM SUPPORTS THE STRUGGLES OF WORKERS AND THEIR UNIONS BECAUSE WE THINK THIS COUNTRY SHOULD BE RUN FOR THE PEOPLE, NOT FOR THE PROFITS OF THE CORPORATIONS. We know that this goal can be reached only if working people gain more economic and political power by standing together.

EVERYBODY IN NEW HAVEN, EXCEPT THE BOSSES, WILL SUFFER IF THE UNION LOSES THE STRIKE AT OLIN, because Olin's contract helps set the pattern for all wages and working conditions in the area. Other companies in New Haven will try to weaken the unions at their plants, and attack the gains workers have won. AIM believes that solidarity is very important. Working people all over the city have to support the workers at Olin because we're all fighting the same battle and need each others help.

THAT BATTLE HAS MANY FRONTS BECAUSE THE CORPORATIONS USE THEIR POWER IN MANY WAYS TO HURT WORKING PEOPLE.

—they can raise their prices and wipe out our wage increases.

—they use their politicians to get them more tax breaks and put the tax burden on the wage-earner.

—high interest rates give the banks fat profits and make housing impossibly expensive.

—The big corporations pollute our air and water and then make us pay to clean them.

—they try to keep unemployment high, which forces workers – particularly black and white – to fight over jobs that are open.

IN ALL THESE AREAS, AIM THINKS ALL WORKING PEOPLE HAVE TO FIGHT TOGETHER TO SOLVE THE PROBLEMS WE FACE

If you want to contribute something in the next issue, (write, work, anything), or if you have other ideas for projects, give us a call.

American Independent Movement
148 Orange Street
787-0123

Editorial, petition signed by businesses, ministers and community leaders and letter to the editor, American Independent Newsletter. *Images are courtesy of the Local 609 files.*

Negotiations To Resume Today

Dinner Held For Olin Strikers

By RICHARD ANTHONY
Journal-Courier Staff Reporter

The Fair Haven Betterment Association hosted a dinner Tuesday night for about 200 Olin Corp. strikers and their families at the East Pearl Methodist Church.

The dinner, which was attended by all four New Haven mayoral candidates as well as the strikers, came on the eve of renewed negotiations in the 15-week-old Olin strike.

About 3,000 Olin employes, members of Victory Lodge 609, International Association of Machinists (IAM), have been on strike since July 16.

Today's bargaining session, which was called by the federal and state mediators involved in the dispute, will start at 10:30 a.m. at Howard Johnson's Motel in Hamden.

Tuesday night's dinner was made possible through donations of food and money by Fair Haven merchants, according to Tom Tripp, vice president of the association.

The dinner was prepared free of charge by Bob Maranti, an instructor at the Culinary Institute, Tripp added.

The association's aid to the striking workers is part of what appears to be a growing effort on the part of city groups and agencies to at least provide assistance to the IAM members.

According to George Poulin, IAM international representa-

Journal-Courier Photo by Robert C. Child III

Serving line at East Pearl Methodist Church.

tive, the union in the last week has been promised aid by major church and social welfare groups in the city.

Earlier, an issue of the American Independent Movement's (AIM) "Olin Strike News," a bulletin put out periodically by AIM, listed the names of 120 businesses supporting the union in the dispute.

Most of the businesses were shops along Chapel and Orange Streets, Dixwell, and Grand Avenues. An AIM spokesman said the shopowners had agreeds to let their shops be distribution points for the strike bulletin.

The union has also received the backing of numerous unions in the state, and IAM locals elsewhere in the country. Poulin said about $15,000 has been contributed to the strike fund by labor groups.

Poulin also said union advertisement that appeared in The Register and Journal-Courier did not represent a change in strategy for the union, which has generally refrained from publicizing its position.

Instead, he explained, it was the results that have been made quests that hav been made for for the union leadership to speak on the strike issues.

"We've had so many requests we haven't been able to fulfill," Poulin said, "that we felt we could cover some of this with an ad."

The full-page advertisement laid out the union's position on the issues and called on the company to move towards a settlement.

FAIR HAVEN BETTERMENT ASSOCIATION, Inc.

Fair Haven
P.O.Box 44

New Haven, Conn.
06513

October 8, 1969

Members of Victory Lodge 609
International Association of Machinists
965 Dixwell Avenue
Hamden, Connecticut

Dear Members of I.A.M. Victory Lodge 609:

The Fair Haven Betterment Association supports the strikers at the Olin plant.

We would like to express our solidarity, not only in words, but with some concrete action. As such, we are planning to hold a dinner for Olin strikers and their families, who live in Fair Haven. We have decided to have a planning meeting on Sunday, October 12, 7:30 P.M. at the FHBA headquarters, at 244 Poplar Street, New Haven. We would be extremely happy to have any interested Olin workers from Fair Haven come to this meeting and assist us in planning the dinner.

The FHBA feels that this is a minor contribution to the efforts of the strikers and we will be very happy and honored to assist you in any other ways in your struggle with Olin. There are suggestions of collections of food and canned goods. We have also thought of participating in a large protest meeting, if the strikers desire it.

We are encouraging other community groups to come to the support of Olin strikers to build a city wide movement in favor of the workers.

We would like very much to hear your reactions to our ideas.

Sincerely yours and good luck,

The Fair Haven Betterment Assoc.

90

Still, some longer-term benefits may have resulted. New Haven teacher Matt Borenstein, later the president of the New Haven Federation of Teachers, Local 933, felt that a helpful precedent had been set that averted a strike when the next contract came up for negotiation four years later. He cited "significant gains in pension, insurance and sick pay benefits" in the 1973 contract, and noted that the new agreement "came as a great surprise and relief to the union, which fought through a bitter strike in 1969 trying to obtain some of the benefits which were only won this time around." In addition to "major gains in benefits," the 1973 contract offered a wage increase of "5% the first year and 5½% the second year...particularly important since they were won from one of New Haven's largest employers."[72]

103 DAYS!!

Today marks the one hundred & Third day that the members of the International Association of Machinist and Aerospace Workers, AFL-CIO, Victory Lodge 609 have walked the picket line since the Company forced Olin workers into the street.

Community support is growing daily for the strikers and their families. The reason for this solid community support is clear — The Community supports the Unions position on the Key issues in this long dispute.

103 DAYS—And the main issues still remain unsettled

THE ISSUES ARE:

1. PROTECTION OF NEGOTIATED RATES OF PAY FOR ALL JOBS DURING THE LIFE OF THE CONTRACT.
2. ELIMINATION OF THE INCENTIVE SYSTEM.
3. HOURS OF WORK.
4. SENIORITY IMPROVEMENTS.
5. PRODUCTIVITY LANGUAGE.

MONETARY ITEMS

A. WAGES
B. COST OF LIVING
C. HEALTH & WELFARE
D. PENSION PLAN
E. SICK LEAVE
F. MILITARY LEAVE WITH PAY
G. JURY DUTY
H. FUNERAL LEAVE
I. HOLIDAYS & VACATIONS
J. JOB INEQUITIES

OTHER AREAS OF DISAGREEMENT

HELPING THE COMMUNITY

THE UNION STANDS READY TO END THIS LONG COSTLY STRIKE AND REQUESTS THAT THE COMPANY ENGAGE IN IMMEDIATE MEANINGFUL COLLECTIVE BARGAINING.

PAID FOR BY VICTORY LODGE 609
Through Community Contributions

Images from Local 609 files.

Western Union Telegram

850A EST OCT 27 69 BB003
SS B117 B NVA011 FE PDF 6 EXTRA NEW HAVEN CONN 27 735A EDT
LOUIS ROMANO PRESIDENT VICTORY LODGE 609 75 DLY
INTERNATIONAL ASSOC OF MACHINISTS
965 DIXWELL AVE HAMDEN CONN
DEAR MR ROMANO
I AM WRITING YOU IN MY CAPACITY AS PRESIDENT OF THE NEW HAVEN BOARD OF ALDERMAN AND THE DEMOCRATIC CANDIDATE FOR MAYOR. THE OLIN STRIKE HAS CONTINUED SINCE JULY 15,1969. THREE THOUSAND PEOPLE HAVE BEEN OUT OF WORK AND WITHOUT INCOME IN THE CITY OF NEW HAVEN FOR OVER THREE MONTHS. THE ECONOMY OF NEW HAVEN AND THE VERY EXISTENCE OF OLIN'S NEW HAVEN-BASED EMPLOYEES ARE IN PRECARIOUS POSITION. LEADERSHIP AND SOCIAL CONSCIENCE ARE REQUIRED TO BRING THIS STRIKE TO AN END. I FEEL SO STRONGLY ABOUT THIS MATTER, WHICH IS OF CRISIS PROPORTION, THAT I WOULD RESPECTFULLY REQUEST THAT I BE INVITED AS A PARTICIPANT IN FUTURE MEETINGS OF THE CONCERNED PARTIES. IT MAY VERY WELL BE THAT THE INTERVENTION OF A THIRD PARTY INTERESTED IN THE WELFARE OF THE PEOPLE OF NEW HAVEN MAY PROVE TO BE THE CATALYST FOR BRINGING THIS MATTER TO AN IMMEDIATE AND SUCCESSFUL CONCLUSION
BARTHOLOMEW GUIDA 100 FOSTER ST NEW HAVEN CONN
757).

AIM
148 Orange St.
New Haven, Conn. 06510
787-0123

STRIKE NEWS
No. 5 12/2/69 **published by the American Independent Movement**

The Strike is Over But the Fight Goes On

Members of IAM Lodge 609 are slowly returning to work at the New Haven Olin plant. On Nov. 11 they voted to accept a settlement of the 112 day strike. About 400 of the 3000 workers will not go back to Olin because of cutbacks in the ammunition department. Some of the former incentive workers feel that they have gotten a raw deal with new, tougher working conditions and a cut in pay from the last wages they received just before the strike.

The union feels that the "on the job protection" written into the contract is a major gain. The New Haven plant is now the only one in Olin's Winchester-Western division with full arbitration rights on any productivity changes and changes in job classification by Olin. The wage gains were in line with other union contracts won this year—about 7% a year, which is a little ahead of the current rate of inflation. The gains in pension payments and medical provisions were small. (See chart for details of contract settlement.)

Layoffs in Ammunition

Olin claims that it did not bid on government ammunition contracts during the strike. Several hundred workers, after striking for over 17 weeks, were told by Olin that they no longer had a job. Those workers laid off in ammo are given first bid by seniority on open jobs in other parts of the plant. There is also talk about tooling jobs which would provide jobs for a limited time.

The battle is not over!

going into a higher labor grade or by increasing his production), his pay now is based upon an average of the higher and lower wages. In this particular case, although the yearly salary goes up, the benefits of improved skill or higher job classification are partially wiped out under the new contract.

Example
$4.50 an hour July '68 to Dec. '68
5.00 an hour Jan. 69 to July '69
$4.75 is the average
the worker's increase is based on the 4.75 average, not on the 5.00 rate

Incentive System Ended

The following is a summary of the major features of the new contract:

1. Wages

Across the board increases for non-incentive workers:
7.5% the first year
6.0% the second year
7.0% the third year

A shift premium is an additional hourly bonus for work on second and third shifts:
Second shift: 12¢—old 20¢—new
Third shift: 16¢—old 25¢—new

The new contract ends the incentive system. Each worker formerly on incentive will earn more than his average for

FINAL

The New Haven Register

WEATHER
TONIGHT: Rain
TOMORROW: Mostly Cloudy
(Full Details on Page 2)

163RD YEAR NO. 82   NEW HAVEN, CONN., 06503, MONDAY, MARCH 24, 1975   15 CENTS

City Offers Olin $6 Million Plan

Package Involves 80 Acres

By STANLEY J. VENOIT
Staff Reporter

The City of New Haven's efforts to keep Olin-Winchester operations in New Haven could involve a massive $6 million spending program to achieve a plant of up to 1.5 million square feet for the world-renowned company.

The program is but one of several unveiled by the city on March 6 at a meeting with company officials here in New Haven. The plans have been kept under wraps, but Mayor Bartholomew F. Guida has now issued invitations to various people to attend a public display of the proposals.

The session is to be held Wednesday at 10 a.m. in the Knights of Columbus Building.

The impressive presentation prepared by the New Haven City Plan Department and the Redevelopment Agency outlines various programs to achieve a varying degree of space to meet the needs of the Winchester operation. The firm has taken an option for a site in the East Haven Industrial Park at the Tweed-New Haven Airport.

A major proposal of the City of New Haven is that the administration is prepared to carry out acquisition, demolition, relocation and site improvement activities necessary to provide Olin-Winchester with a fully expanded Olin "Super-Block" to accommodate a plant of up to 1.5 million square feet, plus related research and development uses and peripheral parking sites.

The project would include construction of three parking

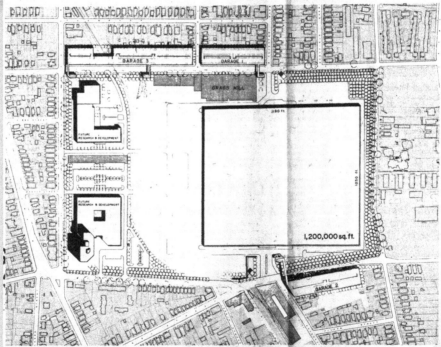

Details of massive "SuperBlock" development plan proposed for Olin-Winchester would involve construction of three parking garages, closing of Winchester Avenue between Munson and Division Streets, and relocation of Canal Line rail tracks.

Defenses Crumble, Viet Severed

New Haven Register, *March 24, 1975, p.1. From Local 609 files.*

8

BUSINESS AS USUAL IN THE 1970S

As contracts for armaments receded after the U.S. war in Indochina ended, weapons makers all over the country suffered. At Winchester, according to the figures cited in the *New Haven Register* and *Strike News,* employment had risen from about 2,000 production workers at the time of the 1962 strike vote to about 3,000 during the 1969 walkout but had shrunk to 1,350 by 1979 at the time of Local 609's third and final strike.

CONCESSIONS

In 1975, the Olin Corporation began to speak of moving its Winchester Division to East Haven, and New Haven responded by "unveiling a 'superblock' plan, which included the development of a new complex for the arms manufacturer and the closing of a segment of Winchester Avenue."[73] The *New Haven Register* reported that after the company "took out an option for a site in the East Haven Industrial Park at the Tweed-New Haven Airport," the City presented "various programs" privately at a meeting with company officials on March 6th and in a public presentation on March 26th "to achieve a varying degree of space to meet the needs of the Winchester operation. A major proposal of the City of New Haven [was] that the administration [was] prepared to carry out acquisition, demolition, relocation and site activities necessary to provide Olin-Winchester with a fully expanded Olin-Winchester 'Super-Block' to accommodate a plant of up to 1.5 million square feet, plus related research and development uses and peripheral parking sites."[74]

The new plant was not built until nearly 20 years later. The only part of the plan that was carried out immediately was the closing of Winchester Avenue between Munson and Division Streets, supposedly to allow for plant expansion, a decision that upset many Newhallville residents because it restricted residential traffic in the area.[75]

NUDGE, NUDGE. WINK, WINK.

From 1976 to 1978, Olin-Winchester came under investigation for illegally selling guns to apartheid South Africa, like its closest competitor, Colt Firearms. Reported the *New York Times,* "The company, which has owned Winchester since 1931, had acknowledged in a no-contest plea to a 21-count federal indictment that employees of its firearms division submitted fraudulent export documents to the State Department over the destination of 3,200 non-automatic and semi-automatic rifles and 20 million rounds of ammunition."[76] The sales were in violation of the U.S. Neutrality Act of 1963.

Target *(company newsletter for Olin employees in New Haven and Branford. January 28, 1977, Vol. 12, No. 1)*

In 1976, a temporary secretary at the company, Marcia Biederman, published a story in the New Haven Advocate *that revealed that Olin Winchester had other customers in addition to its loyal clientele in the United States.*

Marcia Biederman wrote in the *New Haven Advocate* that "White South Africans are buying out all the guns sporting goods stores have to offer and are rushing to form pistol clubs in response to demonstrations of blacks and mixed-race persons demanding an end to apartheid, the government supported system of segregation. Blacks and 'coloreds' fighting with machetes and stones are now very likely facing the barrels of two of our state's most famous products: Winchesters and Colts, which have been shipped to South Africa from New Haven and Hartford, respectively: There is no question," she wrote, "that the Winchester and Colt shipments are illegal. The Mutual Security Act (or Neutrality Act) of the United States code states that munitions can only be exported to countries on the approved list... The Republic of South Africa has not been on the approved list for U.S. munitions since 1963. Nevertheless, elaborate transshipment schemes have been used to run Winchesters and Colts to South Africa secretly." Ms. Biederman characterized federal involvement as a "nudge, nudge, wink, wink situation." She said she was aware from the beginning of her employment that there was a Grand Jury investigation underway, while, at the same time, "there was also a lot of shredding of documents" occurring just in advance of the arrival of federal agents.[77]

In March of 1978, after the company pleaded "No Contest" to the charges of "conspiracy" in the case lodged against it, Judge Robert C. Zampano of

"I decided to write the article [about Winchester selling guns to South Africa] because I saw a documentary... about how horrible conditions were [there]. I was scared to do it [at first] but this documentary changed my mind."

MARCIA BIEDERMAN

How did she come to work at Winchester?: A Bridgeport native, Biederman attended college in Pennsylvania and then lived in California for about 7 years. She returned to Connecticut in 1975, settling in New Haven because she heard it had "a vibrant women's community," with institutions such as the New Haven Women's Liberation Center. "It was tough to get jobs because there was a recession," and especially hard for women. She was placed as a substitute secretary in Winchester's International Division from December 1975 to April 1976, and again in July of 1976.

How did she feel about working at a gun factory?: "I didn't care. I wanted to make enough money to pay my rent and buy food. Not that I liked guns, but I had no moral qualms about it." Like many of her co-workers, she mostly thought of the guns as sporting items.

The "moral qualms" came later. She was aware from the beginning that there was a federal investigation going on. Then she happened to see a documentary called "Last Grave at Dimbaza," about "how horrible conditions were in South Africa." She was scared at first to begin the investigative reporting effort, "but this documentary changed my mind."

What about her co-workers?: They "felt betrayed..." Unlike Biederman, a temporary agency employee, "they really worked for Winchester. It looked bad for them that they had socialized with me. I felt bad about that for a long time. But I felt this was more important."

The Makeover: Biederman published a novel called *The Makeover* in 1984. It is the story of Muriel Axelrod, a secretary at a fictional munitions plant in San Francisco, who learns that her bosses are running guns to South Africa and undertakes her own investigation.

Federal District Court assessed a $45,000 fine plus $500,000 to be paid as "voluntary reparations" to the City of New Haven. The funds were to be allocated by a five-member panel known as the New Haven Community Betterment Fund (set up by the company itself) to 25 charitable organizations by February of 1979. Zampano stated that, having been told by "some Olin employees" that they were "embarrassed" by the conviction, his order to the company to set up the charity fund "was an attempt to restore community confidence in one of our most respected corporations."[78]

But the panel was criticized for its lack of "transparency" to the community, and the penalty itself was deemed by many as too lenient for the severity of the crime. Richard Blumenthal, who was at the time the United States Attorney for Connecticut, termed the fine "nominal" and "said that 'the government is not wholly satisfied with the sentence.' He said that Olin could claim an extensive tax deduction for its 'voluntary' charitable contribution."[79]

Richard Blumenthal, who was at the time the United States Attorney for Connecticut, termed the fine "nominal" and "said that 'the government is not wholly satisfied with the sentence.'"

A coalition of 20 community groups calling itself the Community Renewal and Action Committee, led by the Black Coalition, the Latino Development Corporation and Downtown Cooperative Ministries, had formed before the disbursements were announced to urge that the fines levied against Olin be used "in some way" to benefit blacks in South Africa, who were the primary victims of the company's malfeasance. After Zampano had made his decision and Olin had established the New Haven Betterment Fund at his behest, the group wrote in a prepared statement that its position remained unchanged: "Any monies that are to come to this community as a result of Olin's transgressions in South Africa should be used in some way to benefit those who are dealt the most harm. Obviously those people are the Black South Africans."[80]

The group also criticized the composition of the five-member New Haven Community Betterment Fund panel, noting that its president, Dr. Michael L. Fezza, an ophthalmologist, was a friend of the Judge, and also that the awards given included monies for organizations with which panel members were affiliated. Even the Mayor of New Haven, Frank Logue, complained that "the panel did not welcome outside recommendations, and the only way I could get my views to them, views that were rejected, was to write them a letter."[81]

Hundreds of applications were submitted to the fund from a variety of charitable and educational organizations, and when the 25 recipients were announced in February of 1979 after a year's deliberation by the panel, C.R.A.C. asked the State Attorney General's Office to investigate the disbursements: "In a letter to Attorney General Carl Ajello, [the group] questioned the roles of two of the fund's directors, Emma Ruff, principal of Hillhouse High School, and Rev. Raymond J. Barry, pastor of St. Martin de Porres Church, since Hillhouse got a $20,000 grant and St. Martin's Church School got $40,000."[82]

Because of the strong community reaction and the fact that school board policy had not been followed in applying for it, Superintendent of Schools Gerald Tirozzi rejected the $20,000 grant offered to Hillhouse High School. While commending Mrs. Ruff for her efforts on behalf of the school, Tirozzi also said that he would "find it difficult to justify the acceptance of a $20,000 gift to one particular high school, when the system has three other high schools, each of which could benefit from the purpose for which the grant was intended."[83]

In June, Mrs. Ruff and Father Barry were officially absolved by the State Attorney General Carl Ajello of mishandling the money under C.R.A.C.'s conflict of interest charge.[84]

THE 1979-1980 STRIKE

In July of 1979, Local 609 workers again went on strike. It was a bitter, protracted event, lasting until January of 1980, involving the entire New Haven community, pitting some members against others as the city police force was deployed to protect "scabs" (workers who crossed the picket lines) and replacement workers hired by the company, and to "keep order." There were numerous arrests of striking workers and community supporters.

The crucial issue was that the company wanted to eliminate the hard-fought Article IV of the union contract which protected workers against daily quotas set by management and was especially important to older workers. In particular, the company wanted to set individual production quotas and fire those who did not meet them.

Since 1969, the company had repeatedly threatened to shut down or move out of New Haven to back up its demand for increased production with no increase in pay. It renewed this threat repeatedly during the strike, announcing that it would not reopen its brass mill.

In their continuing struggle, the members of Victory Lodge Local 609, International Association of Machinists, have faced police clubs, a hostile court, and the threat of a plant shutdown...

The Winchester workers are still facing up to these pressures, aided by other IAM locals, the state and city labor councils, the New Haven area UE locals and an active community support committee. The entire labor movement in New Haven sees Olin's attempt to break the union at Winchester as a threat to every union local in the area.[85]

—"IAM Members at Winchester Fighting Incentive Demand," *UE News*, vol. 42 no. 2 (January 1, 1980), 9.

Craig Gauthier, above, was a Chief Steward of Local 609 during the 1979-1980 strike. He became President of the Local in the late 1980s. Photo is from the Local 609 files.

The company spared no efforts to break the 1979 strike and Local 609: it obtained an injunction that mandated no more than 20 picketers at one time and required them to register with police; it took out full page ads in the local papers; and it engaged the local police force to escort strike-breakers across the picket lines. Arrests were made in August of seven picketers. Thousands of workers from throughout New England came to New Haven to march and support the strikers at the end of that month. New Haven's mayor, Frank Logue, ordered all access to the plant closed in an attempt to end the confrontations between police, strikers and "scabs" who crossed the lines.[86]

On January 20, 1980, after six months on strike, workers voted to accept a compromise contract which provided some protections for elderly or disabled workers if they couldn't meet speed-up requirements as well as pay raises and improved pension and medical benefits for all. But the company won the right to set production standards and to fire workers that it alleged were unproductive if an arbitrator's decision was not reached within 45 days.[87]

Craig Gauthier started work at Winchester in 1973, becoming shop steward in 1979. During the 1979 strike, he was also Chair of the Citizens Ad Hoc Committee to Support the Winchester Strikers, which helped to

> **"I was not always confrontational (although some people might disagree) but I was not going to let [the company] violate the union contract."**

CRAIG GAUTHIER

Gauthier worked at Winchester for 23 years, from 1973 until 1996.

Early years in New Haven: Born and raised in Louisiana, he first came to New Haven in 1966, just out of the military. "To me, New Haven was the most exciting place to be, politically."

From 1966 until 1970, he worked mornings at Yale-New Haven Hospital and the 3–11 shift at Pratt and Whitney in North Haven. He became interested in the Black Panther party and volunteered with their children's breakfast program and helped to administer its clothing distribution program: "We had garages on Sylvan Avenue and Orchard Street where people could go" to pick up clothing. In 1967 and 1968, he helped organize housekeeping workers at Yale-New Haven Hospital and met members of the Communist Party who worked alongside Local 1199 organizers. He "was pleased to meet progressive union people." He joined the CP in 1970.

Back to Louisiana: He went home to Louisiana in 1970 to care for his ailing mother. "In many places in Louisiana at the time, there was still 'Jim Crow' stuff going on."

While there, he helped start the Young Workers Liberation League, which worked with the Meat Cutters Union "trying to organize plantation workers...We took people to Washington to testify about [being] locked in to the plantation lifestyle."

Return to New Haven: He came back to the city in 1973, first getting a job as a machine operator at another company, but then went to work at Winchester in the Barrel Shop.

At the same time, utilizing his Veterans' Benefits, he attended South Central Community College: "I went to school full time and worked full time from 1973 to 1976. I loved it because it fit into my political work."

Working with Local 609: "When the union came in, a lot of changes took place, slowly... I loved 609 because [it] had a strong presence in the Central Labor Council and in the state of Connecticut. The Machinists Union was a progressive union even though some of the leaders [were not.] 609 to me was very powerful...With 1800 workers... you bring a lot of votes [to the table and] you can move things."

He eventually became Shop Steward for the Barrel Shop, then Assistant Chief Steward and finally Chief Steward. He became president of Local 609 in the late 1980s. "What I did to prepare for the presidency was I studied the history [of the union.] I give the initiators a lot of credit." His greatest aspirations as president were to "be able to implement the High Performance Work Organization" [plan] "and also to get more workers actually involved in union business...We had to participate at the state level [as well], and Black members had to be involved in that."

Celebrating Martin Luther King Day in the Winchester lunch room.

At Winchester, the union initiated the celebration of Martin Luther King Day every year. "The union had a certain power for the company to shut down production from 2 to 3 p.m."

The union also started the Winchester Fund, whereby members donated money out of their paychecks to organizations such as the Dixwell Community House, the United Way and "Rev. Bonita Grubbs' organization," Christian Community Action. About $60,000 was donated to community groups.

Greatest challenges as Local 609 President: "I was not always confrontational (although some people might disagree) but I was not going to let [the company] violate the contract.

"The biggest problem I had [among the membership] was the trades-people because they always felt they should get all the gravy... The company would play [them] off against the machine operators... The most senior people were white men."

Working at Winchester: **"Winchester was a family. People knew each other. [It] was a place where young people could see people going to work, and leaving work talking to each other. I liked going to work. Winchester was an integral part of the community, and the people who worked there were respected: 'Those are special workers who keep a plant running 24 hours a day, seven days a week.'"**

Support the Workers
ON STRIKE AT OLIN

A PLANING COMMITTEE MEETING
WILL BE HELD FOR A COMMUNITY
—— SUPPORT RALLY ——

MEETINGS: Thursday, August 9
Thursday, August 16

TIME: 7:30 P.M.

PLACE: LINCOLN BASSETT SCHOOL CAFETERIA
CORNER of SHELTON and BASSETT STREETS

Rally - THE COMMUNITY RALLY WILL BE HELD
ON Thursday, August 23, 1979

SPONSORED BY: THE COMMUNITY LABOR ALLIANCE
GREATER NEW HAVEN CENTRAL LABOR COUNCIL
MACHINISTS UNION LOCAL 609 DISTRICT 170

All images and photographs were found in the Local 609 files.

Journal-Courier **STATE & CITY**

WEDNESDAY, OCTOBER 10, 1979   Suburban 16, Obituaries 21   15

Cross High student needed just one look to realize he'd taken the wrong route to school

Staff Photo by KENNETH A. RANDOLPH

Police strategy curbs Olin strife

By JANET KIPPHUT
Staff Reporter

A well-organized shell game put into play by New Haven police Tuesday morning defused a potentially violent confrontation between police and striking Olin Corp. workers.

The plan, devised by Chief Ed Morrone and Patrol Commander John O'Connor, was to emphasize strategy instead of trying to overwhelm by brute force the approximately 300 pickets outside the Newhallville plant's gates.

Also, according to just-released figures, the cost of police protection at the site is estimated at $100,000 since the July 16 start of the strike by Victory Lodge Local 609, District 170, International Association of Machinists and Aerospace Workers.

Morrone said the department's overtime budget, about $170,000, will be exhausted by the first of the year. Tuesday's manpower costs alone were between $8,000 and $10,000, the chief said.

The strategy Tuesday was to use all resources, particularly communications capabilities, to isolate pickets in small groups at the perimeters, while directing management employees and strikebreakers into continually changing routes. This strategy left pickets to play "guess which gate the strikebreakers are using."

With this approach, Morrone said, about 80 percent of the work force was able to get into the plant. The number of strikebreakers has been placed at 85.

Further aiding the department was the relatively small number of pickets on hand. Authorities also were helped by the psychological advantage of the riot gear worn by uniformed police as they formed human chains to serve as blockades. This is the first time the gear — helmets, clubs and gas masks, the latter in sacks hanging from belts — has been worn at the scene of the 13-week-old strike.

Other firsts were firemen manning hoses directed at the north and south gates from inside the complex and ambulances stationed at the top of Hillside Place.

Police came close to outnumbering pickets, as upwards of 200 city police were deployed outside the plant's gates and at key intersections. Approximately 50 state troopers were stationed nearby, but their presence was not needed.

Both sides have publicly stated they feared bloodshed if Olin tried to bring in strikebreakers. And, police said they received information that union machinists from factories all over the area would be on hand this morning to support pickets.

Memories haunt him
Armband resented

John Tonishefski, who for 31 years has been with the company once known as Winchester and now Olin, says he particularly objects to a court order requiring striking machinists to wear identifying armbands because it reminds him of the time he spent in a Russian concentration camp.

Tonishefski, who listed his age as older than 55, said he spent nearly two years in a contentration camp in Siberia and saw almost his entire family wiped out when similarly incarcerated. His father and six of seven children died of starvation in the camps, Tonishefski said.

As he stood on the picket line in the early-morning mist Tuesday, Tonishefski fingered the pastel cloth, the hated symbol tied to his umbrella and recounted the events that led him to Siberia.

Born in Jersey City, N.J., Tonishefski found himself in Poland during World War II because his father, who later was jailed as a capitalist, moved the family to their Polish homeland.

"When the war started, my father told me to go back to the U.S., but can go no place. Germans on one side and Russians on the other," he said, with more than a trace of an accent.

So, he stayed in Poland, a one-way ticket to the Russian camps. Why did they take him to the camps? "No reason," he said.

His American citizenship was no help, either. "I showed them my American papers and they tore them up and threw them on the ground."

He said he finally was released because his father, who later was released because the armband which deeply resents the armband which company's Newhallville plant. And, others would agree. An area legal association has labeled the order a violation of pickets' rights.

SHARON ROSENTHAL
JANET KIPPHUT

Troopers go from tornado to strike

First a tornado, and now a potential melee.

That pretty much characterized the situation early Tuesday morning as a convoy of state troopers — many just completing tornado cleanup duty in and around Windsor Locks — settled into Fort Nathan Hale to await word on whether they'd be swept word on whether they'd be needed to help squelch anticipated violence at the Olin Corp. By 5 a.m., about 50 troopers had claimed the Coast Guard station as "command headquarters" for the duration.

"I was warned before I went to bed last night that all these state cops were coming in and that I should just direct traffic," Seaman Russell Jones confided. He said he had enough problems worrying about being a man reported overboard Monday afternoon.

The atmosphere tingled with urgency, efficiency and power. A radio kept the post in constant touch with New Haven's police department. State Police Commissioner Donald Long, in a three-piece Glen plaid suit, conferred solemnly with aides before breaking away to

tell a reporter the men would soon be getting their second briefing on the situation since they were pulled from barracks all over Connecticut.

"I hope nothing happens," Long said. "We're here to aid New Haven if they require assistance. We've been aware of the strike situation since it began, but were only officially apprised a week ago."

Troopers seemed to discuss everything except the Olin affair over coffee and doughnuts that morning. One trooper was overheard joking how much another resembled teen-idol Donny Osmond. Another fretted over his weight.

A group of medics was debating the ideal pulse rate during exercise. "These people are all seasoned and when policemen get together they talk about a lot of different things," one officer explained.

As things turned out, the buses standing by to transport the troopers to the Newhallville plant never rolled Tuesday.

SHARON ROSENTHAL

THE NEW HAVEN REGISTER, MONDAY, JULY 16, 1979

staff photo by JOHN MONGILLO JR.

A Human Blockade

About 100 striking production workers gather outside the main entrance to the Olin Winchester plant here, in an attempt to keep strikebreakers from the plant this morning. The picketing was boisterous at times, but peaceful. The workers voted overwhelmingly Sunday to stage the strike. (Story, other photo, on Page 1)

Journal-Courier

Olin talks due as confrontation continues

Union calls reinforcements

By SHARON ROSENTHAL
and SHEILA RUBIN
Staff Reporters

Steelworkers OK pact with Farrel

By ROBERT W. SHORTELL
Staff Reporter

Koch orders 'John Hour'

No records missing in break at CETA

By ELEANOR LEVITT

Journal-Courier

3-year agreement ends Olin strike

Recall of workers to begin Wednesday

By SHARON ROSENTHAL
Staff Reporter

organize a Christmas party for workers' children as well as many other community efforts to support his fellow union members. In 1984, he became assistant to the Chief Steward, and was elected president of Local 609 in 1987, leaving Winchester in 1995. He also served as the second vice president of the Greater New Haven Central Labor Council and was a member of the Greater New Haven Peace Council's Amistad Committee.

Gauthier commented on the 1979 strike in an interview conducted by Dorothy Johnson and Lula White of the Greater New Haven Labor History Association: "It was a hard strike because the company had the media and the city on their side…The company felt that the union had become too powerful because of its strength within the Central Labor Council and the state. It wanted to break the union's strength."

When the union learned that the company was bringing in workers by bus to cross the picket line, "we decided that we weren't letting the scabs in."

When the union learned that the company was bringing in workers by bus to cross the picket line, "we decided that we weren't letting the scabs in." Some of the strikers started rocking the bus. Leonard Gallo, then a New Haven police officer who later became the police chief in East Haven, led a "team" who "attacked us; they cornered us between two cars and beat us up. I ended up in the hospital."

Still, Gauthier felt that the strike "not only brought the union together stronger, it brought the community together stronger." The community mobilized to support the strikers. "We couldn't have survived if we didn't have the Central Labor Council and the community behind us."[88]

Re: the 1969 strike: "It was bitter. A lot of things were happening because they were bringing outside people in to work. They tried to break us. But we wasn't going to let them do that. We knew we had to stick together."

BARBARA J. BUTLER

Interview conducted on July 12, 2010 by Dorothy Johnson (No photo available.)

Barbara J. Butler was born in Jonesboro, Georgia where her grandparents were farmers. Her mother was a waitress and her father a cook for the Southern Railway. She has lived in New Haven since 1956. On October 14, 1966, after marrying a man who had been at Winchester "since the union came in 1956," she began working at the plant making ammunition on the "graveyard," or 11-7 shift, working her way up to the day shift. Then, the company decided "they didn't want to make ammo" and sent that work to Chicago.

The company was vast, with seven floors including the basement. Ms. Butler worked on gun assembly and did piece work for a while, "but I didn't do too good on piece work. I was slow." Finally, she ended up doing "checkering" on the stocks, which she liked. She continued to do wood-work for much of her time there: [The wood] "may come in split and you have to patch it...I worked with white wood and that's when I learned that white wood has fleas..." She also worked with dark wood. "You have to try to match the forms and put them together." She liked this work and found it interesting, but did not do the staining. Safety masks were not mandatory, and "one of my friends died. She got that stuff on her lungs."

Another job Ms. Butler did not do: "I never was a shooter, I never wanted to be," although she said she later joined the rifle shooting team for recreation, and got up early Saturday morning to practice. "I had to buy the shells but I used their gun."

Although she held no office in the union, she was eventually picked by the company to be one of the "safety persons." The company provided the training.

Although both her husband and her sister-in-law left the plant, she remained working there until it closed in 2006. Several times, she did consider leaving. In fact, she was laid off for two years, during which she worked at the Sargent Company, but she could not keep up with the piece work and was relieved to receive a telegram from Winchester telling her to return to work.

BITTER STRIKES, "REPLACEMENT PEOPLE"

The company tried to break strikes by bringing in "replacement people," or scabs. In 1969, the strikers held firm and won pay increases and some of their other demands. It was a bitter strike, and "they tried to break us. But we wasn't going to let them do that. We knew we had to stick together."

During the 1979-1980 strike, supervisors joined replacement workers and the company was "bringing in beds for people to sleep. Some of the supervisors didn't go home. We found the beds there when we went back to work." There was daily picketing in shifts and all strikers were expected to walk the line. She took the 6-10 am shift. After the long strike ended and the regular workers returned, some of the "replacement workers" also remained, while others did not. "A lot of things were said back and forth" (between the scabs and the regular workers) "but I kept my mouth shut because what came out of my mouth I might have heard about later on."

MARTIN LUTHER KING DAY

Until mandated by state law, Martin Luther King Day wasn't an official holiday. Workers had the option to stay home if they chose, but without pay.

"I didn't go to work that day. I didn't get paid for it but I stayed home...We got off for Columbus Day, why not Martin Luther King Day?"

"This company is going to go down."

The company was always pushing for "givebacks," but according to Ms. Butler, "the union said 'No, why should we give up what we fought to get?'"

By the time she left, employment had dwindled from the 10 to 15,000 people she remembered when she started to below 200.

Although it was obvious that work was being outsourced to a plant in South Carolina, the immediate plant closing came as a "shock... We went in and went to work and they told us to pack our stuff and go home...I didn't know anything about it." But she and her co-workers did "know something was going on" in advance..." As a wood inspector, she saw that a lot of inferior wood was coming in from Panama: "It was sorry. When you touch a piece of wood, you're supposed to feel some life in it... I rejected it and within days they used it. [She knew] 'This company is going to go down.'..."

"During the 1979-1980 strike, supervisors joined replacement workers and the company was "bringing in beds for people to sleep. Some of the supervisors didn't go home. We found the beds there when we went back to work." There was daily picketing in shifts and all strikers were expected to walk the line. She took the 6-10 am shift. After the long strike ended and the regular workers returned, some of the "replacement workers" also remained, while others did not. "A lot of things were said back and forth" (between the scabs and the regular workers) "but I kept my mouth shut because what came out of my mouth I might have heard about later on"

—Barbara J. Butler

BOARD OF ALDERMEN

Stephen Wareck
Alderman, 18th Ward

President

135 Cliff Street
New Haven, Conn. 06511

Telephone: 562-3848
562-9973

September 2, 1983

Mr. Louis Romano
President
Victory Lodge #609
International Association of Machinists
958 Dixwell Avenue
Hamden, CT 06514

Dear Mr. Romano:

I am writing in my capacity as Chairman of the Winchester Avenue Reopening Study Committee, established by order of the Board of Aldermen to recommend a street reopening timetable, to invite you or your designee to provide testimony to the Committee at our next meeting about your union's position on closed street access along Winchester Avenue between Munson and Division Streets.

In your remarks, you may want to take into account some of the items the Committee has taken into consideration during its period of deliberation, namely, the effect of the street closing on the Newhallville Community, the impact reopened access will have on immediate development plans in the area (ie. U.S. Repeating Arms, Science Park Development Corporation); and other related issues.

I've enclosed a copy of the Aldermanic order, for your information, which established this Committee. Although not yet scheduled, I expect that our next meeting will be held the week of September 12th. If you would call Bryan Anderson, of the City Development Administrator's office, at 787-8333 he will be glad to make necessary meeting arrangements.

Thank you for your cooperation. I look forward to hearing from you about this matter.

Sincerely,

Stephen A. Wareck
Stephen Wareck
President
Board of Aldermen

Enclosure

TO ALL DISTRICT 170 DELEGATES:

If you are a delegate to District 170 who has not been attending any monthly meetings, I would advise you to either start attending meetings or consider resigning and let one of the alternate delegates take your place.

In the past few months, meetings of the District could not be held due to the lack of a quorum.

Delegates to District 170 from 609 are:

L. Romano   R. Bassett
P. LaTorraca   C. Gouthier
T. Ford, Jr.   A. Gambardella
J. Brown   J. Jones
D. White   F. Tolson
C. Carmon   D. Wright
J. Council   R. Iannuzzi
J. Smith   C. Leake
E. Gomes

CREDIT UNION MEETING

The annual meeting of the Science Park Federal Credit Union will be held on:

Date: Thursday, June 10th
Time: 7:30 p.m.
Place: Hamden Elks Club
School St., Hamden

Members should attend the meeting to hear what is happening with the Credit Union and take an active part in the election of its Board of Directors and Credit Union Board.

T-SHIRT KING BACK AGAIN

Due to an emergency, the T-shirt King was not able to attend the April meeting of the Lodge. He will, however, be attending our May 22nd meeting. Since it will be some time before I can schedule him to come to another meeting, it is important that any member wishing to order a jacket, hat or t-shirt, be at the meeting on Sunday.

RETIREMENT REPORT

The Greater New Haven Chapter of the National Council of Senior Citizens finalized plans for its first annual outing, to be held on Monday, June 20, 1983 at Sun Valley Acres in Branford.

The Activities Committee, appointed by Chapter President Frank Durante are:

Joseph LaPuma
Margaret DeFrancisco
Anthony Cietanno
Arletha Young

Club members attended events sponsored by the Greater New Haven Senior Citizens Clubs Council in the Month of May, which included:

* Bloomfield Senior Band concert, May 11th at Conte School
* May 16th "Festival on the Green" featuring entertainment & exhibits
* May 23rd & 26th - free bus tours of New Haven, sponsored by Travel and Convention Center of New Haven.

Culminating the month of May observance was a luncheon at the Park Plaza, New Haven where members of various senior clubs were honored, including Joseph Maillet who was named Chapter's "Senior of the Year".

CENTRAL LABOR COUNCIL DELEGATES

At the April membership meeting of the Lodge, the following members were nominated and elected as delegates to the Greater N.H. Central Labor Council. They will serve as delegates until a new election is held in February, 1985.

I. Abrams   J. Palmieri
L. Council   J. Smith
E. Gomes   T. Turek
J. Jones

The Council meets the first Monday of every month at 7:00 p.m. at the Council's hall at 45 Water Street, New Haven.

* WALK AMERICA MARCH OF DIMES *

One of our members - Ella Smith - who took part in the Walk America March of Dimes has asked me to thank all of the members of 609 who helped her raise over $165 for this very worthy cause.

... Victory L...
CT 06514   Union

Victory Lodge 609 Newsletter

Victory Lo...

958 Dixwell Ave., Hamden, CT 06514   Union O...

FROM YOUR PRESIDENT

I want to report that the first meeting between the Company and the Union for the purpose of trying to negotiate a new Labor Agreement was held on Wednesday, May 18, 1983 at 10:00 a.m. A full report concerning the results of that meeting will be made at Sunday's meeting.

As your President, I am hoping to see as many members as possible in attendance at the meeting, not only there to hear the report, but to show the Negotiating Committee that the membership has their complete confidence in them.

My complete report will be made at Sunday's meeting.

Always remember - "United we Stand....
Divided we fall"

Fraternally,
Lou
Lou Romano, President

BUY US SAVINGS BONDS

LODGE 609 SUPPORTS SAVINGS BOND DRIVE --

You will soon be contacted (or already have) by your Area Steward to explain to you the benefits of the Payroll Savings Plan. They will be encouraging you to sign up for EE Savings Bonds, explaining the new interest rate system and answering any questions about this means of saving and the status of their old Bonds.

Lodge 609 has always supported the U.S. Savings Bond Drive and we urge all of our members to do the same and make this campaign a huge success.

THE NEXT MEMBERSHIP MEETING:

SUNDAY, DECEMBER 18, 1982
HAMDEN I.A. CLUB
COLUMBUS ST., HAMDEN

10:00 A.M.

EXECUTIVE BOARD - 9:00 A.M.

NEXT MEMBERSHIP MEETING WILL BE:

DATE: SUNDAY, MAY 22, 1983

PLACE: HAMDEN I.A. CLUB
COLUMBUS ST., HAMDEN
(First left off Morse St. after Railroad crossing)

TIME: 10:00 A.M.

EXECUTIVE BOARD WILL MEET AT 9:00 A.M. SHARP!

NOTICE TO STEWARDS

All Stewards are to pick up the Dues Cards of all members in their areas and return them to the Union Office no later than Tuesday, May 31st so they can be brought up to date. Members who fail to give their card to their Steward will be required to bring it to the Union Office themselves.

Corinne

CONTRACT NEGOTIATIONS BEGIN MAY 18, 1983

In accordance with Article 39, (Duration) of the Labor Agreement, the Union notified the Company on April 25, 1983 of its request to terminate our present Agreement which expires on 7/15/83.

On April 29, 1983 the Company notified the Union that it had received our letter requesting to terminate our present Agreement and that for the purpose of negotiating a new Agreement, they would like to confirm the morning of Wed., May 18, 1983 as our first bargaining session.

Since the Union had no objection to meeting on that date, the meeting was held.

FROM YOUR PRESIDENT

To open my report, may I take this opportunity, on behalf of the Officers, Chief Stewards and our members and their families a very Merry Christmas and a Happy and Healthy New Year!

We all know that 1983 was a very bad year for most of us with the economy the way it is, but the good news is that if predictions are right, 1984 will be much better. What is even more encouraging is the fact that the Company has informed me that approximately 100 to 125 laid off members will be recalled to work after the first of the year. I know our members out on layoff will be happy to hear this good news.

I also hope by the time you receive this newsletter, the new in-plant parking area for the employees' cars will be ready. As you know, the Company just received the lease from Olin and is presently working on the area which will accommodate approximately 80 cars. The rest of my report will be made at Sunday's meeting.

Fraternally,
Lou
Lou Romano, President

RETIREMENT REPORT

On Tuesday, December 13, the New Haven Chapter of the National Council of Senior Citizens held their first annual Christmas party at the 95 Steak House on State Street, North Haven.

As President of Lodge 609, I was invited as an honored guest, representing 609. There were more than 65 retirees and their guests in attendance and a good time was had by all. The next meeting of the Chapter will be held on Monday, January 9, 1984.

COMPANY TO SHUTDOWN FRIDAY, DECEMBER 23

The Company has informed me that all production operations will be curtailed on Friday, Dec. 23. Notices of the shutdown have been posted throughout the Plant.

In answer to many questions - this is not a paid holiday. The Company is applying the temporary curtailment clause in the Labor Agreement for this shutdown.

Membership Monthly Dues:

At Sunday's meeting, I will be making a full report regarding our monthly dues and the increase in per capita tax we are required to pay to the Grand Lodge.

All concerned members should be at the meeting to hear the report and have any questions they may have concerning our dues, answered.

The District would like to take this opportunity to thank all the members of Lodge 609 for the support you gave to the striking members of Lodge 212C in their fight against the Geometric Tool Company. The strike was successfully ended with a new 3-year Agreement which includes increases in wages and fringe benefits, along with increased protection in their seniority provisions.

The year 1983 will go down in history as one in which our Country's greatest resource, the working people have been through a most devastating year, with high unemployment and the continual pressure by corporate America to force concession bargaining - backed by President Reagan's economic policies which has made negotiations most difficult, to say the least. But District 170 is proud to state that in the 15 new Labor Agreements negotiated this year, no concessions or "take backs" were given. This was made possible through YOU, the members of our District - by your strength and dedication to our Union.

AMERICAN IS BEAUTIFUL
Buy American... and look for the Union Label!!

9

THE 1980S—WHIRLWINDS OF CHANGE

USRAC AND THE BEGINNING OF SCIENCE PARK

The company had already begun its process of disengaging from New Haven by 1979, when it moved its Brass Mill to East Alton, IL. In November 1979, during the strike, the *New Haven Register* reported that the New Haven Board of Alders took up the question of whether or not to reopen the portion of Winchester Avenue that had been sealed off from the Newhallville neighborhood for nearly four years, "as the first step in a city project designed to allow Olin to expand its operations here. That expansion has not yet come about and some question whether it ever will." Prior to the meeting, the City Plan Commission submitted a report that confidently predicted that Winchester operations would continue in New Haven. The Commission recommended that the question be tabled for 18 months, citing "Winchester reports of $11.7 million for capital investments since 1976." Another report, sent to the Newhallville Neighborhood Corporation by Richard D. Wolff, research economist for the Greater New Haven Central Labor Council, AFL-CIO, in advance of the aldermanic meeting, had a different take:

> Wolff said that in 1978, Olin did $1.56 billion in business, of which Winchester-Western accounted for less than 19%…[He] said that Olin had budgeted and spent $162 million in capital construction for 1978, and roughly the same amount again in 1979. 'Despite these large spending programs, nothing of these sums was spent for renovation or expansion in New Haven, nor could anyone promise that such spending was even planned in Olin's capital spending program for 1977-81, planned at $1 billion.'

> Wolff observed that a serious binding commitment could have been demonstrated by the "allocation of just a few million as a down-payment" on the proposed "super-block" expansion.

He said, "Giving Olin tax and other [financial incentives] is a pointless waste of New Haven tax revenues."[89]

OLIN WINCHESTER BECOMES USRAC

At the end of January 1980, Mayor Biagio DiLieto announced that the City of New Haven, Yale University and the Olin Corporation had decided to build a "Science Park" on the 60 acres occupied by Winchester in the Newhallville neighborhood. Reported the New Haven Register, "A key part of the plan would be construction of a new Olin arms plant. There are, however, no specific plans for a new plant yet, and the company said a new facility couldn't be undertaken until the Winchester division has 'improved the profitability of its business.' Olin's Winchester Group President, Phil H. Rickey, did say, however, that the company's intention is to remain in New Haven and work out the future of its arms operation here. The company carefully stated it was only 'considering' building the new plant."[90]

Following on a decision made five years earlier but not yet acted upon, the city purchased seven acres of land (which included a building owned by the departed United Nuclear Corporation) at the corner of Mansfield and Division Streets, in August of 1980, paying $416,500. This was intended to give the Science Park triumvirate an 80-acre tract of land to work with.[91]

At the same time, the city administration was aware that Olin was considering "severing its sporting arms division." The incentive package plan the city put together with the assistance of the Connecticut Department of Commerce to convince the company not to do this was generous, to say the least, reported the Register, including "city support of a $10 million self-sustaining industrial revenue bond for construction of a new Winchester arms plant; a new 20-acre site [to be sold to Olin at 50 cents a square foot] at the corner of Shelton and Munson Streets (part of the so-called Olin Science Park); a city-Olin application for an urban development action grant to provide $1 million of low-interest financing at 9% for 10 years; development of a $350,000 job training program…; abatement of 80% of Olin's real and personal property tax liability for five years after a certificate of occupancy for a new plant is issued…; [and] technical assistance provided to Olin in all project-related matters, including financing, city zoning, permits and lighting.[92]

Nevertheless, by the end of 1980, Olin announced that it was placing the Winchester plant up for sale, and the city scrambled to find a buyer in order to save the 1300 or so jobs at stake. Mayor Biagio DiLieto said, "We have to work like hell," adding that any prospective buyers would be offered the same incentive package.[93]

In July of 1981, Olin sold the company to an 11-member consortium, including a group of executives at the Winchester plant as well as some local and out of state business interests. They offered $24 million for the sale, to include division facilities, inventory, materials, machinery, equipment, and the licensing of the Winchester name. A key provision of the sale was that the plant would remain in New Haven.[94]

> The plant's new management in the short term did have a relatively pacific relationship with the union, which, for nearly three years, repeatedly agreed to concessions and even layoffs to try to keep production in New Haven.

The new managers set up the U.S. Repeating Arms Corporation, retaining 90% of the old company's management. Hugh Fletcher, one of eight division managers who moved from Olin Winchester to USRAC, became the new company's president. Fletcher averred that his success plan would involve consolidation of operations with "construction of a new, 400,000 square foot, one-story plant in the southwest corner of the proposed University Science Park, an 80-acre industrial park for research and high technology firms jointly supported by the city, Yale, and Olin," reported the *New Haven Register.* The newspaper added, somewhat sarcastically, "Fletcher said the company is counting on the continued cooperation of the work force—the same force that struck over a productivity clause during contract negotiations two years ago."[95] Fletcher and his wife would face significant legal trouble later in the decade for actions taken while he was still the president of USRAC.

The plant's new management in the short term did have a relatively pacific relationship with the union, which, for nearly three years, repeatedly agreed to concessions and even layoffs to try to keep production in New Haven. Local 609's first concession occurred right after the purchase, when it agreed to delay the 30-cent-per-hour pay raise and cost-of-living adjustments provided for in its contract.[96]

But the union concessions didn't prevent the quick, precipitous decline of the workforce. 75 people were given permanent layoffs in December 1982, during the annual (but extended now from two to five weeks) Christmas furlough. There were repeated layoffs in the next few years, some permanent, including a "first time ever" reduction by 20 people from the salaried, white collar force in March of 1983 and cuts of another 45 hourly workers. The layoffs reduced the total employment at the plant to 755, with 670 remaining in the Local 609 bargaining unit—the lowest level since before U.S. entry into World War II. Louis Romano, the president of Local 609, blamed the layoffs on the larger economic picture, not the company, and told the *New Haven Register* with no apparent sense of irony in a season purportedly dedicated to world peace that "Right now it's so bad that all we can do is hope it turns around—to put money in people's pockets so they'll be able to buy guns."[97]

In May 1983, the city agreed to a year's extension on its $1 million loan to USRAC, with a reduction from a 14% to an 8% interest rate, with a company official stating that the gun industry was "facing the worst recession in 50 years."[98] The union signed a three-year contract that summer, and the *Register* estimated that about 570 people remained in the Local 609 bargaining unit.[99]

In April 1985, the Board of Alders approved a third loan to USRAC from the city, "the third time the city has loaned federal community development funds—for a total of $1.5 million—to help keep the gun company afloat... The loan is part of an $8 million package of government and bank loans being sought by the company. It intends to return $500,000 to the city when the package is complete, reducing its debt to $1 million," the *Register* reported.[100]

1985: THINGS COME TO A HEAD

Some of those laid off during the 1981-1983 period came back to work slowly in 1984, bringing the production workforce back up to about 700. Early in 1985, the union membership had apparently had enough of making concessions, at least in the short term. The company, euphemistically citing a "cash-flow problem," asked to delay by six months a 5.5% wage increase provided for in the union contract,[101] but the union refused to do so, a move that angered the company and had repercussions for the workforce later in the year.

The immediate crisis was sparked when the company, pleading poor, announced, in late October of 1985, that it was placing employees on a six-week furlough, beginning two days before Thanksgiving and taking away the seven paid holidays that the union had already negotiated into the regular two-week December furlough. Said the *New Haven Register*, "Production employees at the Winchester Avenue plant have agreed to concessions twice since a group of executives purchased the company from the parent Olin Corporation in 1981, but the company's decision to stretch out a Christmas furlough this year and withhold holiday pay has the union talking about a Las Vegas divorce..."[102]

The *Register* article suggested that workers would each lose about $450 in pay. Thomas Krajewski, the company's personnel director, estimated that an average production worker would make about eight dollars an hour, thus, the company would save about $278,000 by not giving out the holiday pay, and "a total of nearly $1.1 million for the entirety of the 28-day layoff. He said the company needs these savings to remain viable." But the Local 609

The shift lets out Tuesday afternoon at U.S. Repeating Arms Co. on Winchester Avenue in New Haven.   *Staff photo by Mara Lavitt*

'Honeymoon' ends at gun plant
No bonus, extended furlough sour union on management

business agent, John Palmieri, felt that the company's decision to withhold holiday pay was "revenge" for the union's refusal, earlier in the year, to accept the delay of the scheduled pay raise, pointing out that this had been the first time workers had refused concessions to help keep the newly-constituted USRAC afloat.[103]

The union responded to the crisis by calling a special meeting of its membership for October 25th, and Richard M. Pelton, USRAC president, wrote a letter to the 609 president, Lou Romano, objecting to the "inflammatory" tone of the meeting notice, "with [its] obvious intent to incite Union members to some form of action against their company," warning that "you and the union will be held fully accountable for any illegal actions taken by the membership against its employer." He added that "the company is in its darkest hour financially. We are trying to rally the necessary financial support to keep going."[104]

More union concessions were on the way, as USRAC filed for bankruptcy protection in mid-January 1986. The union held a meeting on January 26th in which its membership voted for further compromises in order to save their jobs.

Local 609 President Louis Romano greeted his members at the Saturday morning meeting with the grim remark, "You are probably facing the biggest crisis you have ever faced." The Local told its members that, under bankruptcy law, the company could go to court and have the current union contract invalidated, since it could claim

RALLY

SUPPORT

I.A.M.
VICTORY LODGE 609

THE 800 WORKERS AT U.S. REPEATING ARMS IN MANY WAYS
HAVE BENT OVER BACKWARDS TO ASSIST THIS NEW COMPANY.
NOW THE COMPANY IS REFUSING TO PAY THEM 7 PAID HOLIDAYS
OF WHICH THEY HAVE BEEN RECEIVING, FOR MANY YEARS,
AT THE DECEMBER SHUTDOWN. THEY ARE BEING PLACED ON A
SO-CALLED "FURLOUGH", FOR SIX WEEKS, TWO DAYS BEFORE
THANKSGIVING.
I.A.M. VICTORY LODGE 609 HAS BEEN A STEADFAST UNION IN
OUR COMMUNITY FOR OVER 20 YEARS. <u>LETS RALLY IN SOLIDARITY
TO EXPRESS OUR ANGER ABOUT THIS INJUSTICE.</u>

Winchester Ave. gate of U.S. Repeating Arms

TUESDAY NOVEMBER 26th 4:30

FOR MORE INFORMATION CONTACT WARREN GOULD AT 777-2756
SPONSORED BY: GREATER NEW HAVEN CENTRAL LABOR COUNCIL, AFL-CIO

Greater New Haven
CENTRAL LABOR COUNCIL

AFFILIATED WITH THE AFL-CIO AND
THE CONNECTICUT STATE LABOR COUNCIL, AFL-CIO
Address: 267 Chapel Street, New Haven, Conn. 06511
TELEPHONE 777-2756

PRESIDENT
FRANK CARRANO
New Haven Federation of Teachers
Local 933

FIRST VICE PRESIDENT
JOHN PALMIERI
IAM & AW District 170

SECOND VICE PRESIDENT
NICHOLAS MELLO
Amalgamated Clothing
Workers Local 125

SECRETARY-TREASURER
LOIS O'CONNOR
AFSCME Council 4
Local 478

TRUSTEES
GARY ANDERSON
United Rubber Workers
Local 91
DOMINIC PURCO
Office & Professional
Employees Local 153
HUGH MORRIS
Utility Workers Union
Local 470
FRANK PERRELLI
Painters Union
Local 186
IRMGARD WESSEL
AFSCME
Local 1919

EXECUTIVE BOARD
FRANK ANDERSON
Federation of University
Employees Local 35
CAROL BAUSCHER
Office & Professional
Employees Local 752
PAT LOFRANCESCO
Office & Professional
Employees Local 153
JOHN DIRZJO
Postal Workers Union
EMANUEL GOMEZ
IAM & AW
Lodge 609
GRETCHEN GOODWIN
AFSCME Local 884
PETER GROSSI
American Federation
of Government Employees
Local 1674
JOHN KUBUC
United Food & Commercial
Workers Local 371
WILLIAM MORICO
Hospital & Health Care
Workers District 1199
ELLEN THOMSON
Hotel Employees &
Restaurant Employees
Local 217

PRESS ANNOUNCEMENT

A RALLY FOR THE WORKERS AT U.S. REAPEATING ARMS, WHO
ARE REPRESENTED BY THE INTERNATIONAL ASSOCIATION OF
MACHINISTS VICTORY LODGE 609, WILL BE HELD TUESDAY NOVEMBER
26TH 4:30 AT THE WINCHESTER AVE. PLANT GATE.

ENCLOSED IS A FLYER INVITING LABOR AND COMMUNITY TO
ATTEND.

FOR MORE INFORMATION CONTACT:

WARREN GOULD 777-2756
Political Action Director
Greater New Haven Labor Council

JOHN PALMIERI 787-4125
District Representative for I.A.M.
District 170

UNION EARNED WAGES ON AMERICAN UNION LABELS AND SERVICES

U.S. Repeating Arms Company
275 Winchester Avenue, Post Office Box 30-300
New Haven, Connecticut 06511 (203) 789-5000

October 24, 1985

Mr. Louis Romano
Victory Lodge 609
958 Dixwell Avenue
Hamden, Connecticut 06514

Dear Mr. Romano:

The notice of Union Meeting on October 27, 1985 has been
brought to the attention of U. S. Repeating Arms Company
management.

I will point out to you that the language of the "notice"
is clearly and unnecessarily inflammatory with the obvious
intent to incite the Union members to some form of action
against their company.

As you full well know, the announced shutdown for the
month of December is clearly legal and well within the terms
and conditions of the contract we now operate under. The
clear language of that same contract imposes no obligation on
U. S. Repeating Arms Company to pay holidays to the union
members while on shutdown.

The company is struggling to meet its legal financial
obligations. We are in no position to obligate our company
to pay holiday payments not required by our contractual
agreement.

I believe you are leading the membership toward an
unnecessary and no-win confrontation with their company. You
and the union will be held fully accountable for any illegal
actions taken by the membership against its employer.

The company is in its darkest hour financially. We are
trying to rally the maximum financial support to keep going.
All the rhetoric in the world will not change the situation.
Only the combined efforts of all will keep us going.

Mr. Louis Romano
Page 2
October 24, 1985

Your approach to our problems as exemplified by the
meeting "notice" can only lead to unnecessary confrontation
with the high possibility of disaster for all of us.

We urge you to take a calm and thoughtful approach to
this situation.

Very truly yours,

Richard M. Pelton

Richard M. Pelton,
President

ATTENTION!
SPECIAL-CALLED MEETING
FOR ALL THE MEMBERS OF
LODGE 609 IAM

THE EXECUTIVE BOARD OF LODGE 609 HAS CALLED FOR THIS <u>SPECIAL</u> <u>MEETING</u> TO
DISCUSS THE COMPANY'S UNSCRUPULOUS ACTION OF PLACING ALL PRODUCTION AND
MAINTENANCE EMPLOYEES ON LAYOFF STATUS FROM NOVEMBER 27, 1985 THROUGH
JANUARY 5, 1986.

THIS LAYOFF ENCOMPASSES SEVEN (7) NEGOTIATED HOLIDAYS. THE COMPANY
UNMERCIFULLY AND MALICIOUSLY PLOTTED THIS LAYOFF WITH THE FORETHOUGHT
OF REFUSING TO PAY OUR UNION MEMBERS THEIR NEGOTIATED HOLIDAY PAY.

THIS SPECIAL MEETING WILL BE HELD PRIOR TO OUR REGULAR SCHEDULED MONTHLY
MEETING.

<u>PURPOSE:</u> TO HEAR A FULL REPORT FROM THE EXECUTIVE BOARD

<u>DATE:</u> SUNDAY, OCTOBER 27, 1985

<u>TIME:</u> 9:00 A.M. SHARP !

<u>PLACE:</u> WILBUR L. CROSS HIGH SCHOOL
            181 MITCHELL DRIVE, NEW HAVEN

YOU OWE IT TO YOURSELF AND YOUR FAMILY TO BE AT THIS MEETING --
IF <u>YOU FAIL TO ATTEND THIS MEETING</u> - YOU WILL BE TELLING <u>USRACO THAT</u>
<u>YOU AGREE WITH THEM. THAT YOU SHOULD NOT BE PAID FOR YOUR SEVEN</u>
<u>NEGOTIATED HOLIDAYS.</u>

EXECUTIVE BOARD
LODGE 609

Louis H. Romano
PRESIDENT, VICTORY LODGE 609

---

*Union responses to the
six-week furlough and
wipe-out of holiday pay at
the end of 1985. From the
Local 609 files.*

WE NEED
YOUR MONEY

TAKE-A-WAYS

There Is No Santa Claus!

MANAGEMENT
SCROOGE

Dear Santa Claus,

We the members of Victory Lodge 609, employed at the U.S. Repeating Arms Company,
have negotiated seven of our paid holidays into the month of December to enable
us to properly celebrate the Christmas season. We have enjoyed these paid holidays
and have celebrated the Christmas season in this manner for many years.

In the year 1985, we were looking forward to celebrating the Christmas holidays,
but, on October 15, 1985 the USRACO has crushed this year's Christmas spirit when
they announced that they were shutting down the plant and taking away our seven paid
holidays.

The Company stated that they were taking away our paid holidays because they needed
the money for themselves *** ISN'T THAT THE PITS ????

Who could believe that after all the sacrifices we, the employees of USRACO made for
this Company that they would mistreat us like this.

IT'S HARD TO BELIEVE -- BUT IT'S TRUE !

Sincerely yours,

The membership of Lodge 609

REMOVAL DATE - 10/31/85

U.S.R.A.C.O. OR SCROOGE ???
YOU BE THE JUDGE !

FACTS:

THURSDAY, OCTOBER 15, 1985, COMPANY CALLS IN UNION EXECUTIVE BOARD FOR A
MEETING AT 10:00 A.M. AND ANNOUNCES: "ALL PRODUCTION AND MAINTENANCE OPER-
ATIONS WILL CEASE ON WEDNESDAY, NOVEMBER 27, 1985 AND WILL NOT RESUME UNTIL
MONDAY, JANUARY 6, 1986 AT 7:00 A.M."

THE EXECUTIVE BOARD, VERY UPSET WITH THIS NEWS, CALLS A CAUCUS AND AGREES
TO ASK FOR THE FOLLOWING:

1. THAT THE COMPANY PAY FOR ALL NEGOTIATED HOLIDAYS ON
   NOVEMBER 27, 1985.

2. THAT DUE TO PAST CURTAILMENTS, THE COMPANY SHOULD GUARANTEE
   VACATION PAY AT 40 HOURS PER WEEK OF VACATION ENTITLEMENT.

THE COMPANY LISTENED TO THE UNION'S PROPOSALS AND RESPONDED AS FOLLOWS:

"WE CAN UNDERSTAND THE UNION POSITION ON HOLIDAY AND VACATION PAY
BUT...WE WANT TO MAKE THE FOLLOWING POINTS VERY CLEAR TO YOU AND YOUR
UNION MEMBERS:"

1. "IT'S TIME YOUR UNION MEMBERS MAKE THEIR SACRIFICES FOR THIS
   COMPANY AS THE SALARIED EMPLOYEES HAVE."

2. "THE MONIES FOR YOUR HOLIDAY PAY IS NEEDED BY THE COMPANY,
   THEREFORE, WE WILL <u>NOT</u> PAY FOR THE SEVEN HOLIDAYS IN THE MONTH
   OF DECEMBER."

3. "WE ALSO WANT MORE PRODUCTIVITY FROM THE UNION MEMBERS, ALONG
   WITH BETTER QUALITY WORK."

4. "WE ARE HIRING A CONSULTING FIRM TO ENABLE US TO GET THIS
   PRODUCTIVITY."

IN RESPONSE TO THE UNION'S QUESTION ON FOREMEN AND SALARIED EMPLOYEES
THE COMPANY SAID:

1. "THE FOREMEN AND SALARIED EMPLOYEES <u>WILL</u> RECEIVE THEIR HOLIDAY PAY.

2. "IT WOULD NOT BE RIGHT TO TAKE AWAY THE FOREMEN'S HOLIDAY PAY.

NOW YOU KNOW WHAT KIND OF COMPANY YOU WORK FOR AND WHAT THEY THINK OF YOU !

DON'T BE FOOLED BY THEIR "GOOD WILL AMBASSADOR".

"We gave up pay raises for about three years…They said they didn't have any money…That's how we kept the plant running…It was devastating when they told us they were closing."

CLARETHA MCKNIGHT

Born in South Carolina; came to New Haven in 1964 because she had aunts there; just out of high school. Worked for Kelly Services and A.C. Gilbert Company; went to Winchester in 1973 and was there until the plant closed in 2006.

On working at Winchester: She worked as a machinist for 27 years, making side arms for shot guns. She liked her job: "I never thought of leaving. I loved going to work. The people I worked with were nice."

About the union: She was never an officer, but worked on the health and safety committee. She felt the union "somewhat improved life" for its workers "in terms of wages and holidays. "In dealing with the company, the union would "support you as far as they [could] go."

On the repetitive company strategy: "We gave up pay raises for about three years… They said they didn't have any money and so we would take a cut. They would say [if we didn't agree] that they would be leaving."

Several departments closed and moved the work out of state. Some of the New Haven workers had the option to go, but "a lot of them took the buy-out."

On the plant closing in 2006: "In the end they said they were paying too much taxes" in New Haven.

"In January 2006, they told us they would be closing in March. They were supposed to give six months' notice, but they only gave three." The city of New Haven "contacted the Governor [then Jodi Rell] but she wouldn't get involved."

The company "still owes us three months' severance pay."

"These big corporations just see us as numbers, not names. They'd just as soon write you off as look at you."

EMMANUEL GOMEZ

Worked at Winchester from 1947 until his retirement in 1991. Why Winchester? It was a family tradition. His mother had worked there during World War I, before she married and had children.

His two sisters, four brothers and brother-in-law all worked there at one time or another: "We all worked between the rolling mill and the casting shop." Also, "I could walk to work. I lived in the Fair Haven Housing Project. It was convenient, really."

On the work he did: "I worked in the rolling mill where they rolled sheets of brass [and in] the mill and casting shop where they made castings of long bars of metal that then get sent to the rolling mills." It was rough work with low pay and so he "fought tooth and nail to go to shot gun assembly."

A few years before retirement, he bid on a higher paying, skilled job and got it, but the company "had someone else in mind" and "they did everything they could to mess me up. They would not train me."

About the union: He was a charter member, and served as conductor and later legislative chairman.

On the repetitive company strategy: "Whenever the union contract was nearly up, the company would say they were about to go bankrupt: 'In order to keep this company going, you have to give [something] up…' This strategy of theirs had been thought out long before they confronted us with it…These big corporations just see us as numbers, not names. They'd just as soon write you off as look at you."

Comparing the 1969 and 1979 strikes: "The 1979 strike is something I'd like to forget. In 1969, we had all kinds of community support, but not in '79. In '79, the company really put the pressure on [the community]."

On New Haven's tax incentives to keep production lines in New Haven: "They'd take it and then they'd move anyway."

Memories of working there: "About all the good memories I have are from being on the Board of the union and the support of the union."

On the end of Winchester in New Haven: "In 2006, we were fighting tooth and nail to keep it open…but the Mayor was dragging his feet."

Mr. Gomez is a member of the Citizens' Ad Hoc Committee which works, among other things, to recoup the three months' severance pay due the remaining 198 workers when the plant closed in 2006.

that its terms were causing further financial hardship. It also transmitted a threat from the firm which represented Manufacturers Hanover (the company bank) that the company would be liquidated if the concession terms were not agreed to, thus "ending all hope for resumption of operations." This firm, Siegal, O'Connor, Schiff, Zagari and Kainen, was noted locally for its "union busting" activities, having been hired by Yale University in 1983 to aid the university's ongoing effort to prevent its clerical and technical workers from forming a union.[105]

Union members voted 280 to 103 in favor of the "deal" their representatives negotiated with this firm, according to the *Register*. The givebacks did not include a wage reduction, although they did include a two year wage *freeze*, the relinquishing of some benefits, including their dental plan and half-hour paid lunch break, the reduction of the number of union stewards on the shop floor from 22 to 15, and "a possible employee contribution to medical coverage."[106]

The rest of the 1980s saw a drawn-out, futile struggle on the part of the city and the workers to try to keep this failing company afloat. They involved a tangle of sales, loans, union concessions and givebacks that ultimately failed to save more than an ever-shrinking number of jobs, offering short-lived hope for the company and its remaining workforce.

> "*U.S. Repeating Arms Company is an important employer in this city, and we want to give them all the breathing space they need.*"
>
> —Louis Bowers, New Haven Department of Economic Development, quoted in *New Haven Register*, January 17, 1985.

> "*The next six months is going to tell the story…If they don't get some customers, we may be out on the street. The city can't keep supplying us with money.*"
>
> —Thomas Papa, gun barrel shop worker at Winchester for 26 years, quoted in *New Haven Register*, February 17, 1986.

MEANWHILE, SCIENCE PARK REVS UP

In 1982, the Olin Corporation, which remained a partner in the Science Park triumvirate and still owned much of the land surrounding USRAC, donated the first of a number of parcels agreed upon for the development of the park. The parcel was "located in the northern section of the 80-acre park site in the Dixwell-Newhallville neighborhood," and was to be leased to USRAC on a month-to-month basis until actual construction

1980-1990: THE ROLLER COASTER RIDE AT USRAC

Part 1. 1980-1985

JANUARY 1980: The New Haven Mayor announces the building of a Science Park, a key part of which is to be a new plant for Olin Winchester.

AUGUST 1980: The city purchases seven acres of land vacated by United Nuclear in 1974.

DECEMBER 1980: Olin Corporation announces that it is selling the Winchester Division.

JULY 1981: The division is bought by a group of investors, including former Winchester executives; it is renamed U.S. Repeating Arms; the union agrees to delay workers' pay raise and cost of living adjustments.

DECEMBER 1982: 75 workers receive layoffs.

1983: Layoffs continue throughout the year.

FEBRUARY 1983: The Olin Corporation announces it will move its chemical research laboratories to Cheshire Industrial Park by the end of 1984.

SPRING 1983: USRAC's first president, Calvert Hugh Fletcher, quietly resigns after USRAC learns of his partnership in a commemorative gun company located in Branford, CT.

MAY 1983: The city agrees to a year's extension on its $1 million loan to USRAC.

SUMMER 1983: Local 609 signs a three-year contract. About 570 remain in the bargaining unit.

1984: Some of those laid off previously are slowly returned to work, bringing the workforce back up to approximately 700.

DECEMBER 1984: The regular Christmas holiday furlough is extended to five weeks.

JANUARY 1985: The union refuses the company's request to delay a pay raise provided for in the contract.

APRIL 1985: The New Haven Board of Alders approves a third loan to USRAC.

JUNE 1985: 40 layoffs announced.

OCTOBER 1985: USRAC announces it will place employees on a six-week furlough from Thanksgiving through Christmas and ending January 6, 1986, wiping out additional holiday pay as well. The union objects strongly.

1980-1990: THE ROLLER COASTER RIDE AT USRAC

Part 2. 1986-1990

EARLY 1986: Furlough extends to 14 weeks.

JANUARY 1986: USRAC files for bankruptcy protection; union members agree to more concessions in order to "save their jobs."

FEBRUARY 17, 1986: $3 million "city and state package" enables USRAC to obtain loans, recall 260 workers from a 14-week furlough.

FEBRUARY 26, 1986: USRAC opens "job center" to help those not recalled.

JUNE 1986: State auditors challenge the practices involved in obtaining the previous (1984) state loan guarantee of $500,000, charging that the program under which it received help was intended for small businesses.

JULY 1986: The company now employs 515 hourly workers out of the 685 furloughed; a federal investigation is launched into "business irregularities" of USRAC managers.

DECEMBER 1986: Company's current managers are cleared in probe. Three years later, the first USRAC president, Calvin H. Fletcher, and his wife are sentenced to prison terms and fined $10,000 each for tax fraud.

JULY-AUGUST 1987: Three "players" file separate plans for company "reorganization;" one, filed by Massachusetts businessman Peter Alcock, is favored by the city; calls for an "employee incentive plan" whereby the city and state will forgive the $3 million loan at a rate of $400,000 a year for each year the plant keeps full time employment at 400, with an additional $1000 for each additional worker retained, to a maximum of $500,000 per year. Alcock's plan prevails.

NOVEMBER 1987: Sale is briefly delayed because of "unknown extent of environmental hazards "at the plant site.

DECEMBER 29, 1987: In a five-hour closing, USRAC is sold to a group of investors including the Browning America subsidiary of Fabrique Nationale Herstal of Belgium. G.L. "Peter" Alcock becomes the president of the new company.

OCTOBER 26, 1990: Peter Alcock resigns as USRAC president in order to "'pursue other interests.'" 500 workers are laid off as the company "seeks new financing;" A company letter to the city warns that the plant will close "indefinitely...unless timely financing is provided."

NOVEMBER-DECEMBER 1990: Fabrique Nationale buys out the other stockholders, becoming full owner; Jack Mattan becomes new president, predicting a financial turnaround in the coming year; workers "trickle back" to the plant.

began. "The city's current Science Park acreage and the area donated by Olin are soon to be supplemented by a donation from Yale of more than three acres at Prospect and Division streets. Roughly 14 acres will represent the first phase of the park's development," the *New Haven Register* reported in October of that year.[107]

The growing reality of Science Park also involved the clean-up and renovation of a former United Nuclear building, a project to be funded by a $2.5 million urban development action grant from the Department of Housing and Urban Development, a $6.3 million first mortgage "provided by five union pension funds and one union health and insurance fund, all affiliated with the Greater New Haven Building Trades Council," and a $1.3 million contribution from a private investment group known as Science Park Associates. The building, once renovated, would be known as 1 Science Park Center, and would be the "flagship for the park."[108]

As Amended and Approved April 4, 1983

ORDER OF THE BOARD OF ALDERMEN RE SCIENCE PARK

WHEREAS: this Board of Aldermen has approved a Science Park Municipal Development Plan, loan agreements with New Haven Development Corporation and U.S. Repeating Arms Corporation, community development block allocations an Urban Development Action Grant, and fixed assessment agreements for the purpose of developing the Science Park; and

WHEREAS: a special Planned Development District is proposed designating a 35 - acre tract in the Newhallville community for primarily industrial use, including research and development, high tech-nology, light manufacturing and related office use; and

WHEREAS implementation of the plans for the Science Park development is to occur over the next five years; and

WHEREAS: there are components of the development which will have direct bearing on the surrounding residential areas, which components have been articulated and identified by community residents and representatives, namely: traffic and access concerns, the site development timetable, continuing community involvement, and the acquisition and relocation of twenty-four residential structures and two businesses located on Munson Street and Shelton Avenue; and

WHEREAS: it is the desire of the Board of Aldermen to ensure that these concerns are addressed.

NOW, THEREFORE, BE IT ORDERED BY THE NEW HAVEN BOARD OF ALDERMEN THAT:

1. The City Plan Commission - recommended actions regarding the widening of Division street be implemented, and further that the entire Division Street project design be contracted for immediately, with Phase I, (Prospect Street to Winchester Avenue) to be completed within FY 1983-84 and Phase II (to Shelton Avenue) be completed by January 1985.

2. The Mayor immediately appoint a Committee on the Reopening of Winchester Avenue for the purpose of establishing a schedule for the reopening of Winchester Avenue, said Committee to include a representative of the U.S. Repeating Arms Corporation, the New Haven Development Commission, City Department of Traffic and Parking and The Dixwell - Newhallville community as well as four aldermen to be named by the President of the Board of Aldermen among whom shall be aldermen from the area most immediately affected, and which committee shall report back to the Board of Aldermen with a proposed plan within 90 (ninety) days of the adoption of this order.

PAGE 2
ORDER OF THE BOARD OF ALDERMEN RE SCIENCE PARK

3. The Science Park Municipal Development Plan be modified in accordance with Section 8-200 of the Connecticut General Statutes to add two existing businesses to the twenty-four identified residential structures to be acquired and relocated as provided in the Science Park Municipal Development Plan adopted on July 27, 1981 and that the appropriate City agencies, including the Office of Family and Business Relocation, take steps either to begin acquisition proceedings immediately or to make the decision not to acquire these properties and amend all plans accordingly in order to resolve the uncertainty facing the owners of these structures.

BE IT FURTHER ORDERED THAT a copy of this order be sent to the New Haven Development Commission, Science Park Development Commission, U.S. Repeating Arms, the Office of Economic Development, the Office of Family and Business Relocation, and the Department of Traffic and Parking.

Image is from Local 609 files.

High Performance Work Organization

Partnerships

High Performance Work Organization manual from the Local 609 files.

10

THE 1990S—FINAL EFFORTS

In 1990, Fabrique Nationale Herstal of Belgium, which had previously owned 44% of USRAC through its Browning America subsidiary, bought out the two other shareholders, G.I. "Peter" Alcock, Jr., former president (44%) and Robert Hernreich (12%). Jack Mattan became its new president.[109] The company was now wholly owned by Fabrique (whose parent company was GIAT of France), a development that initially was greeted with enthusiasm by Local 609, which wanted to implement the High Performance Work Organization plan being promoted by the International Association of Machinists.

The 1990s also saw the completion, in 1994, of the new factory building that had been discussed for years, advanced by city, state and private funds, as part of uneven progress toward the development of Science Park. For USRAC workers, a period of renewed optimism in the first part of the decade gave way to a repetition of the pattern of company financial difficulties, reduction in employment, intransigence toward employee efforts, and, this time, the final beginning of the end.

Belgian native Jack (Jacque) Mattan, the new president of the once again reconstituted USRAC, declared at a press conference with New Haven Mayor John Daniels in October 1990 that "'this company must be profitable next year,'" and expressed confidence that this goal could be reached. He added that he was "'feeling pretty good to be able to save'" the jobs of those production workers who would be returning to the reopened plant by late January 1991. At this point, the *Register* put the number of workers still to return at 385.[110] The current Local 609 president, Craig Gauthier, told the newspaper on December 13, 1990 that between 90 and 125 of his current membership of 470 had already returned to work, with the remainder to be recalled by January 28, 1991.[111]

By June of 1991, Gauthier reported that "things look more stable. This is one of the few times it looks like we're going to work the whole year." By October, the company announced it would be *adding* 65 workers, thanks to a new, two-year grant of $324,478 from the U.S. Department of Health and Human Services. The grant was actually given to the Science Park Development Corporation, which would administer it. The company was "'to spend the money to provide job and basic skills training, move and install new equipment, implement the new 'total quality management' concept of production and assist community outreach programs to find low-income residents to work in the plant,'" according to the Corporation president, William Ginsberg, who had been appointed to the position after its former president, Henry S. Chauncey, a long-time administrator at Yale University, had resigned in 1988.[112]

> "*Number one, we want them (USRAC) in New Haven. And number two, we want them in Connecticut.*"
>
> —State Economic Development Commissioner Joseph McGee

> "*The company has brought in a lot of new equipment. All of this is positive. The un-positive thing is whether the city and state can come up with the funding to keep them in-state.*"
>
> —Local 609 President Craig Gauthier

> "*We're talking about enticing them to not pick up their stuff and go, and we do that by virtue of making an attractive offer to them (USRAC). The attractive offer is to come from ultimately the taxpayer. The very people we're talking about helping are the very ones who are paying for it.*"
>
> —State Rep. William R. Dyson, D-New Haven, co-chair, State Assembly Appropriations Committee

(All quoted in *New Haven Register*, February 14, 1992)

USRAC'S RACE TO THE FINISH, 1990-2006

Part 1. 1990-1995. Building a New Plant in the "New Culture"

DECEMBER 1990-JANUARY 1991 The plant reopens under ownership of Belgian company, Fabrique Nationale de Herstal.

JANUARY 30, 1991 Winchester back up to full production; announces it wants to build a new, "streamlined" plant (the plan that Olin was forced to scrap in the 1980s due to financial constraints.)

SEPTEMBER 1991 City development officials predict the new factory could create 200-250 new jobs; environmental issues for demolition of old buildings are key concern.

1992 Two-day off-site union-company seminar held to discuss "shop floor rethink" and formulate a joint vision and mission statement under the High Performance Work Organization plan.

FEBRUARY 1992 *New Haven Register* article reports the company is considering moving "some or all" operations to Wallingford or out of Connecticut altogether. City and state officials try to negotiate terms to keep them in New Haven.

MARCH-MAY 1992 "Whoops of joy" in Newhallville: USRAC announces it will stay; deal with city includes tax breaks and forgiveness of $1.5 million loan made in 1987. Yale University and Olin Corporation to contribute $570,000 toward the new plant project, and United Illuminating grants $1.25 million in subsidies. Olin Corporation undertakes demolition of old buildings and site clean-up.

MAY 1992 City of New Haven grants USRAC a new 20-year tax cut reducing its tax liability by half in exchange for commitment to keep the workforce at 400 or above.

1993 Memorandum of agreement between Local 609 and USRAC spells out how the parties will implement the "partnership" mandated by the High Performance Work Organization.

FEBRUARY 1993 The federal Occupational and Safety and Health Administration fines USRAC $279, 800 for 114 worker-safety violations. Ground is broken on new plant.

APRIL 6, 1993 USRAC gets $92,000 more from state to finish demolition of tunnels at its old factory building; construction at new factory had been delayed five months until completion.

MARCH 3-4, 1994 Two-day event for the High Performance Work Organization at USRAC, addressed by IAM President George Kourpias. Includes "mandatory rally."

AUGUST-OCTOBER 1994 235,000 acre plant construction is complete; workers move in. Grand Opening October 15.

FEBRUARY 1995 Off-site "Refocus Seminar" of company and union representatives to discuss "bumps in the road" in the progress of the HWPO partnership. Verbal commitments by both sides to "continue moving forward" despite difficulties.

The optimism evoked by its announcement in 1991 that the "new" USRAC wanted to finally build the streamlined plant with its hoped-for new jobs, an endeavor discussed but stalled since the 1980s, was mitigated somewhat by the company's backsliding on the issue in early 1992. Instead, it floated the idea of moving the bulk of its operations to an abandoned building in Wallingford's industrial park, and also pondered a directive from the new owner of the Herstal Group, GIAT of France, to consider consolidating its operations at a sister plant in South Carolina, FN Manufacturing, Inc. It also worried, as had its predecessors, about the extent of the environmental cleanup required by the demolition of the old Olin-owned buildings. But more city concessions along with the contributions of Yale, Olin, and the United Illuminating Company brought the project to fruition, and the plant was finally opened in the fall of 1994 with a workforce, according to the *New Haven Register*, of 600 (up again, from 535 in 1992.) An article in the *Register* called the concessions a "sweetheart deal," "valued at between $10 million and $20 million over 10 years," and the new president of the company (now officially entitled Browning/USRAC-Winchester North America), Donald Gobel, said at the opening ceremony, "'Without the incentive package, we would not be here today.'"[113]

THE HIGH PERFORMANCE WORK ORGANIZATION AT USRAC

HPWO was, in part, the IAM's response to the hard reality that markets for munitions had shrunk, and that product diversification might be a necessary survival mechanism, as would increased efficiency and productivity. To achieve these ends, workers would need to partner with management and management would have to be willing to share decision-making. The International Association of Machinists had begun to discuss diversification in its industries in the 1980s, and had met with some success, although not at companies as deeply entrenched in weapons production as, for example, the U.S. Repeating Arms Company in New Haven. Diversification doesn't appear to have seriously been on the table there, and, although the early rhetoric of USRAC's new managers suggested that they would be open to the kind of partnerships with workers that were proposed (and, in fact, written into union contracts in the 1990s) the effort did not succeed for very long at the Winchester plant.

When Jack Mattan was brought in in 1990 to head the company by its new owner, Fabrique Nationale of his native Belgium, a subsidiary of a French company known as GIAT, he said publicly that he was optimistic that the company could become profitable again. But it was his successor, Don Gobel, who took over in late 1991, whose words seemed to line up most neatly with the goals of the HPWO. Gobel spoke of the need to end conflict between workers and managers, introduce management-production worker teams, and retrain employees. "'So much of manufacturing is going down the tubes,'" he told the *New Haven Register*. "'In the "good old days" we could tell them (workers) what to do. We didn't listen...Now we have to do something different.'"[114]

In the early 1990s, the IAM moved ahead with its stated goal to "define a new work system which draws on the insights and talents of front-line workers and [determine] how they will play a key role at the workplace." It provided training for union leaders and asked them to negotiate HPWO agreements in their shops. The agreement was to include the following elements:

- The IAM and the employer will draft a Partnership Agreement which outlines their commitment to share decision-making in a Labor-Management relationship focused on changing the enterprise and its work system for mutually beneficial gains...

- ...The IAM and management will engage in joint determination of the methods, processes, and means of manufacturing.

- Worksite education and training will be budgeted and managed jointly by the employer and the union...

- Labor and management will jointly design, select and introduce technology which will be worker-centered and skill based. The technology will improve production while saving and creating jobs.

- The IAM and management will jointly explore and create new markets, brainstorm product development, and work out the methods and processes needed to offer new products and services.

- Financial and technical information will be shared with the IAM to determine all costs from prototype to production, administration, marketing and sales, as well as units of wage and profit...

- The work system created by the High Performance Work Organization will protect the employment of current workers, promote new job opportunities, and compensate for skill enhancement. Ultimately, decisions made under the HPWO Agreement will avoid diluting the bargaining unit or checking its natural growth.[115]

These lofty aspirations were never reached, to the disappointment of Local 609 leaders.

HWPO'S NEW HAVEN ENDEAVOR

"We went after [the HPWO] whole hog. Not only would it keep the company here, but it would allow us to diversify...and maintain a highly skilled, educated work force.

"It was a plan to increase production and maintain quality...[For example], in the Assembly Shop we decided to ask the workers how to improve production. [Within] three weeks they had redesigned the whole Assembly Shop. Their production went from 300 guns to 600 guns a day.

"We had big plans to keep the plant here."

— Craig Gauthier, former president, Local 609

Published in August 1998, the *High Performance Work Organization Partnerships Field Manual* issued by the International Association of Machinists described the history of HPWO's endeavor at USRAC until about 1995. According to this document, the company's new management had "tried to implement Total Quality Management (TQM) and cellular manufacturing in 1990 but failed because the union was not involved."[116] Mattan "approached the union saying that the company and the union had to begin talking to each other and that a partnership was needed if USRAC was to survive. In 1992, a two-day off-site joint union-company seminar was held to discuss the concept of 'shop floor rethink,' and to develop a joint vision and mission statement." The facilitator was "chosen by the company with input from the union. Stewards, union leadership, including District 170 Directing Business Representative John Palmieri, attended, along with the top management of the company and production supervisors."[117]

The seminar developed a joint management-union vision statement and a mission statement, neither of which talked about "diversification" from firearms production. Quite the contrary. The joint vision statement read: "Utilizing the strength of the Winchester brand, U.S. Repeating Arms Company will become a world leader in the sporting firearms business." The six-part mission statement was formulated around achieving this goal:

> *The mission statement focuses first on the customer and the 'quality and value' of the product. The next four points center on the union, the company, the workplace, and the workers: 'The union relationship should be an asset.' The mission statement acknowledges that GIAT industries should realize a profit, and that '...employees should receive competitive wages, share*

company knowledge, and be involved in decision making.' The company's positive relationship with the community is also included in the mission statement, which stresses that USRAC...'should be a good neighbor and one of the community leaders' and respect 'the long term relationship of the local community and Winchester firearms, which has contributed to our success...' All of the points of the Mission Statement build on the importance of positive relationships between the company, the union and the community and the development of an educated, flexible and committed workforce that will achieve 'World Class Manufacturing.'[118]

In 1993, the two parties signed a Memorandum of Agreement which "spelled out how the partnership would be implemented. The MOA provides for equal representation for the union in joint decision making on an Operating Steering Committee (OSC), Area-Wide Union Committees (called Rethink Committees), and Special Task Forces. The company pays for lost time for worker involvement on the various committees, as well as for a full-time Union Coordinator—the Local Lodge President. The MOA clearly specifies that all grievances related to this process and the contract will be treated under the normal grievance procedure set forth in the contract."[119]

At the beginning of March 1994, International Association of Machinists Union President George Kourpias visited the Winchester plant for a two day event which included a general meeting of all USRAC employees; conferences among union leaders, USRAC management and New Haven's mayor, John DeStefano; and a mandatory rally.[120] According to the IAM Field Manual, Kourpias' speech to the "entire workforce" about the "importance of the new partnership between the IAM and USRAC" was greeted positively by the company, which "saw [the] speech as a strong endorsement of the developing partnership and a visible commitment to that partnership from the highest levels of the IAM. According to management representatives, union support is vital for the partnership to proceed. They are convinced that the improvements made thus far could not have happened without the advocacy and strong involvement of the union.

"As IAM President Kourpias committed the union to a new way of doing business, Don Gobel, President of USRAC, set a similar example for management by communicating with managers on the importance of the new relationship with the union and by insisting on union involvement in the change process." The field manual emphasized that "**this clear signal to management that workers and their union had an important role in the company was necessary because, although product managers were committed to the partnership, some shop floor supervisors were less than enthusiastic about sharing traditional management prerogatives with the hourly workforce.**

U.S. Repeating Arms Company

INCORPORATED

275 Winchester Avenue, Post Office Box 30-300
New Haven, Connecticut 06511
TELEPHONE (203) 789-5000

WINCHESTER.
LICENSEE

Georgianna

Mr. George Kourpias, International Machinists Union President
Visit to USRAC/Winchester - March 3 & 4, 1994

Suggested Agenda

Thursday 3/3 PM	❖	Arrive in New Haven Check into Marriott/Residence Inn Hotel
7:00 PM	❖	Dinner at Gennaro's Restaurant (State St. New Haven) Attendees: George Kourpias, George Poulin, John Palmieri, Craig Gouthier, Don Gobel, Bob Kuskowski, Dave Rich, Georgianna Coleman (party of 8)
Friday 3/4 8:30 AM	❖	General meeting with all employees ◆ Opening remarks - Don Gobel, President USRAC ◆ Remarks by New Haven Mayor John DeStefano ◆ Speech by George Kourpias, International President Machinists Union (Introduced by John Palmieri)
10:00 AM	❖	Tour of Plant
Noon	❖	Buffet lunch in board room with Don Gobel/Bob Kuskowski Staff, Union Executive Committee
1:00 PM 2:30 PM	❖	Board Room: Review of USRAC 5-Year Plan and New Plant

SPECIAL ANNOUNCEMENT

Make It Happen Together

THE MARCH 4TH RALLY

THE MARCH 4TH RALLY

Mr. GEORGE KOURPIAS,
the International Machinists Union President,
will be our guest speaker at this company–wide event.

Time: 8:30 AM - 10:00 AM
Place: Community Out Reach Center
Date: March 4, 1994

Your attendance is MANDATORY!
BUS TRANSPORTATION has been arranged for
ALL EMPLOYEES .
DO NOT TAKE YOUR VEHICLE!

➡ **ALL HOURLY & SALARIED EMPLOYEES** ⬅

Report to work as usual and go to your work area.
You will be advised of the DEPARTMENT RELEASE SCHEDULE.
For more detail information see your supervisor, or steward.

Weekly meetings continue to be held with supervisors to share information and talk about their concerns regarding the partnership."[121] (Emphasis added.)

In retrospect, the plan seems hopelessly optimistic as it relates to USRAC. The manual's narrative blamed the delay in "complete implementation of the partnership" on the disruption caused by the opening of the new plant in 1994. It also claimed that USRAC's decision was "most importantly" based on its realization of the "importance and value of its skilled workforce," making only secondary the role of the considerable financial help the company received from the State of Connecticut and City of New Haven.[122]

The manual reported positive changes but at the same time acknowledged difficulties: "The development of a joint partnership has resulted in significant improvements in how work is done and in the relationship between the company and the union. The number of grievances has been cut in half, and most are now about overtime instead of contract language violations. Despite this progress the road has not always been smooth as the roles and responsibilities of both sides evolve." But, without directly pointing the finger at management, it continued, "Some decisions concerning production, training, and the introduction of new equipment, which were supposed to be joint, were done in a unilateral manner. There have been problems at times with communications." Still, at a "Refocus Seminar" held in February 1995, an off-site meeting between company and union representatives "to re-examine their commitment to the change process and the problems encountered in the development of a change process," the parties "jointly decided to continue moving forward in spite of the bumps in the road."[123]

Craig Gauthier says there was ongoing management resistance to the HWPO plan "because they felt we were taking power away." It seems obvious that the commitment to the process was uneven at best among all levels of management, especially when it became clear that the ultimate goal of the Herstal group was to dismantle and close the plant. It would be interesting to discover who knew what when (both among company management and among IAM leadership) about the company's intentions. In any case, as the decade progressed, new financial troubles emerged and cutbacks in personnel ensued, the HPWO contract language was not upheld. At the start of the new century, the effort waned.

"I am very proud of my father and all that he did to establish that union," (IAM Victory Lodge Local 609.)

CONNECTICUT STATE SENATOR MARTIN LOONEY

Looney is a Democratic State Senator representing Connecticut's 11th district which encompasses parts of New Haven, Hamden and North Haven, CT. He is President Pro Tempore of the Connecticut State Senate, as well as an attorney primarily engaged in criminal defense work and an adjunct professor at Quinnipiac University and the University of New Haven. He was born in New Haven in 1948 while his parents lived at 700 Boulevard in veterans' housing. (His father was a World War II veteran.) He was raised from the age of five on Wolcott Street in the Fair Haven section of the city.

Sen. Looney's parents were born in County Clare, Ireland. Both came from farm families. His father, Martin Francis, had older siblings already living in Fair Haven and joined them in 1927, when he began working for the New Haven Railroad. His mother, Mary, came to the United States two years later, to help her sister who was living in New York. She worked as a governess, and later, at a hotel in the City, where she was a member of the Hotel and Restaurant Workers union. She was encouraged to run for union office, but did not do so.

Martin and Mary Looney met at an Irish dance at Rockaway Beach in 1938 and married in 1942. Martin Francis was 48 when Martin Michael was born. Both parents "were New Deal Democrats who believed in an activist government," a tradition that their son inherited.

MRS. LOONEY AS "ROSIE THE RIVETER"

As he approached 40, in 1940, Martin Francis Looney left the railroad and went to work at the Winchester plant, driving a jitney and operating a forklift. Mary Looney also worked at the plant from 1942 until 1946, doing piece work making bullets and shells. She was known as "fastest" on the machines, and many of her co-workers, also mostly women, wanted to work with her because they knew her skill would help everyone earn bonuses. Looney notes that as "part of the Rosie the Riveter generation," his mother excelled at the work but did not remain at the plant after the war years. After Looney's graduation from Notre Dame High School in 1966, Mrs. Looney went to work as a cook at the St. Rose Convent.

"AN INDUSTRIAL JOB WAS A DECENT PAYING JOB...[ENOUGH] TO SUPPORT A FAMILY."

"Our family's standard of living definitely improved" thanks to the union, Sen. Looney recalls. He was able to attend Notre Dame High School, and later Fairfield University and the University of Connecticut Law School where he received his J.D. His parents were "able to save" a modest amount of money. "An industrial job was a decent paying job ...[enough] to support a family." In addition, higher education was much less expensive "than it is today."

Very few Winchester workers came from the Looney family's neighborhood in Fair Haven. They did not have a car, so Looney, Sr., had to catch a bus every morning at 6:15 a.m. to get to the plant. "I never saw him on a week-day morning until he retired," Sen. Looney recalls. His father worked the 7:30 to 3 shift and got home at 4. "By the time he retired, I was staying up later than he was" in order to do homework.

Because they lived in Fair Haven, the Looneys didn't often mix with too many other Winchester workers and their families, most of whom came from the Dixwell-Newhallville communities, although "we used to go to an outing [there] in the summer" which included barbecues, picnics and ball games.

THE COMPANY IN ITS LATTER YEARS

In Sen. Looney's view, the Machinist Union's attempts to revive product diversification and to implement the High Performance Work Organization at Winchester in the 1990s failed, in part, because "the real control of the company was not local at that point. The [plant] had become a division of a larger group that had other goals and concerns [and] wanted to keep the strongest known Winchester brand—the guns. There was no local autonomy."

Winchester kept its "brand," but the company located in New Haven was owned by many different entities throughout its history. Peaking in the war years, employment began to decline in the mid-1960s throughout the 1970s, and to shrink rapidly in the 1980s and 1990s. Although there were many issues in the bitter 1979-1980 strike, Sen. Looney, who was working at the time as an aide to New Haven Mayor Frank Logue, cites as an important one the growing concern among workers about repeated layoffs and the need to maintain guaranteed levels of employment.

Throughout the 1980s and 1990s, the City of New Haven continued to provide the company with major tax incentives in exchange for promises to keep a certain number of workers employed- but the "guaranteed" numbers kept shrinking. The company repeatedly went to the city to renegotiate its agreement, setting the required numbers ever lower.

Although the Connecticut state legislature passed a bill in the early 1980s requiring companies who employed a certain number of people to give its workers six months' notice before closing, the Winchester plant's "catch-22" to avoid doing this may have been the already small numbers employed there in its last year.

"CONNECTING THE DOTS:" LABOR HISTORY EDUCATION

Because of his background, Sen. Looney says he's been pro-labor throughout his career as a legislator, supporting wherever possible the struggles of organized labor. He believes that the existence of unions has improved the overall social welfare of everyone in this country "because they set a community standard of living that everyone benefited from, union or not."

"The role of labor and its contribution to the quality of life has not been taught sufficiently in schools and families," but is a critical component in education because people "had to strive and suffer" to win the gains that we now have. Nothing that has been achieved to date was a "given...." In all of history, nothing—including the U.S. Constitution—was a foregone conclusion: "Things today are as they are because of the sacrifices people made" in the past. "We need to connect the dots."

MOVING FORWARD

"Without a high level of education," there is "no way to make a good living" today, says Sen. Looney. Most of the new jobs being created are low paid, non-union jobs in the service sector of the economy. The percentage of workers in the private sector who are unionized is down below 10%. "We need a new set of organizing campaigns, like went on in the '30s, '40s and '50s to really motivate people. [There is] a need for a new union movement to create more union jobs to elevate the [general] standard of living."

Overall, "I liked it...I had some hard jobs that weren't fit for a man, much less a woman, but never mind..."
Re: the union, "I always called them 'our lawyer on retainer.' The union was very necessary."

MILDRED HOPKINS

Interviewed conducted on August 28, 2010, by Dorothy Johnson and Mary Johnson

Born and raised in New Haven, Ms. Hopkins lived in New Haven County, including 20 years in West Haven, all her life. Her mother was a "homemaker," and "my father wasn't around very much."

She started at Winchester because one sister already worked there, and worked there for 20 years, "15 at Winchester and five at USRAC," (U.S. Repeating Arms Company, its subsequent name.) Four more sisters also went to work there, and at one point "there were five of us at one time."

Hopkins' first job at the plant, in 1962, involved piece work on the milling machines. "I was young and fast." She also worked in the tube shop, in the woodbine, in ammunition and, after ammunition was outsourced, in armaments, and she was an inspector. Generally, she worked second or third shift, "for the convenience of my children."

Apart from a layoff in 1985, when she went to work at Pratt & Whitney for four years until getting called back, she never really thought of leaving "because of the convenience" (it was close to where she lived). "The money was pretty good and the benefits were pretty good. I was glad to work there." With her husband working at Armstrong Rubber, they were able to "put my kids through private school." Although she was not too involved in the social life among the workers at the plant "because my kids were small," her best memory of the plant is "the people" she worked with, "and some of the bosses weren't so bad."

HER WORK

Overall, "I liked it ...I had some jobs that weren't fit for a man, much less a woman, but never mind...Some of the jobs were hard and heavy... I used to have to bear down" on some "big machines."

STRIKES AND ISSUES

Ms. Butler worked at the plant during the 1969 as well as the 1979 and 1980 strikes, and recalls that the '69 strike "wasn't such an angry strike, but the '79-'80 one was a very angry strike. There was a lot of fighting on the line. Some of our people got knocked around—even on Family Day with children there... It was a hurtful thing to see our policeman doing that kind of stuff." It was a long strike, and in the end, she felt "the company met us more than half way."

Health and Safety: Did people get hurt much on the job? "Not seriously, that I remember...There was one incident [where] one of our people was given a warning because she had an infected finger [because of a piece of metal in her finger] and she was 'cited.' ...The union got that dropped. It was asinine."

Martin Luther King Day was not a paid holiday until after she left, although there was an option to take the day off without pay.

On Company Requests for Union "Givebacks": "They had people over a barrel. [Some people said, 'I'd rather give back than not have a job.'"

THE UNION

"The union was there when I came. (Everyone had to join.) It was a closed shop. They had no choice." Although she never held a union office or was part of a union committee, she felt that "the union was very necessary...I always called them 'our lawyer on retainer.' ...If there hadn't been a union" the company would "run over people."

Because she was "out" for four years on layoff, she lost her "time," but was able to get it back with the help of her union steward, who "did more than the higher ups in the union...'No, we're not going to let that go.' We fought and we won."

"The union was pretty powerful when I was there but it got weaker as time went on."

THE CLOSING

The plant closing occurred long after she left, but she had friends who were still there at the time who "were really devastated. You think you're good to go until you are ready to retire and then..."

"Unions have to start forming again.

"There were good jobs...There is nothing here now, and it's very sad."

NEW HAVEN ✦ INDEPENDENT

Valley Independent Sentinel   La Voz Hispana   🔍

Sections

choose   ▾

Neighborhoods

choose   ▾

Features

choose   ▾

WNHH Radio   ⊙ ▶

BREAKING THE NEWS!
CANNABIS CORNER
DATELINE FRIDAY
DATELINE NEW HAVEN
DEEP FOCUS
ECONOMIC UPDATE
INDEPENDENT PROJECT
JAZZ HAVEN
JOE UGLY SHOW
KICA'S CORNER
LA VOZ RADIO
LOVEBABZ LOVETALK
MAYOR MONDAY!
MORNINGS WITH MUBARAKAH
NHV INNOVATIVE PODCAST
NORTHERN REMEDY
THE MUNICIPAL VOICE
THE PETE MEZZETTI SHOW
THE SHOW
THE TABLE UNDERGROUND
THE TALK-SIP
THE TOM FICKLIN SHOW
URBAN TALK RADIO

Follow Us

f facebook
🐦 TWITTER

NHI Newsletter

📧 SIGN UP

Legal Notices

AGENCY ON AGING
ALDERMEN
HOUSING AUTHORITY
CITY CLERK
OTHER
PROBATE

**Government/ Community
Links**

'r Kids Family Center
1 City/ 80 Days
Agency on Aging
AIDS Project NH
ALIVE
All Our Kin
Animal Shelter Volunteers
Arte Inc
Arts Council
Arts In CT
Artspace
Beth El Keser Israel
Big Brothers Big Sisters
Bike New Haven
Boys & Girls Club
Cancer Support
Chabad of Westville
Chamber of Commerce
Children's Museum
Christian Community Action
City of New Haven
CitySeed
Citywide Youth
Columbus House
Community Action Agency
Community Loan Fund
Community Mediation
ConnCAN
Cornell Scott—Hill Health Center
Creative Arts Workshop
CT BAEO
CT Best Restaurants
CT Tech Council
Data Haven
EcoWorks
Elm City Cycling
Elm Shakespeare
Elmseed
Empower NH
Fair Havan Community Health
Friends Of Wooster Sq.

Winchester Workers Pressure City for Jobs

by **MELISSA BAILEY** | Aug 23, 2006 5:42 pm
(1) Comment | Commenting has been closed | E-mail the Author
Posted to: **Newhallville**

After finding out last week that the sources of their livelihoods were gone for good, former employees of the U.S. Repeating Arms Co. gathered Wednesday outside the plant at 344 Winchester Ave. to call for the city's help in replacing the 186 lost jobs. City officials say they're still at work: "The city has had interest from a potential user and discussions are ongoing."

Wednesday's rally was called after Olin Corp. announced last week it had sold the license to produce Winchester rifles to Browning in Utah, instead of to a buyer that would have produced them in New Haven.

"It's a disgrace that corporate greed won out over integrity, tradition and loyalty to dedicated New Haven workers. But Winchester workers are still here, even if the company is not," said Craig Gauthier (pictured above at right), chairman of the Winchester Citizens Ad Hoc Committee. He called on the city to help regain the 186 jobs that were lost when the plant closed in March after 140 years of manufacturing the Gun that Won the West.

"The city has had interest from a potential user and discussions are ongoing," responded Kelly Murphy, the city's director of economic development. Murphy said the city "exhausted efforts to try and draw a new arms manufacturer to the site and secure the licensure for the rifle's manufacture from Olin. Those efforts produced two positive outcomes: Herstal made good on its financial obligations to the city, and a lengthy effort by a third-party consultant to attract a new buyer produced some good follow-up leads."

Gauthier's group called for a public hearing with the Board of Aldermen to discuss how to bring manufacturing jobs back to Newhallville. The request was granted: A meeting has been set for Sept. 8, announced Gauthier.

John Harrity of GrowJobsCT, a coalition working to keep manufacturing jobs in Connecticut, thanked the city for trying to find a buyer and keep the rifle production in the city. "The mayor of New Haven actually did a lot of work to try and come up with an innovative approach," said Harrity. But "it didn't work."

Harrity and Gauthier want the city to find a new employer and to "distribute the $850,000 collected in back taxes from Herstal Group to Winchester workers, in partial payment of four months' lost pay and benefits denied workers through lack of proper notice of the plant closing." Aldermen have indicated that money has already been budgeted for other uses.

Speakers, including John Reynolds (at left), president of Winchester's Local 609, focused on holding the city accountable for getting the 186 workers' jobs back. Some of that pressure fell on the mayor. Some also fell on those seeking office, like Senate hopeful Ned Lamont, who has been endorsed by the machinist union that encompasses Local 609.

Lamont campaign manager Tom Swan showed up to pledge his candidate's support by demanding federal support of universal health care and trade agreements that kept Connecticut jobs from being taken overseas. "We're willing to stand here and continue to fight with you today, tomorrow and the next day."

Newhallville Alderman Charles Blango pledged aldermanic support. "We're still here for the long haul, for the fight. … I am committed; my colleagues are committed; we're here to see what the end's gonna be." In response to the increased pressure on the city, mayoral spokeswoman Catherine Sullivan-DeCarlo recalled the strides the city has taken to help Winchester workers.

"The City of New Haven took proactive steps that almost no other municipality has ever done to try to secure manufacturing jobs in the city. Staff at the city worked with a consultant, initially hired by the city but paid primarily by Herstal, to work to secure a new buyer for the facility and to acquire the license to produce Winchester rifles. In addition, Mayor DeStefano, working with Congresswoman DeLauro and Senator Dodd's office, expedited Trade Adjustment Assistance Act benefits to USRAC workers."

Share this story with others.

| + More | f Facebook | Twitter | in LinkedIn | ✉ Email | 🖨 Print |

🔴 Recommend Be the first of your friends to recommend this.

Post a Comment

Commenting has closed for this entry

Comment

posted by: THREEFIFTHS on August 24, 2006 4:28am

I Feel For the workers,But I Have to say with All
of the Shootings In Hartford And New Haven And Across The Country, I am Glad That Winchester is closed.I Heard The
preachers and Mayor And The police chief of New Haven Talk About The Responsibility Of Parents Who Kids Have Firearms.
Winchester as Colt,Smith wession,Ruger Are Also Part Of This Problem. These company are noting More Than Merchants of Death.

11

1980-2006 THE BEAT GOES ON...
UNTIL IT DOESN'T

"*It's time to say 'no' to corporate welfare.*"

—Elm City Congregations Organized member Ian Skoggard quoted in
New Haven Register, November 13, 1998.

"*The intent of this notice is not to drive the company out of New Haven.*"

—New Haven Mayor John DeStefano, Jr., quoted in *New Haven Register*,
January 10, 1999.

"*It never ceases to amaze me how calls for the removal of guns from the streets and calls for manufacturing guns are made by the same voices, even at the same time. Witness two front-page stories in one* Register*: one about the senseless killing of a young girl by gun violence, and the other about the city administration's aggressive solicitation of bids from gun companies to purchase the Winchester property.*"

—Joel Marks, Letter to the Editor, *New Haven Register*, July 2, 2006, b2.

"*I feel for the workers, but I have to say, with all the shootings in Hartford and New Haven and across the country, I am glad that Winchester is closed. I heard the preachers and Mayor and the police chief of New Haven talk about the responsibility of parents [whose] kids have firearms. Winchester, as Colt, Smith [Wesson], Ruger are also part of this problem. These [companies] are nothing more than Merchants of Death.*"

—posted by THREEFIFTHS on *New Haven Independent* web site,
August 24, 2006, 5:28 am. https://www.newhavenindependent.org/index.php/
archives/entry/winchester_workers_pressure_city_for_jobs/

USRAC'S RACE TO THE FINISH, 1990-2006

Part 2. 1998-2006. The Very, Very, Very End.

NOVEMBER 1998 USRAC employment has dwindled to 341. Citizens protest its failure to keep employment at 400 level or above per 1992 tax agreement.

JANUARY 1999 Mayor John DeStefano sends letter to company finding it in default.

MARCH 2000 DeStefano asks the New Haven Board of Alders to amend the 1992 agreement to pro-rate the tax amendments based on actual number of employees.

SEPTEMBER 2000 Board of Alders approves amended tax deal.

MARCH 2005 Three year contract signed between union and management, approving a "slight raise" in the final two years, placing on hold for a year a company plan to move 28 jobs out of state, and reaffirming the obligation of both sides to the HPWO program "to work for improved production and to preserve or expand the work force" under the HPWO program.

JANUARY 2006 The Herstal Group announces it will close USRAC, "citing global competition and declining demand;" the remaining work force of 186 will lose their jobs as of March 31st. The new plant built in 1994 will be vacant. Citizens' Ad Hoc Committee demands delay in closing to afford workers the requisite six months' notice before relocation mandated in January 2000 city contract.

JANUARY-MARCH 2006 City attempts unsuccessfully to find a new gun manufacturer to buy the plant.

MARCH 16, 2006 The company claims it has violated no tax agreements because it is closing, not relocating; at a public hearing of the Board of Alders, citizens claim it has in fact relocated machines and jobs to South Carolina.

MARCH 31, 2006 USRAC shuts down for the last time.

APRIL 6, 2006 Workforce Alliance holds session to explain federal Trade Adjustment Assistance benefits, offers job and unemployment counseling. About 75 workers attend.

AUGUST 23, 2006 Olin Corporation announces it has sold the license to produce Winchester rifles to Browning in Utah, ending hope that a new buyer could be found to produce them in New Haven; Winchester Citizens Ad Hoc Committee calls for public hearing to discuss how to bring manufacturing jobs back to Newhallville. A date is set for September 8th.

SEPTEMBER 27, 2006 Beginning of two-day auction at the 344 Winchester Ave. to sell off equipment remaining at the plant. The auctioneer is Thomas Industries, which had previously purchased the items. But "the fate of the lobby's life-size statue of John Wayne has not been decided, USRAC officials said Tuesday. The statue will not be auctioned."

As noted, during the company's long tenure and many different incarnations in New Haven, its officials repeatedly threatened to move production elsewhere, and, as a result of these threats, were able to win tax abatements from the city and concessions from the union.

As we have seen, transfer of key operations to other locations began in the 1970s and escalated in the 1980s, always leaving workers worrying about job security and their futures. In 1980, at the end of the six-month strike, there were 1300 people employed at Winchester. In November of 1985, at the time of the massive six-week furlough discussed in Chapter 9, there were 865 people left. The City of New Haven gave the company an "assistance package" of $4 million in loans in exchange for the company's promise to remain in New Haven and keep employment at the plant at a level above 400. In February 1986, 424 of the laid off workers were recalled.[124]

Even as early as 1959, rumors that Olin-Mathieson might move the Winchester Arms Plant to another venue sparked alarm in New Haven, although they were put to rest with promises of company expansion in town and a visit to the plant by the city's Mayor, Richard C. Lee. Winchester News, January 2, 1959 (Vol. VII, No. 13.)

Armester Galloway
Things will be OK

Helen Haddock
Sitting tight and waiting

Albert Pires
Merger wasn't a surprise

Workers worried about future

By Jackey Gold
Staff Reporter

Workers rushing through the gate for the 7 a.m. shift at U.S. Repeating Arms Co. this morning said they were uncertain about their future with the Newhallville-based gun manufacturer, which is set to merge with a smaller Massachusetts rifle company.

Balancing paper cups of coffee in one hand and clutching sack lunches in the other, USRAC employees talked about the pending merger with some optimism, saying they hoped the company would continue to operate in New Haven.

"Things are going to be OK," said Armester Galloway, an 18-year employee with the company. "It's better for the company to merge than do nothing."

USRAC has been in financial difficulty for months and is currently behind in payments on a $1.3 million loan from the city. It also has stretched out payments to many of its creditors.

The company has been seeking federal approval for an $8 million refinancing package.

"The merger is going to be good for this company and the other company," said Helen Haddock, another employee. "We just have to sit tight and wait. As long as we don't move. Winchester has been here for years and it should stay here," she added.

USRAC, the former Winchester Sporting Arms Division of Stamford-based Olin Corp., announced Monday it would pursue a merger agreement with Savage Industries Inc., a 400-employee gun manufacturer based in Westfield, Mass. The company is expected to result in an $80 million company that officials claim would be the second-largest domestic rifle and shotgun producer in the industry.

The new company would require a 550,000-square-foot building on about 30 acres of land. A

new location has not yet been chosen for the plant. But company officials did say Monday that the combined work force would be cut by as many as 300 employees.

Employee Albert Pires, who has worked 35 years for the company, said he wasn't surprised to hear about USRAC's current plans. "Eventually they were going to leave anyway," he said. "If they are going to move to another gun factory, what would they need me for?" said Pires, who lives in the Newhallville neighborhood on Norton Street. He said that his age would probably prevent him from finding another job in the area.

Sixty-year-old Harold Thompson of Dixwell Avenue agreed. Thompson said he has been with the company for 17 years and would not move to keep his job, even if he had that option. "I guess I'd take early retirement," he said. "There aren't any other alternatives."

USRAC's skilled workers are represented by Local 609 of the International Association of Machinists and Aerospace Workers. The union has worked closely with company officials, and has made several large bargaining concessions to help tide USRAC through its financial difficulties.

But Monday's merger announcement caught union officials completely off guard. "Nobody in the company told us a word," said an angry Louis Romano, president of Local 609. "I've been here 45 years. I've never been treated like this before. We've done so much for this company," he said.

"I don't think the company is being fair," echoed first-year employee David Voytek of Stratford. He and John Degnall of Branford said they would not move to keep their jobs at USRAC.

"I'd look for another job in the area," Degnall said, "but I'm sure it wouldn't pay as much as this one."

Harold Thompson
Considering early retirement

John Degnall
Wouldn't move with company

Staff photos by Lorenzo Evans

Rumors of a merger being pursued by USRAC to help alleviate its financial woes, along with the possibility that the plant would move to Westfield, Massachusetts where the other company, Savage Industries, Inc., was located, fueled worker concerns in 1985. New Haven Register, June 4, 1985. Clipping from Local 609 files.

After USRAC was purchased in 1990 by the Herstal group, things were looking temporarily more promising for the plant's fortunes as we have seen in Chapter 10. The new USRAC announced in January of 1991 that it would like to build the "streamlined" 235,000 square foot plant that had been deferred since the 1980s on Winchester and Division Streets on the site of the old, unused Winchester buildings, and city officials happily predicted that such a plant could create between 200 and 250 new additional jobs.[125]

The plant was indeed built, but not before the company had once again threatened to leave town, this time to move its operations to Wallingford, CT or perhaps even out of state altogether, to its sister shop in South Carolina. Among other issues, it was balking at the extent of the environmental cleanup involved in demolition of the old buildings, and there was an ongoing debate as to whose responsibility this was. After forgiveness of a $15 million loan made in 1987, and the promise of $570,000 from Yale University and the Olin Corporation, along with subsidies totaling $1.25 million from United Illuminating to facilitate the building of the plant, USRAC agreed to stay and Olin took responsibility for the site cleanup and demolition. In addition, the city granted the new owners two 20-year tax abatements in exchange for a commitment to maintain employment at the plant at 400 or above.[126]

A series of loans and further tax abatements followed, including the revision of the original agreement in the year 2000, which allowed employment to go below the 400 level and to pro-rate the abatement based on numbers of employees (the higher the number, the larger the abatement.)[127] But none of these measures achieved their stated purpose of maintaining employment at the plant or preventing the company from leaving town. By the end of 1998, employment was down to 341; by the time the plant closed in March of 2006, it had dwindled to an all-time low of 186.[128]

John Reynolds, third from left, was elected president of Local 609 in 2001. Photo is from Local 609 files.

PARTING SHOTS

"*It saddens my heart to say this, but in the next one to five years, most of us will retire with a pension of less than 1,000 a month after working 30, 35, even 40 years or more. We cannot let this happen to the younger employee coming behind us…Our senior employees deserve all the increases and benefits they can get in the next five years. This can only happen if labor and management can work together for a common goal to keep jobs at Winchester. We are all in this boat together. One cannot win without the other.*"

—Nate McClam, candidate for president of Local 609, in a letter dated October 24, 2001

Loans, concessions, tax abatements and the High Performance Work Organization notwithstanding, whatever uneasy (and unequal) "partnership" may have existed between the company, the union, and indeed the city from 1956 on did not reemerge in the 21st century. The material produced by the Local 609 candidates in their 2001 presidential campaigns reflected disillusionment no doubt shared by workers, both with the union leadership and with their current situation. On paper, candidates John Reynolds and Nate McClam both stated that changes had to be made, and quickly, with new contract negotiations coming up in 2002. They both acknowledged, McClam explicitly, that the union had lost both power and respect in its dealings with

"On the last day, we all gathered around the statue of John Wayne. I had polished him up real good before that. I was the only one who cleaned up John Wayne."

DAVID W.P. ROY

Roy worked at Winchester from 1985 until it closed in 2006.

He was hired because he "was working installing burglar alarms and going to school at night for electronics, tutoring a guy [on layoff from Winchester] whose father was a boss there." When his friend was called back, "I applied there and within a week I was working there. I used to be lucky getting jobs that way."

When he got laid off, Roy bid on another Winchester job, working on a "torturous hot machine" that made metal slugs and hammered them into shotgun barrels. It was work "no one wanted, so I figured...I'd never get laid off" again. It was "nice, though" because there were two shifts, each twelve-hours long, and I "never had time to go to the bank."

Next, he became a maintenance worker, a position he also liked, for a different reason: "In maintenance I was allowed to go out on my own and to work on the job as I saw fit... and make things safe. I liked fixing things and I liked making things better...A lot of people wanted to do a good job but their machines wouldn't work and they didn't trust maintenance because they thought they were being blamed. I tried to find the truth." Once he earned the trust of "the people on the floor," they became long term, "true friends."

Throughout his years there, Roy worked mostly first shift. He met his wife at Winchester, although "she didn't make the first month... She got sick. They said she had missed two days without calling... She [really] got fired because she was a distraction [because of her looks] but they didn't say that."

He lived in Fair Haven when first working at Winchester, usually driving to work. Then, when he and his wife moved to West Haven, he took the bus so she could use their car to get to medical appointments.

SERIOUS HEALTH AND SAFETY ISSUES

"When I first started there, safety [equipment] was a privilege."

Vapors: "There were people in some situations working with vapors [using] a ratty fan that didn't work well. They gave them masks, but they were dust masks, not vapor masks... It was just for show. I told them that."

Electronic Issues: In one case, machines were removed from a room, but the wires were left behind, wrapped up in tape, the power not shut off. The tape came loose and a worker was shocked.

"I got electrocuted twice" while working at Winchester, and had to go to the company doctor in North Haven. He was "not a bedside manner kind of guy. He told me, 'the pain will either go by fast or slow...'"

Old, substandard equipment: Winchester had an on-site nurse "for small things. She was good. She pulled a lot of splinters out of me. We had some old equipment," including old rickety ladders. Much of their equipment was "always operating...just barely."

Indifference: Management was "indifferent to safety conditions... mostly their attitude was that money could be spent better somewhere else." The bosses felt that "maintenance people caused problems." One manager "felt that whatever money he didn't spend on safety equipment went into his pocket."

OSHA was called in. The company had suspicions as to who called OSHA and the man was let go, but the OSHA personnel were there for weeks. "It was like a training center for them."

"We got no support for quality except for quality parts...not quality of life...OSHA had a field day at that place (the old plant.) When we built the new plant," however, "we never saw them."

The one agency that did show up was "water safety." Winchester had been built on a swamp, and when they were cleaning up for the new building, workers dug up old oil tanks that had been forgotten. New condos had been built in the area, but they "couldn't open them up because oil was pouring into the water system."

Outside contractors: "Management really didn't check what outsider contractors did. They were profiting from the contractors..." One contractor told one boss he'd do a $4000 job for $2000, and "he could expect an envelope when the job was done.

"My boss explained to me that you should not tell anyone this."

"One time I was told to disconnect a machine...I went toward a compressor and it went off. [There was] no box to turn off [the] power The only way to turn it off was to go to another building on another block. [There was] no sign saying 'high voltage' or 'danger.' I said, 'You paid these people tens of 1000s of dollars and didn't even look to see if the switch was there!'

ROY AND THE UNION

Did the union intervene in health and safety issues? "That was spotty, especially in the old factory...The union did not get involved as much as they should have."

Roy became active in the union "only in the last few years before we closed."

"The first three contracts I had, we got no raises, for nine years." The next time, everyone in maintenance began picking up their tools and leaving. "We got a raise that year, a good raise."

The last union president that Roy liked and respected was Craig Gauthier. "He was the last one who really fought the company and that I had confidence in...[The] union stopped being a place of hope at the same time I was being drawn towards it out of desperation."

THE END

"I ended up cleaning bathrooms just to keep busy. I cleaned the hell out of them, too."

The Herstal Group, based in Belgium, a "multinational group which owns Fabrique National, an arms manufacturer, and Browning Rifles," bought the company. "When I first started Winchester made almost everything themselves except for castings." Now, parts were made all over the world, although often identified as "American made."

"Right before the last contract [we found out] that the European Union gave Fabrique National 100 million Euros. Today 70% of all small arms used in Afghanistan and Iraq are Fabrique National made."

Two or three years before the company closed, Roy and other workers noticed that equipment was being moved. Returning to work after Christmas the last year, "I ran into one of the janitors who said, 'They moved all the machines out.' This was done during the [Christmas] break. Neighbors saw the trucks come in, but never saw them leave. I don't really know why.

"Later on that week they made the official announcement...The plans had been kept secret. The people who did know what was going on were already busy stuffing their pockets with company money and [had] kept their mouths shut..."

Most of the workers were gone in March of 2006, with about a dozen or so left in the offices and a dozen in maintenance.

A larger-than-life statue of the actor John Wayne had greeted visitors at the main entrance of the plant for decades. On the last day before the final closing, in June 2006, "we all gathered around the statue... I had polished him up real good before that. I was the only one who cleaned up John Wayne."

In a way, the final closing was a relief, because "the last few months with no one walking around were really sad. I ended up cleaning bathrooms just to keep busy. I cleaned the hell out of them, too. They were really clean."

HIS LIFE IN THE AFTERMATH

After the closing, his wife was still sick, and "I was hurt...I just wanted to spend some time with her..." But he needed work. Under the Trade Adjustment program, he went to school, graduated and kept looking for a job. "Half the jobs I went to, they'd already laid off 12 people."

As of this interview in 2010, he remained unemployed.

Why did he agree to do this interview with the Greater New Haven Labor History Association?

"I like history. I appreciate people who take care of history. It's a good calling."

management, especially in the last three to six years. Reynolds wrote that "Together we will stand but divided we will fall—which is what we have been doing for the last six years," noting that "poor leadership has created a real struggle for Local 609." McClam, who had held the presidential office once before, called for "union-management cooperation," while Reynolds' literature stressed the need to "work together for a better union."

John Reynolds won the election, and the union signed a new contract with the company in 2002 and again in 2005. The three-year contract signed in 2005 granted a "slight raise" to be given in 2006 and 2007 and put on hold the company's plan to move 28 jobs out of state. Both gains obviously proved to be meaningless. Ironically,

October 24, 2001

Greetings Brothers and Sisters:

On October 26, 2001, you must choose a President for your local for the next three years. In addition, in March 2002, our Union contract ends and there will be negotiations on a new contract. This is one of the most important contracts in our history, that you, the members of this local will face. Why, because your next President and his cabinet will have the future of your employment in their hands. If you read the newspaper or listen to the news, you can see that it is a sad time for businesses and laborers. People are loosing their jobs, by the hundreds and thousands, even as low as 40 – 50 people in small businesses. Since 9/11/01, our whole way of life has changed. Therefore, it is imperative that your next President understand the issues clearly, is committed to the responsibilities assigned to him with a willingness to work with the company and his cabinet.

I am committed to this Union. I have attended all of our meetings for the last three years. I did not wait to the last year of the contract to attend meetings to quality to run for office. I have attended leadership school, as well as conferences on union and company relationships. In this election, the question will come down to this, who do you trust to represent you for the next three years, to defend your rights and jobs. Why are these people running for President? The last three years, I have watched our Union lose great respect in the management of union matters. I must admit, when I was President, I did make some mistakes. I am not saying that I won't make mistakes again, but I won't make the same ones.

We have lost all respect from the Personnel Department, to the Manager's Office, to the Foreman's Office. We must rebuild the bridge of confidence among our members and in our workplace. During the next five years, most of our experienced members will be at retirement age. There's a great number of younger employees that we will leave here to carry on the work. We need to share our experience with the younger workforce. It saddens my heart to say this, but in the next one to five years, most of us will retire with a pension of less than $1,000 a month after working 30, 35 even 40 years or more. We can not let this happen to the younger employee coming behind us. If elected, I am committed to fight for a better pension plan, better wages and medical. Our senior employees deserve all their increases and benefits they can get in the next five years. This can only happen if labor and management can work together for a common goal to keep jobs here at Winchester. We are all in this boat together. One can not win without the other. Our employees need to know how many jobs are needed for the present sales for the upcoming year, so that we can work without worrying about being laid off.

Let me close with this. It was said that our current President made decisions on his own without the advice of his cabinet. They were elected to do a job for the people. How did they let this happen? If elected, I promise that everyone will do their job, from the President, to the Business Rep, Trustees, Financial Secretary, down to the Stewards. Let no one tell you how to vote. It's your job and your future on the line.

In this struggle with you.
Nate McClam.

VOTE !!

John Reynolds for President Local 609

- Union member for 36 years
- Steward for 5 years
- Chief steward for 10 years, currently holding this position

We need change at the top!

Poor leadership has caused a real struggle for local 609. Elect me as president and I will give members back a local you can be proud of. Together we will stand, but divided we will fall, which is what we've been doing for the last 6 years.

If elected I will:
- Represent everyone fairly, regardless of who they are or what they have done.
- Stand up for my union members in dealing with the company on issues such as job bids, job changes, or job related injuries.
- Assure grievances are heard and the outcome brought back to the grievant as soon as possible.
- Negotiate pension, wages, and insurance in the upcoming contract to the benefit of all union members, including senior workers nearing or planning retirement.

We can work together for a better union. Thanks for your support!!

Both presidential candidates in the 2001 union election acknowledged that changes had to be made in the union. McClam made the case that times had gotten much harder, and Reynolds promised to "give members back a local you can be proud of." Flyers are from the Local 609 files.

When he was asked to join the Ink Spots, "I told them, 'I am not going to give up my job, because I have a family'... but Winchester let me off if I had to go somewhere [on tour.]"

JAMES FOSTER

FEBRUARY 20, 1929 — NOVEMBER 17, 2013

Born in New Haven, Mr. Foster was raised by his grandmother and his aunt, who were domestic workers. He started working at Winchester in 1948 and retired in 1991.

"It was the place everyone was going to work when they were young. [At 18 or 19] all the kids used to sign up."

He did piece work when he started in the barrel shop. "It was up to you how much money you could make. It all depended on how fast you could go."

When he first came to Winchester, the plant was operating 24/7, with three shifts. But over the years, he was laid off "several times...You got laid off, then they'd call you back."

What about the union?: "I guess for some people..." it made a difference. "I wasn't a leader, I was just a member. I just wanted to go to work and go back home."

How effective the union was "all depended on who was the president. Some worked harder for you than others."

Mr. Foster lived for a while in the same building as Carl Johnson, the third president of Local 609. He and the Johnson family were good friends.

How did he feel about working at Winchester as an African American?: "I felt alright. I had no trouble with anyone, nothing I couldn't handle myself. You had some good bosses, and you had some bad bosses."

The first African American man hired in the gun testing department was harassed. "That was a good paying job...It was not open at first to everybody. You had to be the right color."

On joining the Ink Spots while working at Winchester: Someone came up to him at church with the news that the Ink Spots were looking for a replacement tenor: "They asked me to join the group. I told them, 'I am not going to give up my job, because I have a family.'" He didn't have to: "Winchester let me off if I had to go somewhere [on tour]."

Mr. Foster was with the Ink Spots "for over 20 years."

How did he feel about the plant closing in 2006?: "I felt sorry for the people who were still working there. I am just glad I got out. I kept hoping they would do something... but it didn't happen."

> "At the time the pay was pretty decent and my children were pretty small and it was nearby in the neighborhood."

MARIE BOULWARE

Interviewed conducted on August 24, 2010 by Dorothy Johnson. (No photograph available.)

Marie was born in New Haven and her father worked at Winchester for over 20 years in a number of positions including as a gun tester; her brother worked there for eight, as a polisher. Her father retired shortly after she got there, just after the 1979-1980 strike, but she stayed for 26 years, until the plant closed in 2006. She held a number of jobs there, including that of assembly worker and machine operator.

She said she remained there for so many years because "the pay was pretty decent" for the time, and the plant was conveniently located in the neighborhood, a plus especially when her children were small.

She did not hold a union or committee position and mostly wasn't involved in the social life there, although she remembered that "four or five of my co-workers were in a band...the Winchester Specials..." and that there was always a program for Black History Month.

Re: the cutbacks and givebacks demanded by the company, she said that although "they didn't want to...[the union] gave in to the company to keep their jobs."

She was laid off several times, once for a year.

SHUTDOWN, AND THEN CLOSING

Coming off the Christmas shutdown in early 2006, she and her friends met some of their co-workers who told them the plant was closing. They were upset. Where would they go to find jobs? "A lot of my co-workers did not know how to use a computer."

She herself applied for and got a job at Yale New Haven Hospital in December 2006.

How did you feel about working at Winchester?: "It was a job."

What about the union?: "I guess they did the best they could."

the contract also reaffirmed the obligation of both company and management to uphold their commitment to the High Performance Work Organization program, "to work for improved production and to preserve or expand the work force."[129]

By March of 2006, when the Herstal Group shut down the company, having given two months' notice to its employees, Craig Gauthier, who had left Winchester several years previously, headed a Citizens' Ad Hoc Committee to apply community pressure to get those workers the four months' back pay they felt was due them.[130] The committee members argued that the "benefits recapture" clause in the company's 2000 amended tax abatement agreement with the city stipulated that "if the plant relocated or caused the work force to fall beneath 200, the abatements would be cancelled and tax benefits already received would have to be paid back with interest," and also provided that "the manufacturer would have to notify all parties six months prior to a relocation." However, the company continued to claim that it had not "relocated," but "closed." At a public hearing of the Board of Alders at New Haven's City Hall, the semantics battle provoked Alder Jorge Perez to comment, "If it smells like a rat, it's a rat...If you move a machine down to South Carolina, and you move someone down to train workers how to run it—that doesn't sound like a plant closing." Responded Alfreda Edwards, the Alder who represented the part of Newhallville where the plant stood, "It sounds like relocation!"[131]

Why did she stay at Winchester? "It was a job, I had a family to support, and I liked my co-workers. We had fun."

Regarding scabs who stayed after the strikes ended and were therefore required to become union members: "They paid their [union] dues, but that's about it. But they complained. [I said] 'What you complaining about? You came in here as a scab and now you're making more money.'"

EDNA L. HUDSON

Interviewed by Dorothy Johnson and Lula White on June 30, 2010

Ms. Hudson left the company in 1997, long before the closing, but she but was there during both the 1969 and 1979-1980 strikes. Why did she stay for so long? "It was a job, I had a family to support, and I liked my co-workers. We had fun."

During the 1979-1980 strike, she went to school to become a Certified Nurse's Aide. She flew to Florida in the winter with the people she was taking care of, and her employer flew her back to do her picket duty. "I had to be on line," she said, although strikers received only $40 a week for picket duty. The CNA job was "the only way I made it" through the strike.

She was not arrested during the contentious strike, but many co-workers were. She recalls helping to "hide" one striker who was being pursued by the police and attempted to disguise himself by donning a trench coat. "Then I had to get on the plane and go back to Florida."

TELLING THE TRUTH

Some of the "scabs" who were recruited by the company during the strikes remained afterwards, although a lot of them had to leave. Those who stayed had to become union members, and "they paid their dues, but that's about it." Nevertheless, they complained. Her response? "What you complaining about? You came in here as a scab and now you're making more money."

She was at one point a union steward in a department of about 85 people, reporting to the Chief Steward.

She heard complaints about one union president who was a "company man." She told him, "You're supposed to represent the people, the employees, not the company." He said, "I can't get mad at you." She said, "I know you can't, because I'm telling the truth."

AGREEMENTS BROKEN

According to an agreement with the city, the company received tax abatements in exchange for keeping at least 400 people in the work force. But the numbers continued to shrink. "They were supposed to give back that money," but they didn't. "Too many people lost their jobs."

The New Face of Winchester. Image courtesy the New Haven Independent, *June 25, 2015*

12

2006-2019—BACK TO THE FUTURE

Science Park Development Corporation is a not-for-profit corporation established by Yale, the City of New Haven, Olin Corporation, and the State of Connecticut to develop the former Winchester Firearms factory campus in New Haven, CT. Science Park is located just west of Yale's Science Hill and the "Yale Whale" Ingalls Skating Arena. It is home to start up and established biotech and technology companies, Yale University offices, apartments, and not-for-profit organizations serving New Haven communities.

The mission: Complete the development/redevelopment of Science Park and its environs for the purpose of increasing employment in the City of New Haven in general and the Dixwell and Newhallville neighborhoods in particular, increasing the tax base of the City of New Haven, attracting research and technological enterprises to the City of New Haven, *and to the extent compatible with the foregoing, increasing the variety of housing in Science Park and its environs.* (Emphasis added) —https:// www.scienceparknewhaven.org/.

Before and especially after the demise of the Winchester plant, the City of New Haven touted Science Park as a significant new economic anchor. Like USRAC, its development required a tangle of loans, grants, and tax abatements; city, state, and private money; and a series of incentives to keep particularly valued tenants from moving away. Its costly tenants have included a variety of start-up companies, some of which quickly folded only to be replaced by new ones; a luxury apartment building constructed within the "re-purposed" Winchester plant itself, catering largely to high-tech workers as well as graduate students attending Yale's professional schools; and a variety of upscale businesses serving a select, well-heeled clientele. Poor and working-class members of the Dixwell/Newhallville neighborhood in particular and the City of New Haven in general have not realized economic gains from most of these enterprises, which were often underwritten by state and city contributions and tax incentives but have neither employed, housed, or otherwise benefitted large numbers of working class or poor community members.

March, 2012: Ribbon cutting for Higher One, a student financial services "start-up" company begun in New Haven in 2000 by three Yale undergraduates, two of whom, Mark Volchek (left) and Miles Lasater (center, right), are shown here with former Connecticut Governor Dannel Malloy (center left) and former New Haven Mayor John Destefano (far right). Photo courtesy New Haven Independent, *March 20, 2012.*

HIGHER ONE

Higher One, a startup student financial services company begun by three Yale undergraduates in 2000 and located at 25 Science Park, felt it was "bursting at the seams" and wanted room to expand, quickly. With Higher One's promise of "creating new jobs," Science Park Development Corporation and developers Carter Winstanley and Forest City Enterprises received the necessary approval from the City Plan Commission and the Board of Alders in 2010 to proceed with a plan to create its new headquarters in part of the abandoned Winchester Plant. The cost of this project, considered to be Phase One of the planned Winchester redevelopment, was to be $40 million. There was widespread opposition, largely because of the fear that the jobs that were to be created would not employ the community and because there had been minimal local input about the overall project.[132]

"*Sounds like the city had 'good intentions', and once again got taken [for] yet another ride. I wish we had the ability to embed YouTube videos, because there's really only one response to this: Jerry Seinfeld saying, 'That's a shame'.*"
—Posted by RobotShlomo on the *New Haven Independent* web site, April 5, 2016, 11:05 a.m.

HIGHER ONE, WINCHESTER LOFTS, ET AL.: THE 21ST CENTURY ROLLER COASTER RIDE AT SCIENCE PARK

Part 1. The Unicorn: Higher One

JULY 2010 The New Haven Board of Alders approves a plan by Science Park Development Corporation and developers Carter Winstanley and Forest City Enterprises to create a new headquarters for student financial services company Higher One, which has outgrown its headquarters at 25 Science Park, by renovating part of the old Winchester plant entrance building.

MARCH 2012 The "first phase" of the renovation of the Winchester plant is inaugurated, with a ribbon cutting at Higher One, which will occupy two of the plant's former buildings. The company spends $46 million on the project, with the state providing $2 million and the federal government $3.5 million for environmental clean-up; the state also provides another potential $18.5 million in tax credits. Higher One estimates it will employ 368 people by 2018.

DECEMBER 2015 At the conclusion of an investigation by the Federal Deposit Insurance Corporation, it is determined that Higher One and its business partner, Wex Bank (based in Utah) were guilty of "deceptive business practices" by improperly collecting $31 million in fees from students from May 2012 to July 2014.

APRIL 2016 Higher One denies it will leave New Haven, despite its litigious difficulties. The *New Haven Independent* quotes New Haven's Economic Development Administrator Matthew Nemerson: The company is an "'iconic example,'" he says, of "new-economy 'unicorns' drawing billion-dollar investments with big dreams for creating jobs." He adds that "Unicorns are hard to catch," and **"*my focus now is going to be on keeping them in town.*"** [emphasis supplied.]

APRIL 2018 Having "sold itself off in pieces in 2015 and 2016" to finance its mounting restitution debts, Higher One settles a $7.5 million shareholder lawsuit for insider trading. It is replaced in its short-lived Munson Street home by Blackboard/Transact, a company which provides transaction processing systems for students.

MARCH 2019 Blackboard announces that Transact is to be "spun off," having been acquired by Revenue Capital Partners. As of this writing, it is unclear what if any impact this "spin-off" will have on the company's presence in New Haven.

Ribbon cutting for Winchester Lofts, June, 2015. Abe Naparstak, senior vice-president of Forest City, the company that completed this first $60 million phase with the help of a $4 million state CHAMP (Competitive Housing Assistance for Multifamily Properties) grant (which helps subsidize apartments set aside at "affordable" rents) is pictured at the far right. Photo courtesy the New Haven Independent, *June 25, 2015.*

WINCHESTER LOFTS

Just months after the opening of Higher One in its new Science Park location, the "second phase" of the Winchester renovation was put in place. The plan was to make luxury apartments out of the old Winchester entrance building at Munson Street and Winchester Avenue, and tear down two of the other old plant buildings across the street to provide a parking lot and shops for its tenants.[133]

When the official opening of the new apartment complex occurred in June of 2015, Higher One, soon to flounder, was still considered a "success story." Reported the *New Haven Independent*, City Development Administrator Matthew Nemerson noted at the opening ceremony that "dramatic changes" had occurred "since 1983, when the not-for-profit Science Park Development Corporation began retrofitting the abandoned gun factory buildings to serve as high-tech incubator space. Nemerson was the number-two official in Science Park's early days." The *Independent* commented, "The blue-collar Winchester past has given way to a gentrified future."[134]

> "*$4 million of state money to build affordable housing and we get $1300 studios?*"
>
> —Posted by MarkS on *New Haven Independent* web site, June 25, 2015, 6:18 pm

> "*How is this 'expanding the grand list', when one developer comes in, gets tax breaks... then charges rents that nobody can afford so they can pretend they can live in some kind of homogeneous hipster technotopia, and then we all sit around and HOPE we can get a job serving them coffee at Starbucks? And what happens when New Haven, much like Brooklyn, is declared 'dead', and those very same people start leaving because suddenly it's not 'cool'? Meanwhile, you're exacerbating the problem of income inequality. As usual, New Haven and city leaders seem to miss the bigger picture.*"
>
> —Posted by RobotShlomo on *New Haven Independent* web site, July 4, 2015, 12:22 pm

> "*Again, the poor and working poor are locked out.*"
>
> —Posted by THREEFIFTHS on the *New Haven Independent* web site, June 26, 2015, 8:32 am

HIGHER ONE, WINCHESTER LOFTS, ET AL.:
THE 21ST CENTURY ROLLER COASTER RIDE AT SCIENCE PARK

Part 2. Winchester Lofts: The Transformation. With Amenities.

2008 Science Park Development Corporation signs deal with Forest City to develop housing at the site of the former plant. Progress is delayed for several years due to Great Recession.

OCTOBER 2012 "Second phase" of the Winchester renovation begins. The plan is to renovate the former plant entrance at Munson Street and Winchester Avenue to create a luxury apartment building called Winchester Lofts, and to tear down two of the old factory buildings across the street to provide a parking lot and other amenities for its tenants.

SEPTEMBER 2013 Ground is broken on the new Winchester Lofts. City officials doing the shoveling include then CT Governor Dannel P. Malloy and then New Haven Mayor John DeStefano.

JUNE 2015 Official opening of Winchester Lofts, the first phase of its renovation. Abe Naparstak, senior vice-president of Forest City, which renovated the building, cuts ceremonial ribbon.

DECEMBER 2018 Science Park Development Corporation is awarded $200,000 state grant to conduct environmental assessment for second phase of reclamation of abandoned plant for housing from 275 Winchester Avenue up to Mansfield Street.

SUMMER 2019 The winchesterlofts.com brochure heralds "the transformation of a factory space into the finest apartment community in New Haven." Winchester Lofts today offers "market rate" rents ranging from $1260 for a studio to $3150 for a two-bedroom apartment. Studios alone can price as high as $1630. The complex has 158 units, only 32 of which are available as "affordable housing" with rents ranging from $754 (for a studio) to $1407 (for a two bedroom), and a current wait list of 57. Minimum income for the "affordable" ranges from $21,168 with a maximum of $64,330 for a household of one, depending on the rental unit. Prices and terms subject to change without notice.

Tenants as of July 2019 at 5 Science Park on Winchester Ave.

SCIENCE PARK'S CURRENT TENANTS

In 2002, Science Park officially tagged "at Yale" onto its name, at the behest of Lyme Properties, LLC, which had undertaken the renovation of Building 25 two years earlier and was moving ahead with other renovation projects to attract future biotechnology start-up companies. At the opening ceremony for Building 25, then Yale President Richard Levin said, "Part of making it a success is renaming it Science Park at Yale," proclaiming, "This is another event in the unfolding of New Haven's Renaissance."[135] Yale moved 600 employees to Building 25, known as 25 Science Park, and in 2009 projected that it would move another 600 to the 344 Winchester Avenue site once it was renovated.[136]

The new face of Winchester as part of Yale's gentrified New Haven.

HIGHER ONE, WINCHESTER LOFTS, ET AL.:
THE 21ST CENTURY ROLLER COASTER RIDE AT SCIENCE PARK

Part 3. Science Park: Today's Entrepreneurial Technotopia.

The current tenants of Science Park include:

AT 344 WINCHESTER AVE.: Yale Printing and Publishing Services, "which offers offers printing, copying and mailing services to the university community." Its nearest neighbors on that side of the street are a parking lot and several businesses, including "Fussy Coffee" and CrossFit.

AT 1 SCIENCE PARK: Highville Charter School and Highville Change Academy

2 SCIENCE PARK appears to still be under construction.

AT 4 SCIENCE PARK: Connecticut Center for Arts and Technology, established in 2011, a "non-profit career training institution...linked with the hospitality industry and corporate partners who assist in the design of training;" **Precipio Diagnostics,** a commercial specialty diagnostics company founded in 2011; **RxGen,** a specialty biotechnology company; Revegen, a commercial medical research company; **KnockMedia,** a website and app design, development, and marketing company; and **The Literacy Resource Center, with the New Haven office of Literacy Volunteers, New Haven Reads, Concepts for Adaptive Learning and The Literacy Coalition for Greater New Haven.**

AT 5 SCIENCE PARK: Ikonisys, "a cell based diagnostics company that markets the proprietary Ikoniscope Digital Microscope;" **Cybrexa Therapeutics,** a New Haven startup developing a new class of cancer drugs planning to start its first human clinical trial in 2020; **Survey Launch,** offering technical solutions and products for the market research industry; **Arvinas,** "built on the research of Craig Crews, PhD, Lewis B. Cullman Professor of Molecular, Cellular and Developmental Biology and professor of Chemistry and Pharmacology at Yale"; **Valisure,** a lab attached to an online pharmacy; and the **Fitscript Diabetes Training Center.** (The latter was founded in 2012 and moved into Science Park in 2013.)

AT 25 SCIENCE PARK: [Yale] **Information Technology Services; Yale Medicine Care Center, Yale Health Clinical Call Center,** Yale offices formerly housed elsewhere; **Kleo Pharmaceuticals** (a start-up company founded by Dr. David Spiegel, Professor of Chemistry and Pharmacology); **Artizan Biosciences,** "advancing the innovative technology of Yale faculty members Richard Flavell and Noah Palm"; and **Quantum Circuits** (another Yale start-up company, co-founded by Sterling Professor of Applied Physics and Physics at Yale, Michel Devoret, Yale's F.W. Beinecke Professor of Applied Physics and Physics and Luigi Frunzio, a senior research scientist in applied physics).

Science Park has hosted several startup companies along with its other tenants thus far into the 21st century. These companies are often associated with Yale University faculty and graduate students whose efforts to commercialize their scientific research have been nurtured by the Yale Office of Cooperative Research and Yale Entrepreneurial Institute. According to its web site, OCR "assists in every stage of the go-to-market process from patent filing, to market assessment, to connections with partners and funders."[137]

Many enterprises have come and gone from the Science Park site, but an array of high-tech companies currently occupy the former Winchester landscape, along with offices of Yale University, CrossFit Science Park, Fussy Coffee, and a couple of New Haven-based non-profits. The area is now designated the "Winchester Historic District," and the Farmington Canal Greenway Trail runs along the west side of the complex. A short walk down Munson Street leads to one of New Haven's poorest neighborhoods, where the children and grandchildren of many of the Winchester gun factory's former employees still reside, trying to make a living.

Afterword

THE STORY OF WORKERS at the Winchester Repeating Arms Company is an important part of the 20th century history of New Haven, CT, with major implications for the city's past and future. This book, like the exhibit which preceded it, begins to describe and depict the complex interaction between the company, the community members it employed, their union leadership and the city administration.

Personally and politically, the story interested me from the time I arrived in the city. When I began working at the New Haven Women's Liberation Center in 1979, Winchester's workers were in the midst of a prolonged strike that literally involved the entire community. The New Haven police, many of whom were neighbors, relatives or friends of the strikers, were being deployed en masse to escort replacement workers and "scabs" across the picket lines. The police officers were receiving overtime pay for their assignment. The confrontations that ensued were painful on all levels. There were arrests and there was violence. In addition, the community also faced an issue of long-standing: as noted in Chapter 8, a large block of the street on which the plant stood, Winchester Avenue, had been closed to traffic since 1975, restricting access to the primarily black, working class neighborhood of Newhallville, where many of the company's employees lived.

Concerned citizens and organizations mobilized to support the union. With other representatives of like-minded city groups, Women's Center board members and staff attended a public hearing held by the Board of Aldermen (as they were then known) to discuss and vote on resolutions to end the overtime pay for "strike-breaking" and to "open the gate" in order to restore the community right-of-way. We sat for more than an hour waiting for the hearing to start, discovering that the Alders were already having their own, private meeting in a side chamber. Several of us lost patience and stormed the room, which was smoke-filled, to demand that our elected representatives come out and listen to us. In the end, after all the testimony was heard, much of it in favor of the resolutions, the majority of these officials voted against both of them. It was an eye-opening experience for many, to see that the voices of citizens could be so dramatically ignored in the service of a large company's interests.

Full disclosure: as someone whose anti-war beliefs often took me to Groton to protest the building of nuclear submarines at General Dynamics' Electric Boat Shipyard and to other weapons production facilities as well, I did not always find it easy to reconcile the product that was being made at Winchester with the workers' just demands. Much of Connecticut's economy was (and is) based on militarism and war. The Winchester plant played its own role in that dismal economic picture.

However, like most young working class people, I had been employed since about age 15. In my first two years in New Haven, before being hired for the position at the Women's Center, I held three or four jobs, including substitute teaching, cashiering at Macy's Department Store, packing sausage at Perri's, and briefly working as a proofreader, all in non-unionized workplaces. I learned firsthand how nearly impossible it is to support oneself when you have no recourse but to accept whatever poor pay, benefits and working conditions the boss imposes, and how demeaning it is to have no control over your work environment or what is being produced.

Winchester workers, as the book shows, had struggled long and hard to win the right to bargain collectively and to bring a union into their shop to make it a more equitable workplace. They succeeded in doing so after more than half a century. But the company just as determinedly tried to thwart their aspirations and to crush the union once it was in place.

When the Winchester plant closed in 2006, I had been employed as the Archivist/Director of the Greater New Haven Labor History Association for five years. Our primary mission was to document local labor and working-class history. Like the carriage industry, the garment industry, and others before it, Winchester had been a major employer of those who lived in and around New Haven. It had been part of the very fabric of the community. The story of the guns it produced had been told and re-told in books, movies, songs, and exhibits, and were the stuff of legend. Its workers' own stories? The company's management practices and their impact on the community? Not so much.

While the Local 609 records served as a window into the struggles of union leaders and rank and file members, and while local media sources gave a picture of the city administration's interaction with Winchester's various owners, largely missing were stories of individual workers' experiences. With their contacts in the community and as the daughters of the late Edward White, a machinist who had been employed at the plant, Labor History Association Executive Board members Dorothy Johnson and her sister, the late Lula White, began to locate and interview Winchester employees who had either retired, left the company to go elsewhere, or been laid off when the plant closed. They were sometimes assisted by the LHA vice president, the late Mary Johnson. The LHA president, the late L. W. Berndtson, Jr., helped videotape and catalogue the interviews. I conducted only two of the interviews myself, with Marcia Biederman and Sen. Martin Looney. I distilled the content of all the interviews for use in the exhibit. The stories became an integral part of it, as they are of this book.

ABOUT THE BOOK

This book is an attempt to flesh out in more detail, and, in some cases, to clarify, the history we tried to tell in the exhibit. It has required additional research. It is still only a beginning. The gaps are wide; no doubt there are discrepancies or unintentional errors; without a doubt, there are many more stories to tell. While the specifics of Winchester's tenure in New Haven are about one plant in one town, its themes are reflective of a much broader history that has unfolded (and is still unfolding) throughout the United States. It is my hope that some who have experienced that history and those who understand its importance will write more chapters—or, better still, write more books.

JOAN CAVANAGH
Archival Preservation & Historical Research
Archivist and Director, Greater New Haven Labor History Association, 2001-2016

ABOUT THE GREATER NEW HAVEN LABOR HISTORY ASSOCIATION

The Labor History Association was formed in 1988 by teachers, students, and trade unionists. They understood that new generations of workers were coming of age without being taught about the struggles and sacrifices made by their parents and grandparents to win the rights, benefits, and protections in the workplace that we take for granted. They wanted to ensure that current and future generations learned that history and its lesson: the need for continuing struggle to secure and improve labor rights even as the nature of work changed dramatically in the latter part of the 20th century and into the 21st.

We are all workers. Thus, labor history is about all of us. It is about ordinary people who have produced commodities and provided services of all varieties while simultaneously fighting for protections that are systematically being eroded and removed. Unfortunately, an ever-shrinking number of us in the United States work in union shops today. The right to bargain collectively is under siege and must be won all over again.

Until 2016, the Labor History Association held the historical records of several union locals and individual labor activists. These are now available as the Greater New Haven Labor History Association Collection at Archives and Special Collections at the Thomas J. Dodd Center at the University of Connecticut in Storrs, CT. The finding guide to the collection can be accessed at https://archivessearch.lib.uconn.edu/repositories/2/resources/1047.

The records and files of International Association of Machinists Local 609, the union that represented workers at the Winchester plant and many of whose documents are reproduced in the exhibit and in this book, are now housed at the Southern Labor Archives at Georgia State University, the official repository for all International Association of Machinists records. The finding guide, based on inventories done by interns and the former Archivist/Director of the Greater New Haven Labor History Association, can be accessed at https://archivesspace.library.gsu.edu/repositories/2/resources/1769.

While no longer an archival repository, the Labor History Association continues to educate about workers and working-class history and recently contributed to creating a curriculum for Connecticut's public schools on the subject. This can be accessed at: https://portal.ct.gov/ SDE/Publications/CT-Labor-and-Working-Class-History. In addition, the Council/Teachers building at 267 Chapel Street in New Haven, CT, houses a permanent display of portions of the Association's first exhibit, "New Haven's Garment Workers: An Elm City Story."

Sources for Information on the Timelines

UNITED NUCLEAR—IN AND OUT OF NEW HAVEN 1961-1976 (CHAPTER 7)

1948: Coldwar-CT.com

1950: Coldwar-CT.com; Walter Dudar, "64 million Contract Awarded to United Nuclear," *New Haven Register*, April 13, 1970, 8.

1961: Ibid, *Register*, April 13, 1970.

1965: "400 Strike United Nuclear, New Contract Termed Issue," *New Haven Register*, February 13, 1968, 1.

FEBRUARY 1968: Ibid.

APRIL 1970: Ibid, *Register*, April 13, 1970.

FEBRUARY 1972: Walter Dudar, "United Nuclear Wins $60 Million Contract," *New Haven Register*, February 23, 1972, 1.

APRIL 1972: Walter Dudar, "United Nuclear Moving Bulk of its Operation," *New Haven Register*, April 10, 1972, 1.

MARCH 1973: "UNC, Union In Accord On Pact," *New Haven Register*, March 24, 1973, 1.

1980-1990: THE ROLLER COASTER RIDE AT USRAC (CHAPTER 9)

JANUARY 1980: "Olin to get 'Science Park,'" *New Haven Register*, February 2, 1980, 1.

AUGUST 1980: Arthur M. Horowitz, "Olin 'superblock' complete," *New Haven Register*, August 19, 1980, 1.

DECEMBER 1980: Lynne DeLucia, "City seeks buyer for Winchester," *New Haven Register*, December 13, 1980, 1.

JULY 1981: Angela D. Chatman, "Olin reaches accord on sporting arms deal," *New Haven Register*, July 1, 1981, 1; Steve Hamm, "Wage concessions refused," *New Haven Register*, January 17, 1985, 1.

DECEMBER 1982: Robert Weisman, "Repeating Arms axes 45," *New Haven Register*, March 17, 1983, 15.

1983: Ibid.

FEBRUARY 1983: Angela D. Chatman and Lucia Klemovich, "Olin Chemical Labs moving to Cheshire," *New Haven Register*, February 1, 1983, 1.

SPRING 1983: Jon Hall, "Firm investigates Fletcher's deals," *New Haven Register*, A33; Rick Povinelli, "Ex-president of USRAC, wife get prison terms—Judge also fines Fletchers $10,000 each for tax fraud," *New Haven Register*, November 30, 1989, 3.

MAY 1983: Janet Koch, "Extension of loan endorsed for Repeating Arms Company," *New Haven Register*, May 18, 1983, 1.

SUMMER 1983: "Machinists union oks three-year contract," *New Haven Register*, July 15, 1983, 2.

DECEMBER 1984: Steve Hamm, "Honeymoon ends at gun plant: No bonus, extended furlough sour union on management," *New Haven Register*, November 13, 1985, 1.

JANUARY 1985: Ibid.

APRIL 1985: "Aldermen ok loan to help gunmaker," *New Haven Register*, April 2, 1985, 15.

JUNE 1985: October 1985: Steve Hamm, "Honeymoon ends at gun plant: No bonus, extended furlough sour union on management," *New Haven Register*, November 13, 1985, 1. This article came from the Local 609 files; http://exhibits.winchesterworkers.gnhlha.org ("The Christmas Crisis.") Correspondence used in this exhibit panel came from Local 609 files.

EARLY 1986: January 1986: Edward Petriuolo III, "Winchester union oks concessions to save jobs," *New Haven Register*, January 27, 1986, 12.

FEBRUARY 17, 1986: David Hezekiel, "First group of arms employees returns to work as plant reopens," *New Haven Register*, February 17, 1986, 1; David Hezekiel, "USRAC gets $3 million," *New Haven Register*, March 15, 1986, 36.

FEBRUARY 26, 1986: David Hezekiel, "USRAC Jobs Center closes, task done," *New Haven Register*, July 12, 1986, 40.

JUNE 1986: David Hezekiel and Dan Kaferle, "Surprise, relief greet news on loan to USRAC," *New Haven Register*, June 19, 1986, 1.

JULY 1986: David Hezekiel, "USRAC Jobs Center closes, task done," *New Haven Register*, July 12, 1986, 40; Jon Hall, "Federal probe launched into dealings at USRAC," *New Haven Register*, July 14, 1986, 1.

DECEMBER 31, 1986, 1; Nick Povinelli, "Ex-President of USRAC, wife, get prison terms," *New Haven Register,* November 30, 1989, 3.

JULY 1987-AUGUST 1987: Jacqueline Smith, "3 Meet deadline for filing plans in USRAC sweepstakes," *New Haven Register*, July 11, 1087, 4.; Jacqueline Smith, "Funding shortfall scuttles USRAC suitor," *New Haven Register*, July 21, 1987, 33; Steve Hamm, "City, gunmaker forge deal to salvage company," *New Haven Register*, August 30, 1987, a1.

NOVEMBER 1987: Jacqueline Smith, "Hazardous wastes delay USRAC deal," *New Haven Register*, November 24, 1987, 1.

DECEMBER 29, 1987: Steve Hamm, "USRAC changes hands, rises from bankruptcy," *New Haven Register*, December 30, 1987, 17.

OCTOBER 1990: Howard Isenstein, "USRAC lays off 500, seeks new financing," *New Haven Register*, October 27, 1990, 1.

NOVEMBER-DECEMBER 1990: Catherine Sullivan, "Workers trickling back to U.S. Repeating Arms," *New Haven Register*, December 13, 1990, 57; Howard Isenstein, "New exec aims at profits in one year," *New Haven Register*, December 14, 1990, 53.

USRAC'S RACE TO THE FINISH (CHAPTERS 10-11)

PART 1. 1990-1995 BUILDING A NEW PLANT IN THE "NEW CULTURE." (CHAPTER 10)

JANUARY 30, 1991: Howard Isenstein, "Gunmaker has sights on new plant," *New Haven Register*, January 30, 1991, 10.

SEPTEMBER 1991: Howard Isenstein, "Job-loaded plant comes into view: Repeating Arms eyes Olin site in Science Park," *New Haven Register*, September 19, 1991, 39.

1992: *High Performance Work Organization Partnerships Field Manual*, International Association of Machinists, August 1, 1998, 9-75, Local 609 Records.

MARCH-MAY 1992: Catherine Sullivan, "USRAC staying in city," *New Haven Register*, March 13, 1992, 1; Howard Isenstein, "Olin mops up at Science Park," *New Haven Register*, April 1, 1992, 17; Howard Isenstein, "New gun factory clears first hurdle," *New Haven Register*, April 9, 1992, 25.

MAY 1992: Kim S. Hirsch, "Aldermen Ok tax break for gun firm," *New Haven Register*, May 19, 1992, 3.; Mark Zaretsky, "Hearing aimed at keeping gun plant," *New Haven Register*, November 10, 1998, a3.

1993: *High Performance Work Organization Partnerships Field Manual*, International Association of Machinists, August 1, 1998, 9-76. Local 609 records.

FEBRUARY 1993: Mitchell Hartman, "Feds fine gun firm for safety violations," *New Haven Register*, February 9, 1993, 1; Paul Davies, "Gun maker expands city roots," *New Haven Register*, August 24, 1994, 11.

APRIL 1993: Mitchell Hartman, "Gun maker gets $92,000 more to demolish old tunnels," *New Haven Register*, April 6, 1993, a3.

MARCH 3-4, 1994: *High Performance Work Organization (HWPO) Partnership Seminar Manual*, International Association of Machinists, 1994, Local 609 Records, http://exhibits.winchesterworkers.gnhlha.org/.

AUGUST-OCTOBER 1994: Paul Davies, "Gun maker expands city roots," *New Haven Register*, August 24, 1994, f1.

FEBRUARY 1995: *High Performance Work Organization Field Partnerships Field Manual*, International Association of Machinists, August 1, 1998, 9-75.

PART 2. 1998-2006. THE VERY, VERY, VERY END. (CHAPTER 11)

NOVEMBER 1998: Mark Zaretsky, "Hearing aimed at keeping gun plant," *New Haven Register*, "Hearing aimed at keeping gun plant," November 10, 1998, a3; "Mayor urged to zero in on gun maker," *New Haven Register*, November 13, 1998, a3.

JANUARY 1999: Mark Zaretsky, "USRAC stands to lose tax deal," *New Haven Register*, January 10, 1999, a1.

MARCH 2000: Angela Carter, "USRAC tax deal might be changed," *New Haven Register*, March 19, 2000, a3.

SEPTEMBER 2000: Angela Carter, "City amends tax abatement deal with gun maker," *New Haven Register*, September 7, 2000, a5.

MARCH 2005: Damian J. Troise, "Machinists, USRAC, sign pact," *New Haven Register*, March 22, 2005, https://www.nhregister.com/news/article/Machinists-USRAC-sign-pact-11646595.php.

JANUARY 2006: Steve Higgins, "USRAC working to sell gun plant, save city jobs," *New Haven Register*, January 19, 2006, a1; "City, state subsidies fail to save USRAC: A business anchored in 19th century meets its end in 21st," Editorial, *New*

Haven Register, January 19, 2006, a6; Sarah Raymond, "Don't Let the Door Hit You On the Way Out," *New Haven Independent*, January 31, 2006, https://www.newhavenindependent.org/index.php/archives/entry/dont_let_the_door_hit_you_on_the_way_out/.

JANUARY-MARCH 2006: Damian J. Troise, "Elm City brings in big guns to help keep USRAC from closing, *New Haven Register*, February 26, 2006; Damian J. Troise, "Winchester rifle maker still closing March 31," *New Haven Register*, March 17, 2006, d1.

MARCH 17, 2006: Tess Wheelwright, "Plant Closing? Or 'Relocation?'", *New Haven Independent*, March 17, 2006, https://www.newhavenindependent.org/index.php/archives/entry/plant_closing_or_relocation/.

APRIL 6, 2006: Damian Troise, "USRAC workers encouraged to apply for federal aid," *New Haven Register*, April 7, 2006, d1.

AUGUST 23, 2006: Steve Higgins, "Last shot fails to keep Winchester made in U.S.," *New Haven Register*, August 18, 2006, a1; Melissa Bailey, "Winchester Workers Pressure City for Jobs," *New Haven Independent*, August 23, 2006, https://www.newhavenindependent.org/index.php/archives/entry/winchester_workers_pressure_city_for_jobs/; Angela Carter, "Ex-Winchester workers seek public hearing on grievances," *New Haven Register*, August 24, 2006, d1.

SEPTEMBER 27, 2006: Steve Higgins, "Winchester equipment on auction block," *New Haven Register*, September 27, 2006, a1.

THE 21ST CENTURY ROLLER COASTER RIDE AT SCIENCE PARK (CHAPTER 12)

PART 1. THE UNICORN: HIGHER ONE

JULY 2010: Thomas MacMillan, "Amid Barbs, Winchester Project Advances," *New Haven Independent*, July 22, 2010. https://www.newhavenindependent.org/index.php/archives/entry/winchester_factory_re-do_under_fire/; Allan Appel, "Winchester Factory's Renewal Lurches Ahead," *New Haven Independent*, July 30, 2010. https://www.newhavenindependent.org/index.php/archives/entry/winchester/

MARCH 2012: Paul Bass, "Check Out Their Dorm Room Now," *New Haven Independent*, March 12, 2012, www.newhavenindependent.org/index.php/archives/entry/check_out_their_dorm_room_now/)

DECEMBER 2015: *New Haven Register*, Wednesday, December 23, 2015, https://www.nhregister.com/connecticut/article/FDIC-orders-Higher-One-in-New-Haven-to-share-cost-11343080.php)

APRIL 2016: https://yaledailynews.com/blog/2016/04/14/higher-one-sells-two-major-divisions/; Paul Bass, "Shareholders Vote to Sell Off a 'Unicorn,'" *New Haven Independent*, April 4, 2016.

APRIL 2018: https://www.newhavenindependent.org/index.php/archives/entry/higher_one1/; Christopher Hoffman, "Higher One to pay $7.M to settle shareholder lawsuit," *newhavenBIZ*, April 9, 2018. https://www.newhavenbiz.com/article/higher-one-to-pay-75m-to-settle-shareholder-suit).

MARCH 2019: Wikipedia, en.wikipedia.org/wiki/Blackboard_Inc, and https://news.elearninginside.com/blackboard-inc-sells-off-transact-leaving-blackboard-mobile-credentials-behind/.

PART 2. THE TRANSFORMATION. WITH AMENITIES

2008: "State grant may mean more Newhallville housing," *New Haven Register*, December 25, 2018, a3.

OCTOBER 2012: Thomas MacMillan, "50 M. Winchester Ave. Project Advances, *New Haven Independent*, October 18, 2012, https://www.newhavenindependent.org/index.php/archives/entry/50m_winchester_renovation_advances/)

SEPTEMBER 2013: Allan Appel, "Winchester Lofts Launched," *New Haven Independent,* September 11, 2013, https://www.newhavenindependent.org/index.php/archives/entry/winchester_lofts_launched/

JUNE 2015: Paul Bass, "Welcome to Winchester Ave. $3K, Please," *New Haven Independent*, June 25, 2015, https://www.newhavenindependent.org/index.php/archives/entry/the_lofts_win_the_west/

DECEMBER 2018: "State grant may mean more Newhallville housing," *New Haven Register*, December 25, 2018, a3.

SUMMER 2019: https://www.apartments.com/winchester-lofts-new-haven-ct/rq6y9v1/; inquiry of rental office in June of 2019; Brookfield properties brochure, www.winchesterlofts.com.

PART 3. TODAY'S ENTREPRENEURIAL TECHNOTOPIA

AT 344 WINCHESTER AVE.

Yale Printing and Publishing Services
https://ypps.yale.edu

AT 1 SCIENCE PARK

Highville Charter School and Highville Change Academy
https://highville.charter.com

AT 4 SCIENCE PARK

CT Center for Arts and Technology
http://conncat.org/about-conncat/mission-history/

Precipio Diagnostics
http://www.precipiodx.com

RxGen
www.rx-gen.com

Revegen
https://www.manta.com/c/mmyrw4b/revegen-corporation; http://revegencorp.com/

KnockMedia
www.knockmedia.com

AT 5 SCIENCE PARK

Ikonisys
http://www.ikonisys.com/about-us/vision-mission

Cybrexa Therapeutics
www.cybrexa.com/about; https://www.courant.com/health/hc-news-health-cybrexa-clinical-trial-20190103 (*Hartford Courant*, January 3, 2019)

Survey Launch
http://www.surveylaunch.com

Arvinas, Inc.
http://ir.arvinas.com/news-releases/news-release-details/arvinas-secures-1825-million-advance-clinical-programs-; https://www.nhregister.com/business/article/New-Haven-drugmaker-expands-presence-in-Science-12508783.php.

Valisure
www.valisure.com

Artificial Cell Technologies
https://artificialcelltech.com/company/about-us

Fitscript
https://fitscript.myshopify.com/pages/about-us;
https://www.courant.com/business/hc-biz-new-haven-glucosezone-20180308-story.html

Literacy Resource Center
https://www.lvagnh.org

AT 25 SCIENCE PARK

Kleo Pharmaceuticals
https://ocr.yale.edu/news/new-yale-faculty-startup-will-harness-immune-system-fight-disease,
Copyright 2019.

Artizan Biosciences
http://artizanbiosciences.com.

Quantum Circuits
https://news.yale.edu/2019/01/24/yale-quantum-computing-startup-quantum-circuits-inc-opens-lab-new-haven

Endnotes

TIMELINE

1. David Montgomery Papers, Series 3, Folder 5, Greater New Haven Labor History Association Bus Tour 1999, Greater New Haven Labor History Association Collection, University of Connecticut Archives and Special Collections. (Most of the entries on this timeline were originally created by Debbie Elkin for the 1999 Labor History Bus Tour of New Haven. The timeline has been updated after 1979.)

INTRODUCTION

2. https://www.apartments.com/winchester-lofts-new-haven-ct/rq6y9v1/; inquiry of rental office in June of 2019; Brookfield properties brochure, www.winchesterlofts.com.

CHAPTER 1

3. http://exhibits.winchesterworkers.gnhlha.org/panel02.html.

4. "The Winchester Story," *Winchester Life*, July 1942 (Vol. 1, No. 4), 5.

5. Mary Jo Ignoffo, *Captive of the Labryrinth: Sarah L. Winchester, Heiress to the Rifle Fortune.*

6. Op cit., *Winchester Life*, 5; Rollin G. Osterweis, *Three Centuries of New Haven,* New Haven: Yale University Press, 1953, 377-378.

CHAPTER 2

7. *Machinists Monthly Journal*, Vol. X, No. 3 (March 1898), 133.

8. Fifth Vice President Landers' Report, *Machinists Monthly Journal*, Vol. XIV, No. 10 (October 1902), 665.

9. The Unfair List, *Machinists Monthly Journal*, Vol. 14, No. 12 (December 1902), 865.

10. Robert M. Lackey, "How the Winchester Repeating Arms Company Rifles Its Workers," *International Socialist Review*, November 1912. Quoted in Steve Thornton, *A Shoeleather History of the Wobblies: Stories of the Industrial Workers of the World*, September, 2013. http://exhibits.winchesterworkers.gnhlha.org/panel05.html.

11. Report of Organizer G.A. Doyle, *Machinists Monthly Journal*, Vol. XXVIII, No. 1 (January 1916), 61.

12. Ibid.

13. Report of Organizer J. J. Egan, *Machinists Monthly Journal*, Vol. XXVIII, No. 2 (February 1916), 186.

14. Report of Organizer J.A. Wickham, *Machinists Monthly Journal*, Vol. XXVIII, No. 8 (August 1916), 819. The National Association of Manufacturers was founded in 1895. It was organized to oppose labor unions and labor advocacy. Later in the century, it would vigorously oppose the New Deal policies of FDR and lobby relentlessly for federal laws to restrict the power of labor unions. In its 21st century incarnation, it has been funded heavily by rightwing Republicans, most notably the Koch brothers.

15. Report of Organizer J.A. Wickham, *Machinists Monthly Journal*, Vol. XXVIII, No. 10 (October 1916), 1018.

16. Rollin G. Osterweis, Three Centuries of New Haven, New Haven: Yale University Press, 1953, 403-404; "Enemy Aliens Out After Census of 15,000," *New Haven Evening Register*, April 18, 1917, 1.

17. "Aliens Rush to Moyle for Advice; Seek to Learn City Attorney's Interpretation of Order Barring Them from One-Half Mile Zone," *New Haven Evening Register*, October 24, 1917, 1. The text of the article reads, in part: "Since the police authorities have interpreted the special orders from the department of justice to mean that the center of the city within a half mile radius of the armory will be barred to enemy aliens, and that many of the smaller factories making munition parts will have a barred zone, unnaturalized Germans and Austrians have become alarmed. They inform the city attorney that rents have been refused them in many cases and implore him to point out a way whereby they may avoid being deprived not only of their employment and homes, but of being actually driven from the city. The city attorney, of course, is powerless to act, as the regulations are from the department of justice and must be enforced to the letter. However, he may strive to secure a more liberal interpretation of the restrictions. In the meantime department of justice agents and the police are taking the enemy alien census in all territories, which will be known as 'danger zones' after June 1."

CHAPTER 3

18. www.gunslot.com/winchester-repeating-arms; Arnold Guyot Dana, *New Haven's Problems- Whither the City? All Cities?*, New Haven, July, 1937, 111; http://www.b2i.us/profiles/investor/fullpage.asp?BzID=1548&to=cp&Nav=0&LangID=1&s=0&ID=6661.

19. "Today in Union History: President Franklin D. Roosevelt asserts the right of all workers to join unions." www.fairwageonstage.org.

CHAPTER 4

20. *UE News*, vol. 3, no. 21, May 24, 1941, 1, https://digital.library.pitt.edu/islandora/object/pitt%3A31735066250758/viewer#page/1/mode/2up; *UE News*, vol. 3, no. 33, August 16, 1941.

21. *UE News*, vol. 3 no. 22, May 31, 1941, 1, https://digital.library.pitt.edu/islandora/object/pitt%3A31735066250311/viewer#page/1/mode/2up.

22. *UE News,* vol. 3, no. 22, May 31, 1941, 6, https://digital.library.pitt.edu/islandora/object/pitt%3A31735066250311/from_search/d460a2afe0a151502af64a010f3c58e7-9#page/6/mode/2up.

23. *UE News*. vol. 3, no. 27, July 5, 1941, 1, https://digital.library.pitt.edu/islandora/object/pitt%3A31735066250519/viewer#page/1/mode/2up; also *UE News*, vol. 3, no. 52, December 27, 1941, 1. https://digital.library.pitt.edu/islandora/object/pitt%3A31735066251897/viewer#page/1/mode/2up.

24. Memorandum, Michael Jimenez, International Field Organizer, Winchester Organizing Committee, undated, United Electrical Workers Archives, Box 14, Folder 103, Archives Service Center, University of Pittsburgh.

25. Historically, the needs of women workers were also underrepresented in the Trade Union movement. As part of the war effort, because women workers were at least temporarily swelling the ranks of production workers in jobs left vacant by men in the service, UE (and other unions) began to take more of an interest in them. In June of 1942, the UE District 2 Conference included a special luncheon to discuss the "problems of women in UE industry in New England." It was decided to send a questionnaire to representatives at all the UE organized plants, "to collect information on some of the conditions of women" there. The letter was signed by Claire Neikind, an International Field Organizer who apparently worked out of the New Haven office on Congress Avenue. It wanted to know if the company had a training program for women workers or "are women workers given opportunity for advancement to higher paying jobs?" and whether there were "adequate facilities for care of children of working women in your community." It also asked the union representatives how many officers of the local union were female, how many women stewards and/or representatives the local union had, and "Are members of your local encouraged to become active union leaders?" See: Letter to "Brothers and Sisters" from Claire Neikind, June 24, 1942, Box 14, Folder 102, Archives Service Center, University of Pittsburgh.

26. *UE News*, vol. 4, no. 17, March 7, 1942, 12, "Winchester Under Fire For Discrimination," https://digital.library.pitt.edu/islandora/object/pitt%3A31735047439041/from_search/N-2#page/12/mode/2up.

27. *UE News*, vol. 4, no. 12, 1942, 7. https://digital.library.pitt.edu/islandora/object/pitt%3A31735047439074/viewer#page/6/mode/2up.

28. Press Release, United Electrical, Radio and Machine Workers, CIO, April 24, 1942, United Electrical Workers Archives, Box 14, Folder 104, Archives Service Center, University of Pittsburgh. Also: "NLRB Examiner Finds Winchester Guilty," *UE News-Winchester Edition*, April 25, 1942, Box 4, Folder 19, 1, Archives Service Center, University of Pittsburgh; and "Trial Examiner Finds for UE in Winchester Case; Orders Three UE Members Reinstated, *UE News*, vol. 4, no. 18, May 2, 1942, https://digital.library.pitt.edu/islandora/object/pitt%3A31735047438944/from_search/d460a2afe0a151502af64a010f3c58e7-10#page/8/mode/2up.

29. Press Release, Winchester Organizing Committee, UER & MWA-CIO, May 2, 1942. United Electrical Workers Archives, Box 4, Folder 14, Archives Service Center, University of Pittsburgh. Also: *UE News-Winchester Edition*, May 9, 1942, Archives Service Center, University of Pittsburgh; and *UE News*, vol. 4, no. 19, 4, https://digital.library.pitt.edu/islandora/object/pitt%3A31735047438951/viewer#page/4/mode/2up.

30. *UE News*, *Winchester Edition*, May 28, 1942, 1. United Electrical Workers Archives, Box 4, Folder 19, Archives Service Center, University of Pittsburgh; *UE News*, vol. 4, no. 23, June 6, 1942, 8, https://digital.library.pitt.edu/islandora/object/pitt%3A31735047438886/from_search/d460a2afe0a151502af64a010f3c58e7-21#page/8/mode/2up.

31. "Winchester Grievance Procedure: The 'All American Run-Around,'" and "State Rep. Says: 'Organize!', *UE News-New Haven Edition*, June 6, 1942, United Electrical Workers Archives, Box 4, Folder 20, Archives Service Center, University of Pittsburgh.

32. "UE Protests Hitlerite Attack on Union Leader—Company Supervisor Loses Job After Union Takes Action, *UE News-New Haven Edition*, June 20, 1942, United Electrical Workers Archives, Box 4, Folder 20, Archives Service Center, University of Pittsburgh. No further information was given in this article as to the specific nature of or reason for the attack on Mr. Cassella.

33. "Union Victory at Winchester—UE Forces Company to Reinstate Three Workers," *UE News-New Haven Edition*, July 4th, 1942. United Electrical Workers Archives, Box 4, Folder 20, Archives Service Center, University of Pittsburgh.

34. "Rolling Mill Goes Through the Mill" and "Winchester Posts Notice—You're Free to Join UE-CIO- Boak Offers Bonus to Offset Notice But Workers Don't Fall for That," *UE News-New Haven Edition*, July 28, 1942, United Electrical Workers Archives, Box 4, Folder 20, Archives Service Center, University of Pittsburgh. The capitalizations are found in the original newsletter article.

35. Ibid. The term "open shop," as used in the context of this quote, refers to the Open Shop Movement, which was an organized attempt on the part of business to weaken the labor movement by requiring employees to work in an "open" or non-union shop. It developed in response to the growth of labor union membership in the 1920s. Closed shops, which hire only those who are members of a specific labor union, were made illegal by the Taft-Hartley Act of 1947. "Open shop" as used today means that employees in a shop where workers are represented by a union may or may not be members of that union (chosen by a majority of workers) but the union is legally required, nevertheless, to represent their interests in negotiations with management.

36. *UE News*, vol. 4, no. 33, August 15, 1942, 4, https://digital.library.pitt.edu/islandora/object/pitt%3A31735047438779/from_search/d460a2afe0a151502af64a010f3c58e7-3#page/4/mode/2up.

37. Letter to All Local Unions from Martin Hourihan, August 31st, 1942, United Electrical Workers Archives, Box 14, Folder 103, Archives Service Center, University of Pittsburgh.

38. *UE News*, vol. 4, no. 39, September 26, 1942, 1.

39. *UE News*, vol. 5, no. 1, January 2, 1943, 4, https://digital.library.pitt.edu/islandora/object/pitt%/3A31735047441047/viewer#page/4/mode/2up; *UE News*, vol. 5, no.; *UE News*, vol. 5, no. 2, January 9, 1943, 4, https://digital.library.pitt.edu/islandora/object/pitt%3A31735047440965/viewer#page/4/mode/2up.

40. *UE News* (National Edition), vol. 6, no. 17, April 22, 1944, 8, https://digital.library.pitt.edu/islandora/object/pitt%3A31735047444835/viewer#page/8/mode/2up.

41. *UE News*, vol. 6, no. 52, December 25, 1944, 4, "Court Orders UE Member Rehired," https://digital.library.pitt.edu/islandora/object/pitt%3A31735047442987/from_search/d460a2afe0a151502af64a010f3c58e7-7#page/4/mode/2up.

42. "UE Drive to Crack Open Shop at Winchester Wins Support," *UE News*, vol. 8, no. 42, October 14, 1946, 6, https://digital.library,pitt.edu/islandora/object/pitt%3A31735070065697/viewer#page/6/mode/2up.

43. Ibid.

44. "Deny Winchester Injunction Bid to Bar UE Pickets," *UE News*, vol. 8, no. 46, November 16, 1946, 9, https://digital.library.pitt.edu/islandora/object/pitt%3A31735070065739/viewer#page/9/mode/1up.

45. Xeroxed copy of "The Winchester Story," undated and unattributed document. David Montgomery Papers, Series 5, Folder 9, Greater New Haven Labor History Association Collection, University of Connecticut Archives and Special Collections. The original is located at the University of Pittsburgh in the United Electrical Workers archives. Although he could not immediately locate the document in the collection, Zachary Brodt, University Archivist at the University of Pittsburgh, wrote: "My best guess is that the date would be Fall 1946, sometime between September 21 and November 11. It seems to have been delivered at a meeting organized by the UE for the citizens of New Haven. I would imagine that this speech was delivered by someone from the national level of the union working with the Winchester union members, likely Field Organizer Vincent Romeo or International Representative Richard Linsley." The timing makes sense, since we know that the lockout of the brass mill workers occurred in the fall of 1946. There is a discrepancy in the numbers locked out. The *UE News* articles repeatedly say there are 440 people locked out, but this organizer's speech puts the figure at 200, as do the original legal documents filed by the union and later by the law firm which represented the workers after the union withdrew from the case in 1947.

46. Ibid. As noted previously, Boak was a prominent member of the National Association of Manufacturers, founded in 1895, which had vigorously opposed the New Deal policies of FDR and later lobbied extensively for federal laws to restrict the power of labor unions.

47. Ibid.

48. Xerox copy of Memorandum from Marvin Gold, *In the Matter of Winchester Repeating Arms Co.*, November 27, 1948. This copy is in Series 5, Folder 9 of the David Montgomery Papers in the Greater New Haven Labor History Association Collection, Archives and Special Collections at the University of Connecticut, Storrs, CT. The original is in the United Electrical Workers' archives at the University of Pittsburgh.

49. Xeroxed copy of Letter to Alfred Smith, International Representative, UE-CIO, from David Scribner, General Counsel, UER & MWA, re: Olin Industries, Winchester Div. (New Haven), Case No. 1-C-2822, July 22, 1947; Xeroxed copy of Letter to Smith from Scribner, re: Winchester Arms Company (New Haven, Conn.), December 3, 1948; Xeroxed copy of Letter to Scribner from Smith, re: Winchester Arms Company, (New Haven, Conn.), December 6, 1948. These copies of the letters are in Series 5, Folder 9 of the David Montgomery Papers, in the Greater New Haven Labor History Collection at the Archives and Special Collections, University of Connecticut, Storrs, CT. The originals are in the United Electrical Workers Archives at the University of Pittsburgh.

CHAPTER 5

50. The American Federation of Labor (AFL) was founded in 1886 by a group of craft unions which had previously belonged to the Knights of Labor. The Congress of Industrial Organizations (CIO) had formed within the AFL at the end of 1935 and grew throughout the 1930s. It sought to unionize by industry rather than by craft or trade, which had been the AFL's strategy. It argued that industrial organization would make possible the organization of all workers, including those who were not eligible to join trade unions. It was expelled from the AFL. Subsequently, the AFL ventured into industrial organizing as well, often in companies like Winchester where the CIO had already initiated organizing campaigns. Thus, there were many cases where the CIO accused the AFL of "raiding" their members and vice versa. But the two organizations saw the wisdom of merging, despite often profound differences. As early as 1939, they began having "unity discussions." The merger was not finalized until December of 1955, the same month that the International Association of Machinists (an AFL affiliate) was certified by the NLRB as the new bargaining unit for Winchester's hourly workers. The merger included a detailed "No Raid" agreement. Constructing this deal had been a painstaking and lengthy process.

51. *Winchester Life*, September 1949 (Vol. 8, No. 6), 2.

52. *Winchester Life*, April 1950 (Vol. 9, No. 1), 5, and July 1950 (Vol. 9, No. 7), 16.

53. "NLRB Conducts Hearing on Union Petition," *Winchester News*, September 16, 1955, 3.

54. Ibid; "4,147 Vote as Union Wins Election," *Winchester News*, December 16, 1955, 1A.

55. Ibid.

56. "Winchester Goes Union," *The Machinist*, Vol. X, Number 42 (December 29, 1955), 1.

57. Op cit., "4,147 Vote As Union Wins Election," *Winchester News*, December 16, 1955, 1A.

58. "First Contract in 90 Years: 21 Cents, Union Shop Negotiated for 4500 in New Winchester Pact," *The Machinist*, Vol. XI, Number 13 (June, 1956), 1.

CHAPTER 6

59. Melinda Tuhus, "Courtland Wilson's Legacy: A New Beacon in the Hill," *New Haven Independent*, September 5, 2006, https://www.newhavenindependent.org/index.php/archives/entry/courtland_wilsons_legacy_a_new_beacon_in_the_hill/

60. *Winchester News*, August 15, 1958, 4.

CHAPTER 7

61. "Research Center is Dedicated," *Olin News at New Haven*, March 24, 1961, Vol. IX, Number 18, 1.

62. "New Haven Brass Facility Will be Modernized," *Olin News at New Haven,* August 18, 1961, Vol. X, Number 2, 1.

63. "Machinists File Petition to Represent United Nuclear," and "Plans Progress for Formation of United Nuclear Corporation," *Olin News at New Haven*, March 24, 1961, Vol IX, Number 18, 1.

64. Coldwar-ct.com

65. Walter Dudar, "United Nuclear Moving Bulk of Its Operation," *New Haven Register*, April 10, 1972, 1.

66. "Union, Olin Will Resume Negotiations—State, Federal Mediators to be Called Following Rejection of Offer," *New Haven Register*, May 7, 1962, 1.

67. "Pact Approved, Olin Strike Ends," *New Haven Register*, July 16, 1962, 1. See also: "Olin Strike in 6th Week; No End Seen," *New Haven Register*, July 6, 1962, 42.

68. Ibid, *New Haven Register*, July 16, 1962, 1.

69. http://exhibits.winchesterworkers.gnhlha.org/media/GNHLHA_winchester18-01.jpg. Like the other articles, the article by Ruth Meyerowitz, "Workers Strike Profit Hungry Olin," is from the Local 609 records. It is most likely from the newsletter of the American Independent Movement, which had headquarters on Orange Street in New Haven at the time of the 1969 Olin strike.

70. Ibid, Meyerowitz.

71. "The Strike Is Over but the Fight Goes On," *Strike News*, American Independent Movement, 5/12/69, No. 5, 1. According to WorldCat, copies of AIM's *Olin Strike News* [New Haven CT., 1969] are available at the Homer Babst Library at New York University and at the Wisconsin Historical Society in Madison, Wisconsin: https://www.worldcat.org/title/olin-strike-news/oclc/62174967.

72. Matt Borenstein, "Contract Victory Averts Olin Strike," *Modern Times*, undated clipping from Local 609 files, http://exhibits.winchesterworkers.gnhlha.org.

CHAPTER 8

73. "Olin, Yale, City Officials Seek Science Park Help," *New Haven Register*, Friday, May 2, 1980, 1.

74. "City Offers Olin $6 Million Plan," *New Haven Register*, Monday March 24, 1975, p. 1; op cit. *Register*, 1.

75. Ibid.

76. Robert E. Tomasson, "Disbursal of Olin Funds Stirs a Wave of Criticism," *New York Times*, Feb. 14, 1979, 2, https://www.nytimes.com/1979/02/14/archives/disbursal-of-olin-penalty-stirs-a-wave-of-criticism-fully-as.html.

77. Marcia Biederman, *New Haven Advocate*, October 20, 1976, 4, http://exhibits.winchesterworkers.gnhlha.org. Image is from Local 609 files.

78. Bob Greenlee, "Coalition Still Seeks African Aid," *New Haven Register*, June 2, 1978, 1.

79. Robert E. Tomasson, "Olin's Arms Penalty: 'Donation' Plus Fine," *New York Times*, June 2, 1978, 1, https://www.nytimes.com/1978/06/02/archives/olins-arms-penalty-donation-plus-fine-test-of-issue-avoided-olin.html.

80. Bob Greenlee, "Coalition Still Seeks African Aid," *New Haven Register*, June 20, 1978, 29.

81. Robert E. Tomasson, "Controversy Mars New Haven Gifts," *New York Times*, February 18, 1979, 1, https://www.nytimes.com/1979/02/18/archives/connecticut-weekly-controversy-mars-new-haven-gift-olinfunded.html.

82. Bob Greenlee, "Council Asks State to Probe $500,000 Olin Fund Allocations," *New Haven Register*, February 20, 1979, 1.

83. Bob Greenlee, "City Schools Reject $20,000 Olin Grant," *New Haven Register*, February 19, 1991, 1.

84. *New Haven Register*, June 5, 2019, 21.

85. "IAM Members at Winchester Fighting Incentive Demand," *UE News*, vol. 42, no. 2, Jan 1, 1980, 9, https://digital.library.pitt.edu/islandora/object/pitt%3A31735070080662/from_search/d460a2afe0a151502af64a010f3c58e7-4#page/8/mode/2up.

86. http://exhibits.winchesterworkers.gnhlha.org (Local 609 files.)

87. Ibid.

88. Interview with Craig Gauthier, http://exhibits.winchesterworkers.gnhlha.org.

CHAPTER 9

89. *New Haven Register*, Monday, November 5, 1979, 9.

90. "Olin to Get 'Science Park,'" *New Haven Register*, February 2, 1980, 1.

91. Arthur M. Horowitz, "Arthur M. Horowitz, "Olin 'Super-block' Complete," *New Haven Register*, August 19, 1980, 1.

92. Lynne DeLucia, "City Seeks Buyer for Winchester," *New Haven Register*, December 13, 1980, 1.

93. Ibid.

94. Angela D. Chatman, "Olin reaches accord on Sporting Arms Sale," *New Haven Register*, July 9, 1981, 27.

95. Angela D. Chatman, "Winchester owner aims for success as small firm," *New Haven Register*, July 26, 1981, b1.

96. Steve Hamm, "Wage concessions refused," *New Haven Register*, January 17, 1985, 1.

97. Robert Weisman, "Repeating Arms axes 45," *New Haven Register*, March 17, 1983, 15.

98. Janet Koch, "Extension of loan endorsed for U.S. Repeating Arms Company," *New Haven Register*, May 18, 1983, 1.

99. "Machinists Union Oks three-year contract, *New Haven Register*, July 15, 1983, 2.

100. Janet Koch, "Aldermen OK Loan to Help Gunmaker, *New Haven Register*, April 2, 1985, 15.

101. Op cit, *New Haven Register*, January 17, 1985.

102. Steve Hamm, "Honeymoon ends at gun plant: No bonus, extended furlough sour union on management," *New Haven Register*, November 13, 1985, p. 1. This article came from the Local 609 files.

103. Ibid.

104. Letter from Richard M. Pelton, President, U.S. Repeating Arms Company, to Louis Romano, President, Victory Lodge 609, October 24, 1985, http://exhibits.winchesterworkers.gnhlha.org/("The 1985 Christmas Crisis.")

105. "Winchester union okays concessions to save jobs," *New Haven Register*, January 27, 1986, 12. (The law firm's efforts on Yale's behalf had already failed. Local 34 won its first contract at Yale in 1985 after a 10-week strike.)

106. Ibid.

107. "Olin donates site for park," *New Haven Register*, October 13, 1982, 15.

108. Angela D. Chatman, "$2.5 million will refurbish United Nuclear Plant," *New Haven Register*, July 1, 1982, 4.

CHAPTER 10

109. Howard Isenstein, "New exec aims at profits in one year," *New Haven Register*, October 14, 1990, 53.

110. Ibid.

111. Catherine Sullivan, "Workers trickling back to U.S. Repeating Arms," *New Haven Register*, December 13, 1990, 57.

112. Howard Isenstein, "Winchester maker to add 65 workers, upgrade plant," *New Haven Register*, October 4, 1991, 22; *New Haven Register*, February 10, 1989, 56; Steve Hamm, "Search for new Science Park head delayed," *New Haven Register*, June 1, 1988 (accessed through Newsbank at New Haven Free Public Library; no page number identified.) Chauncey, a long-time administrator at Yale University, had moved on to become president of Gaylord Hospital in Wallingford. Ginsberg was the development administrator for the city of New Haven.

113. Catherine Sullivan, "Officials scramble to keep city gun plant," *New Haven Register*, February 14, 199, 23; Paul Davies, "New gun factory debuts in Elm City," *New Haven Register*, October 15, 1994, e12.

114. Howard Isenstein, "Gunmaker eyes new target," *New Haven Register*, May 5, 1992, a1.

115. *High Performance Work Organization (HWPO) Partnership Seminar Manual*, International Association of Machinists (no date on original document, probably 1992), Local 609 Records. http://exhibits.winchesterworkers.gnhlha.org.

116. "'**Total quality management (TQM)**' consists of organization-wide efforts to 'install and make permanent a climate where employees continuously improve their ability to provide on demand products and services that customers will find of particular value.' 'Total' emphasizes that departments in addition to production (for example sales and marketing, accounting and finance, engineering and design) are obligated to improve their operations; 'management' emphasizes that executives are obligated to actively manage quality through funding, training, staffing, and goal setting. While there is no widely agreed-upon approach, TQM efforts typically draw heavily on the previously developed tools and techniques of quality control. TQM enjoyed widespread attention during the late 1980s and early 1990s before being overshadowed by ISO 9000, Lean manufacturing, and Six Sigma." (https://en.wikipedia.org/wiki/Total_quality_management).

"**Cellular manufacturing** is a process of manufacturing which is a subsection of just-in-time manufacturing and lean manufacturing encompassing group technology... A cell is created by consolidating the processes required to create a specific output, such as a part or a set of instructions. These cells allow for the reduction of extraneous steps in the process of creating the specific output, and facilitate quick identification of problems and encourage communication of employees within the cell in order to resolve issues that arise quickly. Once implemented, cellular manufacturing has been said to reliably create massive gains in productivity and quality while simultaneously reducing the amount of inventory, space and lead time required to create a product. It is for this reason that the one-piece-flow cell has been called "'the ultimate in lean production.'" (https://en.wikipedia.org/wiki/Cellular_manufacturing).

117. *High Performance Work Organization Field Partnerships Field Manual*, International Association of Machinists, August 1, 1998, 9-75.

118. Ibid.

119. Ibid, 9-76. Although this field manual was published (or re-issued) in 1998, as noted, it does not describe events at USRAC beyond 1995. It states that "although regular contract negotiations were taking place when the MOA was hammered out, both sides agreed to keep the MOA separate from the collective bargaining agreement. It was felt that since both parties were new to partnering that a more cautious, go slow approach was the best way to proceed. The current contract, which expires in February 1996, is traditional in its form and language."

120. Flyers about March 3-4, 1994 IAM rally at USRAC regarding the High Performance Work Organization, Local 609 records, http://exhibits.winchesterworkers.gnhlha.org.

121. Op cit., *High Performance Work Organization Field Partnerships Field Manual*, 9-76. Emphasis added.

122. Ibid.

123. Ibid, 9-79.

CHAPTER 11

124. David Hezekiel, "First group of arms employees returns to work as plant reopens," *New Haven Register*, February 17, 1986, 1.

125. Howard Isenstein, "Gunmaker has sights on new plant," *New Haven Register*, January 30, 1991, 10; Howard Isenstein, "Job-loaded plant comes into view: Repeating Arms eyes Olin site in Science Park," *New Haven Register*, September 19, 1991, 39.

126. Kim S. Hirsch, "Aldermen Ok tax break for gun firm," *New Haven Register*, May 19, 1992, 3; Mark Zaretsky, "Hearing aimed at keeping gun plant," *New Haven Register*, November 10, 1998, a3.

127. "Mayor urged to zero in on gun maker," *New Haven Register*, November 13, 1998, a3; Mark Zaretsky, "USRAC stands to lose tax deal," *New Haven Register*, January 10, 1999, a1; Angela Carter, "USRAC tax deal might be changed," *New Haven Register*, March 19, 2000, a3; Angela Carter, "City amends tax abatement deal with gun maker," *New Haven Register*, September 7, 2000, a5.

128. "Mayor urged to zero in on gun maker," *New Haven Register*, November 13, 1998, a3.

129. Damian J. Troise, "Machinists, USRAC, sign pact," *New Haven Register*, March 22, 2005, https://www.nhregister.com/news/article/Machinists-USRAC-sign-pact-11646595.php.

130. Oral history, Craig Gauthier, http://exhibits.winchesterworkers.gnhlha.org/.

131. Angela Carter, "Ex-Winchester workers seek public hearing on grievances," *New Haven Register*, August 24, 2006, d1; Tess Wheelwright, "Plant Closing? Or 'Relocation?,'" *New Haven Independent*, March 17, 2006, https://www.newhavenindependent.org/index.php/archives/entry/plant_closing_or_relocation/.

CHAPTER 12

132. Thomas MacMillan, "Amid Barbs, Winchester Project Advances," *New Haven Independent*, July 22, 2010, https://www.newhavenindependent.org/index.php/archives/entry/winchester_factory_re-do_under_fire/; Allan Appel, "Winchester Factory's Renewal Lurches Ahead," *New Haven Independent*, July 30, 2010, https://www.newhavenindependent.org/index.php/archives/entry/winchester/.

133. Thomas MacMillan, "50 M. Winchester Ave. Project Advances, *New Haven Independent*, October 18, 2012, https://www.newhavenindependent.org/index.php/archives/entry/50m_winchester_renovation_advances/.

134. Paul Bass, "Welcome to Winchester Ave. $3K, Please," *New Haven Independent*, June 25, 2015, https://www.newhavenindependent.org/index.php/archives/entry/the_lofts_win_the_west/.

135. Kimberly S. Johnson, "Science Park tags 'at Yale' onto its name," *New Haven Register*, October 31, 2002, c1.

136. Mary E. O'Leary, "Yale will move 600 workers to Science Park site," *New Haven Register*, January 15, 2009, a3.

137. https://ocr.yale.edu/news/new-yale-faculty-startup-will-harness-immune-system-fight-disease, Copyright 2020.

Credits

RESEARCH, WRITING, EDITING AND PRODUCTION OVERSIGHT

Joan Cavanagh | Archival Preservation & Historical Research

CREATIVE DIRECTION, DESIGN AND PRODUCTION

Jeanne Criscola | Criscola Design | www.criscoladesign.com

VIDEOGRAPHY AND PHOTOGRAPHY FOR ORAL HISTORY INTERVIEWS

James Hoffecker and L. W. Berndtson, Jr.

EXHIBIT IMAGE RE-MASTERING AND DIGITIZATION

Cynthia Beth Rubin, Jeanne Criscola

ONLINE EXHIBIT DESIGN, PRODUCTION AND WEB HOSTING

David Cirella

ORAL HISTORY INTERVIEWS

Conducted by Dorothy Johnson, Mary Johnson (1922-2017), Lula White (1938-2019), Joan Cavanagh, Louis W. Berndtson, Jr. (1934-2017) and Frank Annunziato